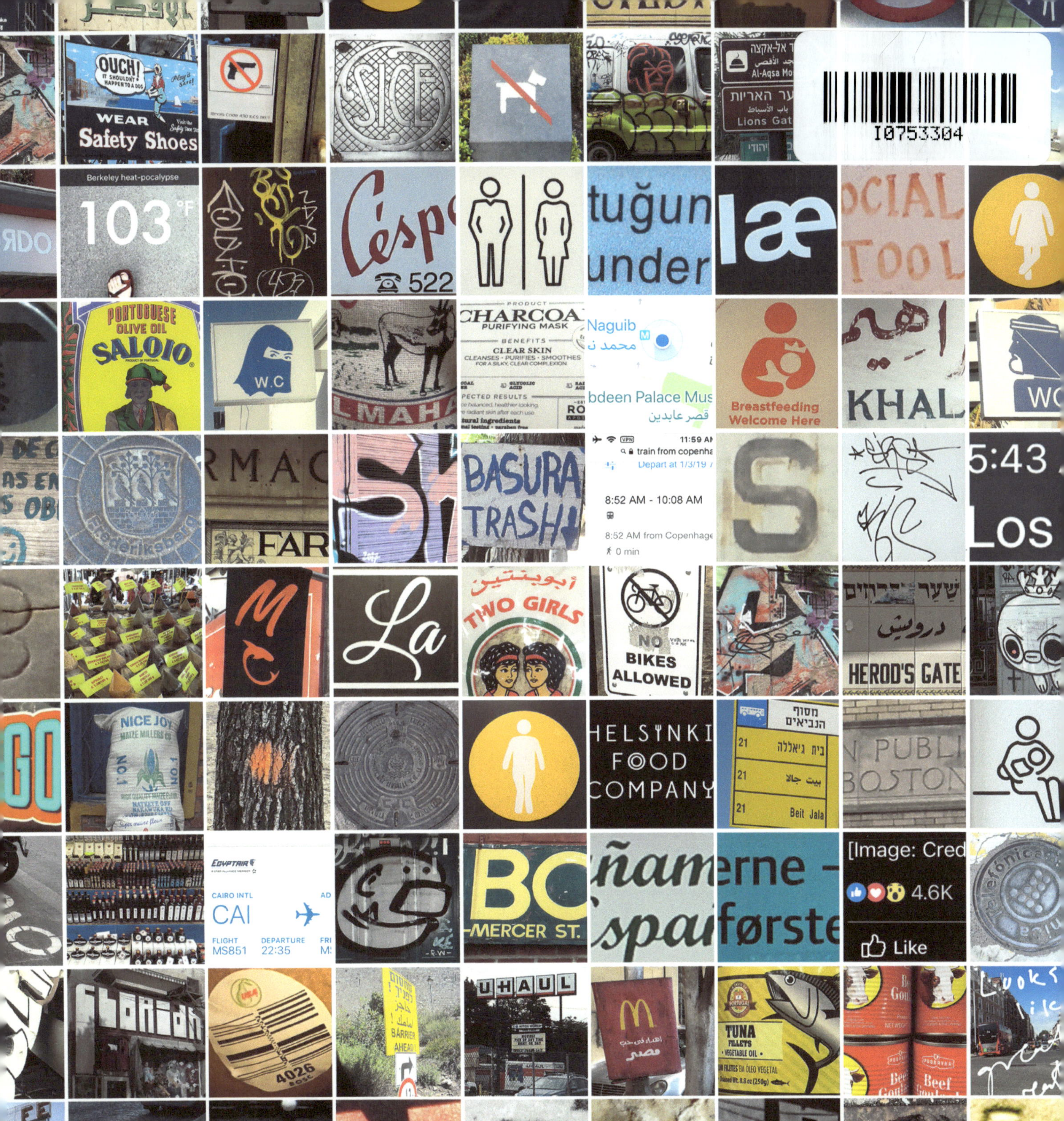

I0753304
OUCH! IT SHOULDN'T HAPPEN TO A DOG
WEAR
Safety Shoes
Al-Aqsa Mo
Lions Gat
Berkeley heat-pocalypse
103 °F
Césp
522
tuğun
under
læ
OCIAL
TOOL
PORTUGUESE OLIVE OIL
SALOIO
W.C
CHARCOA
PURIFYING MASK
BENEFITS
CLEAR SKIN
Naguib
محمد ن
bdeen Palace Mus
قصر عابدين
Breastfeeding
Welcome Here
KHAL
WC
RMAC
FAR
BASURA
TRASH
11:59 AM
train from copenha
Depart at 1/3/19
8:52 AM - 10:08 AM
8:52 AM from Copenhage
0 min
5:43
LOS
La
TWO GIRLS
NO
BIKES
ALLOWED
HEROD'S GATE
GO
NICE JOY
HELSINKI
FOOD
COMPANY
Beit Jala
N PUBLI
BOSTON
EGYPTAIR
CAIRO INTL
CAI
FLIGHT
MS851
DEPARTURE
22:35
BO
MERCER ST.
ñam
spa
erne –
første
[Image: Cred
4.6K
Like
UHAUL
TUNA
FILLETS
VEGETABLE OIL
Beef

Praise for *The Accountant, the King, the Priest, and the Poet*

"This book is a powerhouse of typographic information—well researched, with incredible image documentation, accessible, and well designed. An amazing endeavor, rich with facts, well documented with images, clean, clear, accessible design. An exquisite and important book—accessible, packed with interesting, important and fun facts about the alphabet."
—Jan Fairbarin, Professor of Design, *Maine College of Art + Design*

"Type lovers take note of this unparalled visual history of the Latin alphabet."
—Don Tarello, Professor of Design, *Fitchburg State University*

"A wonderful journey through language, cultures, and time."
—Paulina Banas, Art Historian, *University of Albama at Birmingham*

"This book is a real reflection of its author's lovely nature by sending a message for peace and love within the great information she presents. She is trying to link the world and humanity by finding the origin of the Alphabet which forms languages that link the world together. I love it and I do appreciate her years of research and effort to give us such a very valuable and interesting book full of knowledge and evidence. Thank you Colleen."
—Lamia Afifi, Artist-in-Residence, *Modern English School Cairo*

"Excerpts of this book are being used to teaching Kurdish archaeologists online; it is being referred to it in a series of lectures on literacy for a teacher training university in Phnom Penh; and I am using it with architecture students in Cambodia… investigating origins…vernacular, early technology… How did we start building? When did we start writing? How do ideas travel?"
—Barbara Anello, Art Historian, *Royal University of Fine Arts, Phnom Penh*

"Fascinating."
—Maura McGurk, Writer/Editor

THE ACCOUNTANT, THE KING, THE PRIEST, AND THE POET

Also by the Author

ABCing: Seeing the Alphabet Differently

THE ACCOUNTANT, THE KING, THE PRIEST, AND THE POET

A VISUAL HISTORY OF THE ALPHABET

COLLEEN COMERFORD

WE ARE ONE نحن واحد
PUBLISHING للنشر

JEDDAH CAIRO BOSTON

WE ARE ONE نحن واحد
PUBLISHING للنشر

JEDDAH CAIRO BOSTON

ISBN 979 8 218 80024 6

Library of Congress Control Number: 2025911300

Book design by Colleen Comerford

All photos and illustrations are either created by the author, in the public domain, or credited.

10 9 8 7 6 5 4 3 2 Second Edition.

Cover: Detail from the *Blau Monuments*, 3300–3000 BCE © The Trustees of the British Museum.

To Hannah & Carina

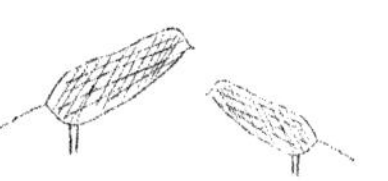

Animal, Grafitti, ca. 78 BCE, House of the Stags, Herculaneum, Italy (IV.21) 83, Abb. 228.

Linguists, artists, visionaries, kings, even novelists and poets, have designed many scripts, but it is missionaries, teachers, traders, administrators and immigrants—both conquerors and refugees—who actually spread them around.
—Robert Bringhurst, *The Elements of Typographic Style*

Just as flowing water follows gravity, letters follow language. Their job is to show sounds of speech. If sounds change, so will letters, in some way, eventually.
—David Sacks, *Letter Perfect: The Marvelous History of Our Alphabet From A to Z*

ACKNOWLEDGEMENTS

This book began an idea in 2006, during graduate school. In 2010, while teaching in Jeddah, Saudi Arabia, this idea began to take shape as three large mind map drawings. By 2017, back in Boston, the project evolved into a list of twenty-six artifacts, an outline, and a very rough draft. A year later, while working in Cairo, Egypt, that draft slowly evolved into the book you are now holding. Over the years, and across several countries, many people have encouraged, advised, and supported me.

As a graduate student, I was fortunate to work with Jan Fairbairn at the University of Massachusetts Dartmouth, who flipped the typographic switch—thank you.

At Dar Al Hekma University in Jeddah, I was grateful for the support of generous colleagues, including Lina Najjar, Cordula Peters, and Emilie Burnham, who offered thoughtful feedback on both early and late drafts—thank you.

In the United States, Don Tarallo invited me into his classroom to share the manuscript with his students and supported the publishing process. Michael Huspek offered thoughtful insights into Socrates, Plato, and the ongoing debate over whether writing is a benefit or a burden to society. Maura McGurk brought a careful eye and valuable suggestions that strengthened the text. Elizabeth DeNoma provided invaluable guidance on the book proposal—thank you all.

During my continued research in Cairo (2018–2023), Lamia Afifi assisted with Arabic translations; Terese Cuff suggested including a glossary; and Omar Mohamed Eissa served as translator throughout Cairo, Alexandria, and Rashid—thank you. Particularly between 2020 and 2023, the digitization of critical historical resources—by the Library of Congress, the Bodleian Libraries at the University of Oxford, the British Library, the Library of Trinity College Dublin, and the Ancient Graffiti Project—along with the work of David Sacks and others, made this project possible.

To the Mass Cultural Council—thank you for your generous financial support in producing the First Edition of this book.

To my students, past and present—you make this journey meaningful and fun.

To my sister, Lynn Comerford, and my niece, Ellie—thank you for your unwavering encouragement every step of the way.

To my daughters, Hannah and Carina, who have watched this book take shape over twenty-five years with patience, encouragement, and love, who make it all worthwhile—I am forever grateful.

CONTENTS

INTRODUCTION 17
ILLUSTRATED MAP 20
LATIN ALPHABET FAMILY TREE 22
I GEOMETRIC SIGNS 24
II PHYSICAL OBJECTS 26
1 PICTOGRAPHIC 28
2 HIEROGLYPHS 30
3 PROTO-CUNEIFORM 32
4 HIEROGLYPHS 34
5 HIERATIC 36
6 EARLY ALPHABETIC 38
7 EARLY ALPHABETIC AND HIEROGLYPHS 40
8 PHOENICIAN 42
9 PHOENICIAN IN ARCHAIC GREEK 44
10 PHOENICIAN 46
11 ARCHAIC GREEK 48
12 ARCHAIC GREEK 50
13 ARCHAIC GREEN AND ETRUSCAN 52

14 ARCHAIC LATIN 54
15 ETRUSCAN 56
16 ARCHAIC LATIN 58
17 ARCHAIC LATIN 60
18 PHOENICIAN AND ETRUSCAN 62
19 CLASSICAL GREEK 64
20 HIEROGLYPHS, DEMOTIC, AND HELLENISTIC GREEK 66
21 EVERYDAY (VULGER) LATIN AND GREEK 68
22 CLASSICAL LATIN 70
23 MEDIEVAL LATIN 72
24 OLD ENGLISH 74
25 SPANISH 76
26 AMERICAN ENGLISH 78
AFTERWORD 80
GLOSSARY 82
LIST OF ILLUSTRATIONS 85
BIBLIOGRAPHY 87
COLOPHON

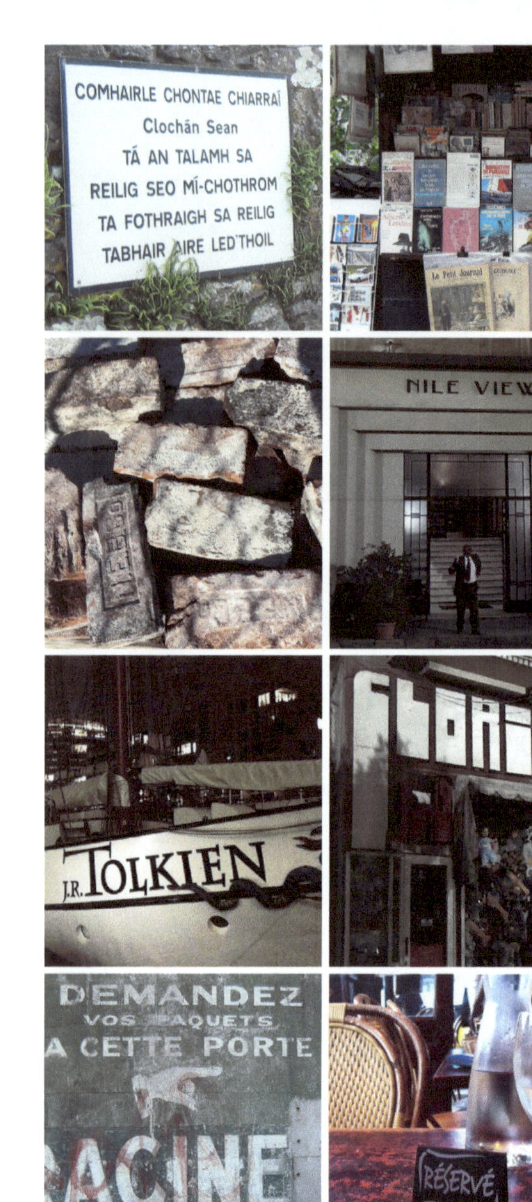
COMHAIRLE CHONTAE CHIARRAÍ
Clochán Sean
TÁ AN TALAMH SA
REILIG SEO MÍ-CHOTHROM
TA FOTHRAIGH SA REILIG
TABHAIR AIRE LED'THOIL
NILE VIEW
J.R. TOLKIEN

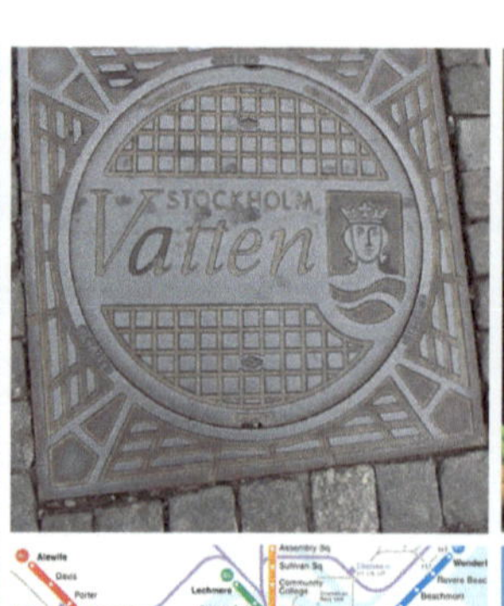
STOCKHOLM
Vatten

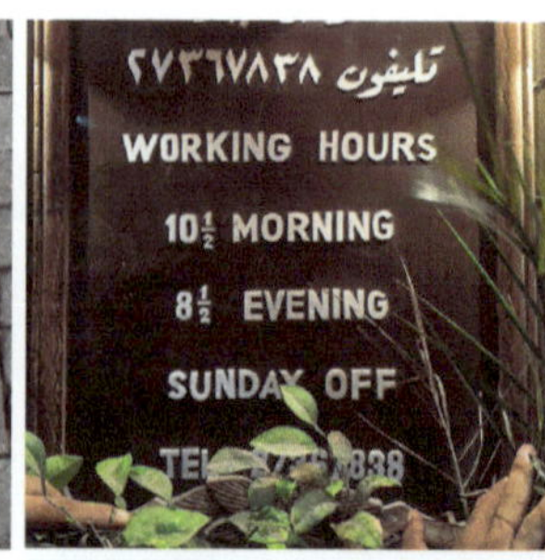
تليفون ٢٧٣٦٧٨٣٨
WORKING HOURS
10½ MORNING
8½ EVENING
SUNDAY OFF

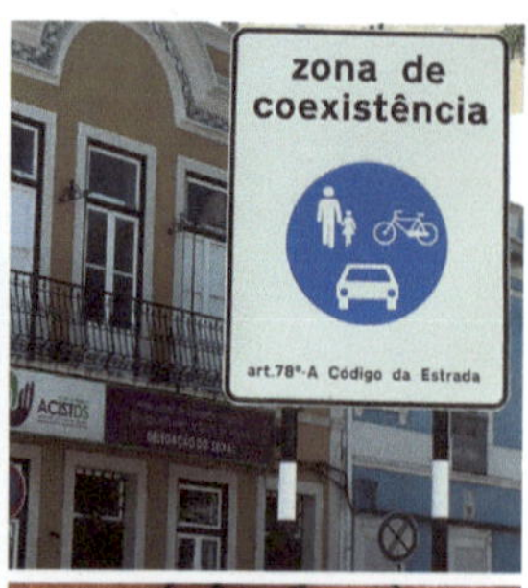
zona de
coexistência
art.78º-A Código da Estrada

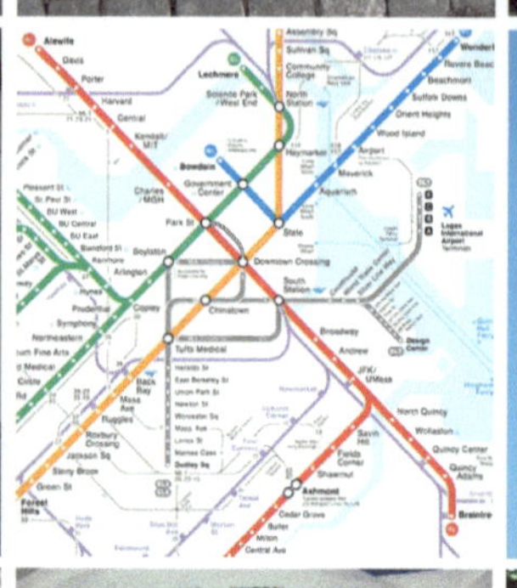

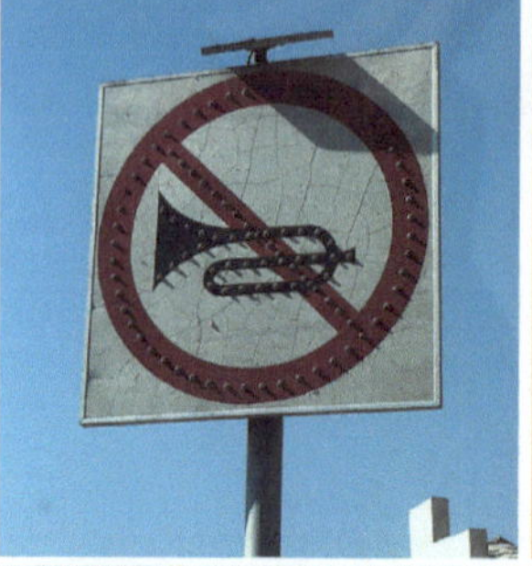

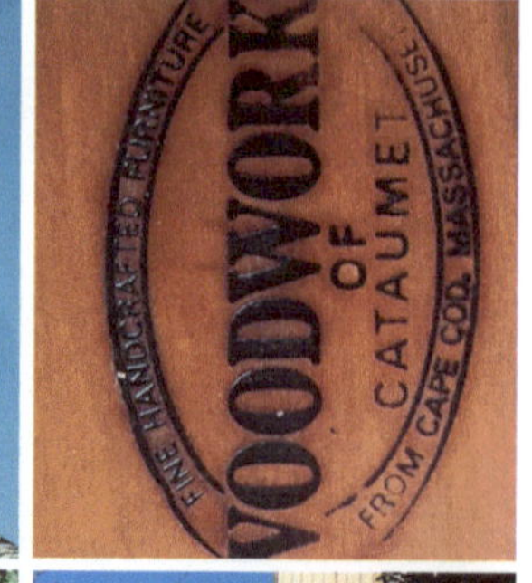
WOODWORK
OF
CATAUMET
FINE HANDCRAFTED FURNITURE
FROM CAPE COD, MASSACHUSETTS

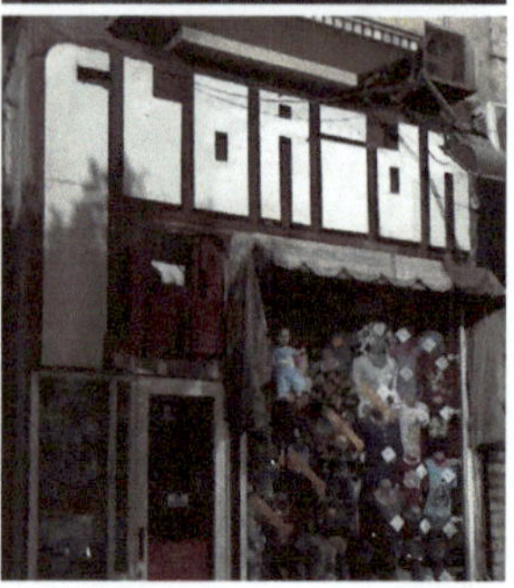

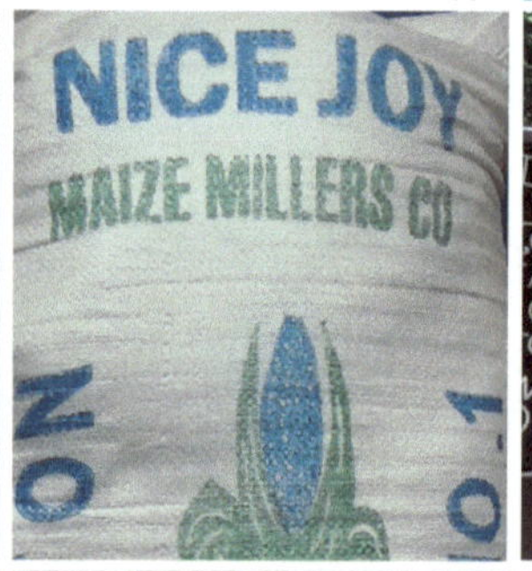
NICE JOY
MAIZE MILLERS CO

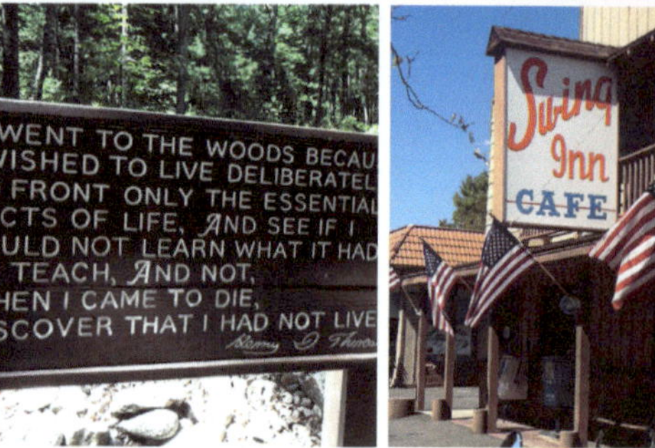
I WENT TO THE WOODS BECAU
WISHED TO LIVE DELIBERATEL
O FRONT ONLY THE ESSENTIAL
ACTS OF LIFE, AND SEE IF I
OULD NOT LEARN WHAT IT HAD
O TEACH, AND NOT,
WHEN I CAME TO DIE,
DISCOVER THAT I HAD NOT LIVE
Swing
Inn
CAFE

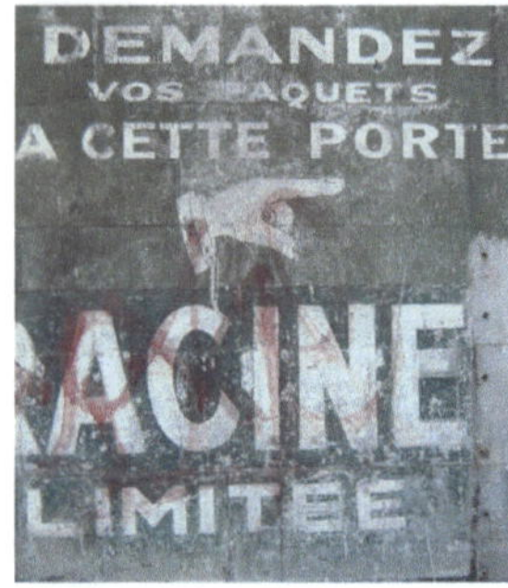
DEMANDEZ
VOS PAQUETS
A CETTE PORTE
RACINE
LIMITÉE

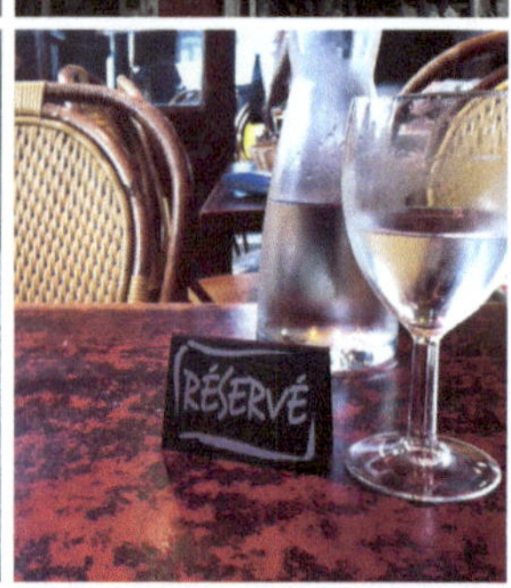
RÉSERVÉ

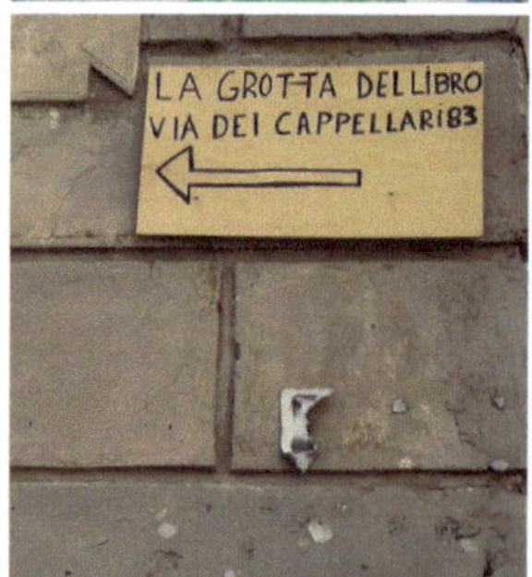
LA GROTTA DEL LIBRO
VIA DEI CAPPELLARI 83

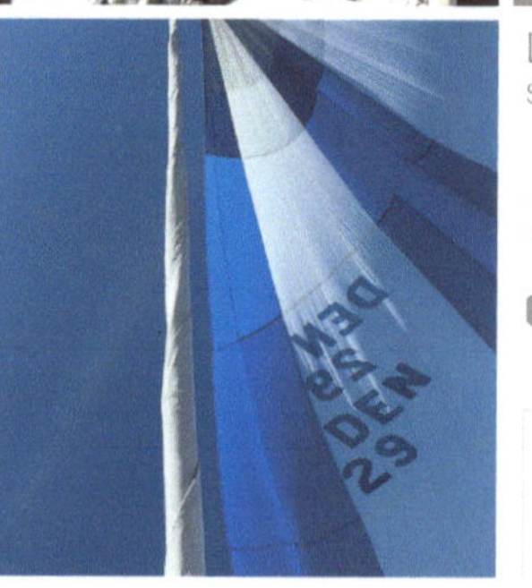

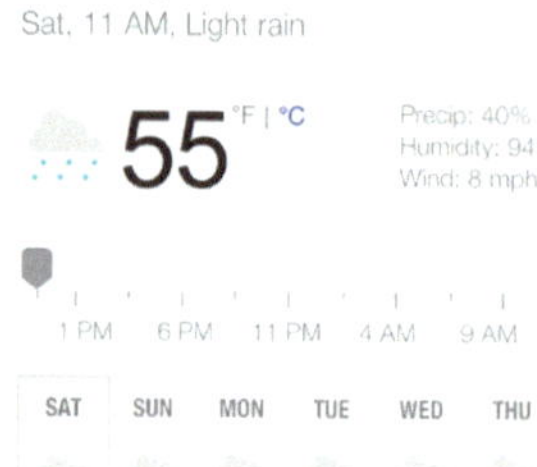
La Gruyère
Sat, 11 AM, Light rain
55 °F | °C
Precip: 40%
Humidity: 94
Wind: 8 mph
1 PM 6 PM 11 PM 4 AM 9 AM
SAT SUN MON TUE WED THU
70° 70° 66° 64° 68° 73°

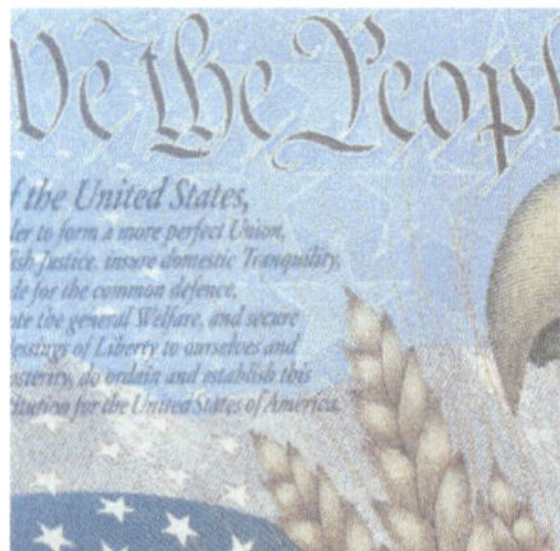
We the People

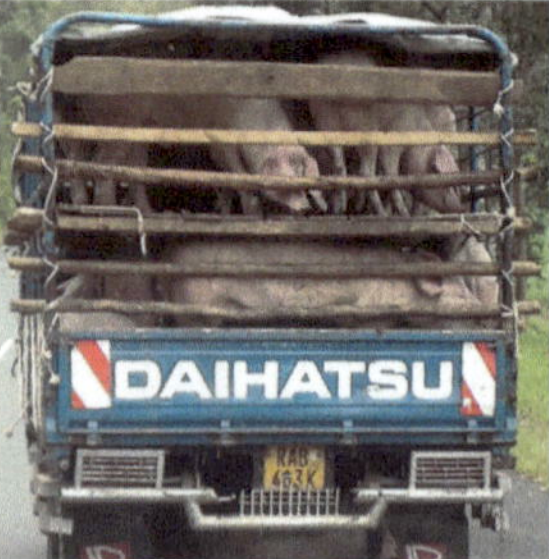
DAIHATSU

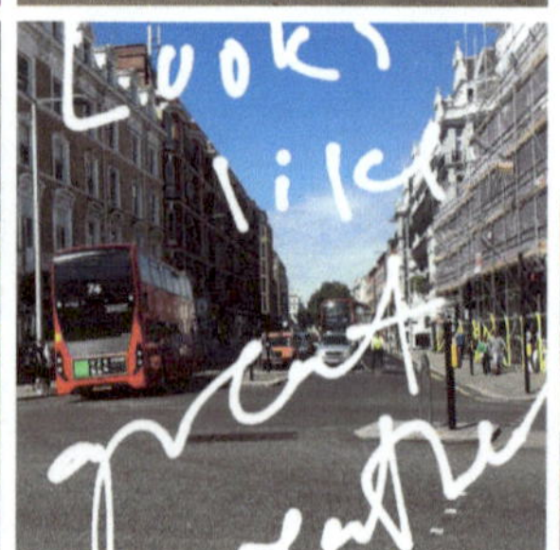

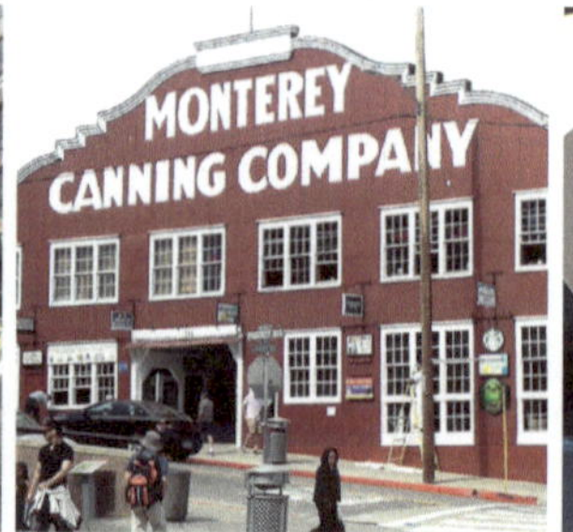
MONTEREY
CANNING COMPANY

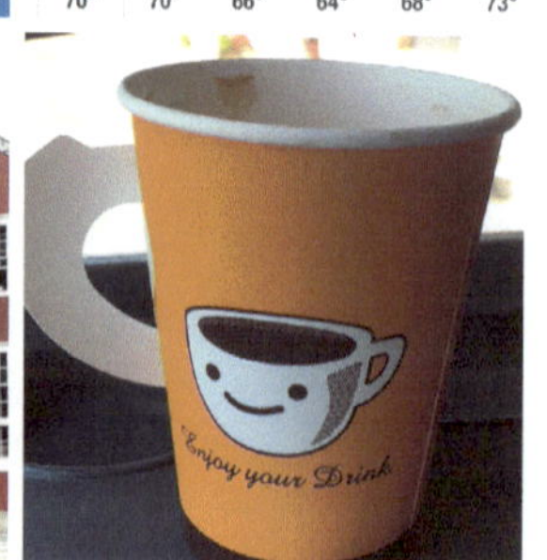
Enjoy your Drink

INTRODUCTION

The word *alphabet* appears in Latin as *alphabetum*, first mentioned by scholar and writer Tertullian (ca. 155 - 230 CE) and by Saint Jerome (ca. 340 - 420 CE). Etymologically it comes from the first two letters of the Phoenician alphabet: *aleph, beth*. When the Greeks adopted the Phoenician alphabet, they called it *alphabetos* from the first two letters in their alphabet: *alpha, beta*.

At this moment in history, humans speak over six thousand languages. Of those, more than one thousand use Latin-based alphabets, representing over two billion speakers. From Romance languages such as Portuguese, Spanish, and French, to Germanic languages including German, English, and the Scandinavian tongues, all rely on the Latin alphabet. Disparate languages such as Afar—spoken in Djibouti, Eritrea, and Ethiopia—and Zazaki—spoken in eastern Turkey, northern Iraq, and Iran—also employ Latin-based alphabets. These alphabets are used by all twelve Slavic languages not written in Cyrillic, as well as by languages like Navajo, Hopi, and Swahili, and across many Polynesian and Southeast Asian language groups. Nearly wherever you go, you see these alphabetic forms—either alone or alongside local scripts. The Latin alphabet is the most adaptable and adapted alphabetic system in the world.

But where do these letters come from?

I wrote *The Accountant, the King, the Priest, and the Poet* to satisfy my curiosity about that very question. In graduate school, I taught a typography course to undergraduate graphic design students. One of their first assignments was to choose a single letter from the Phoenician, Greek, Etruscan, or Latin alphabets and to create an informative poster about it. Pretty basic stuff. But at the time, I knew little (nothing) about early typographic history. When I discovered that nineteen of our twenty-six modern letters could be traced back—in shape, sequence, and even sound—to their Phoenician counterparts from three thousand years ago, I was compelled to learn more.

My search deepened four years later, while teaching Latin Typography at a women's university in Jeddah, Saudi Arabia. I was struck by how my students and colleagues—raised in the region where writing first emerged—already possessed a deep awareness and appreciation for how their rich histories and cultures were intertwined with the evolution of the alphabet. Their perspectives inspired me and fueled my desire to see more, learn more, and better understand the alphabet's origins.

Though I include a brief introduction to geometric signs and physical tokens as symbols of pre-writing, this story begins in Sumer—modern-day Syria, Iran, and Iraq—around 3500 BCE, with the abstract idea of pictures representing sound. It ends in the United States with the formal acceptance of the letter J into Noah Webster's *American Dictionary of the English Language* in 1828. This book offers a broad and accessible historical overview of where, when, why, how, and by whom the alphabet was developed. It is intended to provide design students with a deeper appreciation of the alphabet's origins—offering historical context for design decisions and connecting ancient forms to contemporary visual communication.

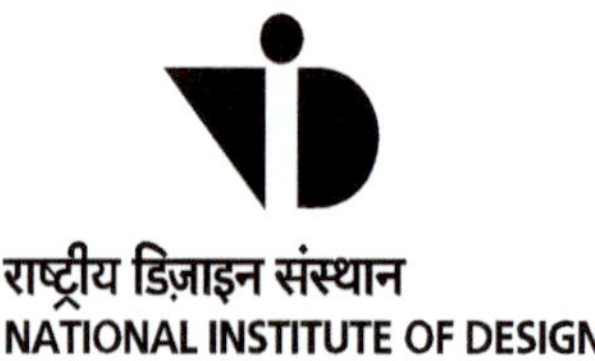

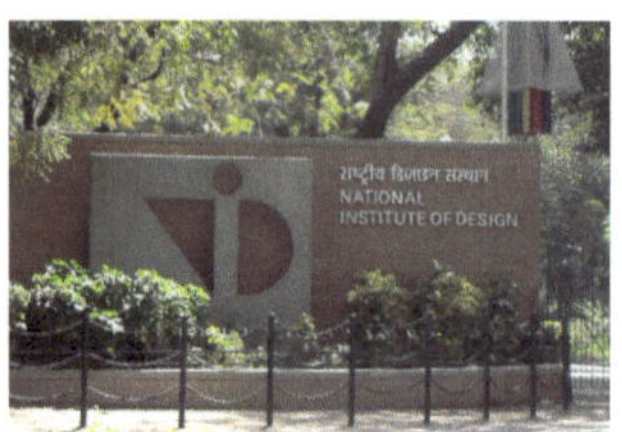

The entrance to the National Institute of Design, Ahmedabad, India.

Swiss type designer Adrian Frutiger (1928–2015) was invited to design a new visual identity for the school, as well as a new Devanagari font (see above photo). His goal was "to simplify the sacred characters, without compromising their ancient calligraphic expression." It was during this time in India, as he shared with Matthew Carter, that he improved his English.

Early in his career, Frutiger moved from his birthplace of Unterseen, Switzerland to Paris in 1952 to work for the type foundry Deberny & Peignot. Over the course of his career, he designed numerous visual identities and more than thirty typefaces—including the one you are reading, Avenir. Like the Phoenicians, Greeks, Etruscans, and Romans before him, he traveled and exchanged ideas with others, contributing to the advancement, clarity, and beauty of letterforms.

As Robert Bringhurst wrote in *The Elements of Typographic Style*:

> *Typography never occurs in isolation. Good typography demands not only a knowledge of type itself, but an understanding of the relationship between letterforms and the other things that humans make and do. Typographic history is just that: the study of the relationships between type designs and the rest of human activity—politics, philosophy, the arts, and the history of ideas.*

This book begins with an illustrative map showing twenty-six numbered artifacts spanning five thousand years of alphabetic history. Each artifact is featured on the left side of a spread, highlighting a specific period of development, while the right side reflects contemporary practice. These artifacts trace the alphabet's evolution from preliterate, oral societies to ones that documented trade, law, religion, and literature. The forms evolved from Sumer, moved to Egypt, spread through the Levant and the Mediterranean, into Europe, and finally to the Americas. Whether carved, incised, painted, or written, each artifact reflects the human need to record time, to teach, to learn, and, to tell stories. They document victories, treaties, love stories, births, deaths, marriages, rituals, tax records, and trade agreements—each a testament to human creativity, innovation, and problem-solving.

As Egyptologist Barry Kemp wrote in *Ancient Egypt: Anatomy of a Civilization*:

Chronology enables us to follow changing patterns over time and to chart progress towards our own modern world. But too great a concern with 'history'—with dates and the chronicling of events—can become a barrier to seeing the societies and civilizations of the past for what they really were: solutions to the problems of individual and collective existence which we can add to the range of solutions apparent in the contemporary world.

This book distills the history of the alphabet into twenty-six objects across twenty-six spreads, showing how societies evolved through the progression of writing. When we talk about writing, we're also talking about language and sound. Each object, whether innovative or everyday, is a record of how writing systems and spoken language evolved over time.

Among the twenty-six artifacts, five are bilingual or trilingual, reflecting two key ideas:

1. When a text appears in multiple languages, scholars can better decipher unknown scripts by comparing sounds and forms—*The Rosetta Stone* being the most famous example.

2. Such texts reflect multilingual societies and the ongoing interaction between cultures over millennia.

In my research, I found dozens of bilingual documents—from Adelaide's *Bilingual Mandate* (1109 CE), written in Greek and Arabic (see page 69), to Erasmus's *Novum Testamentum* (1519 CE), written in Greek and Latin (see page 73). In Pompeii (79 BCE), Greek and Latin appear side by side, and in southern Egypt near today's Sudanese border, Greek graffiti (593 BCE) is etched into the colossal sandstone leg of Ramses II (see page 51). Whether through colonization, trade, religion, or war, these cultural interactions introduced new ideas, technologies, and innovations—that shaped the development of the Latin alphabet.

As the alphabet was adopted across the Mediterranean, many variations arose. The twenty-six artifacts presented here—aside from the *Rosetta Stone*—trace what would ultimately become the modern alphabet. Some are ordinary in form and function (like the clay wine jug, or *oinochoe*, with the Dipylon Inscription, ca. 740 BCE, page 44), while others are rare and extraordinary (like the golden cloak pin, known as the *Praeneste Fibula*, ca. 650 BCE, page 50). Their survival is a testament to both human ingenuity and historical luck.

This book offers a *weltanschauung*—a broader worldview—of our alphabet and a tool for exploring it more deeply. As Sheila Levrant de Bretteville wrote in an announcement poster for the CalArts School of Design (1970):

> *If the designer is to make a deliberate contribution to society, he must be able to integrate all he can learn about behavior and resources, ecology and human needs; taste and style just aren't enough.*

This book serves as a starting point for students of graphic design and curious readers alike—anyone interested in gaining a deeper understanding and appreciation for how the alphabet came to be. It offers an opportunity to honor all those, both known and unknown, who contributed to its evolution: the accountants, kings, queens, priests, priestesses, and poets.

Colleen Comerford

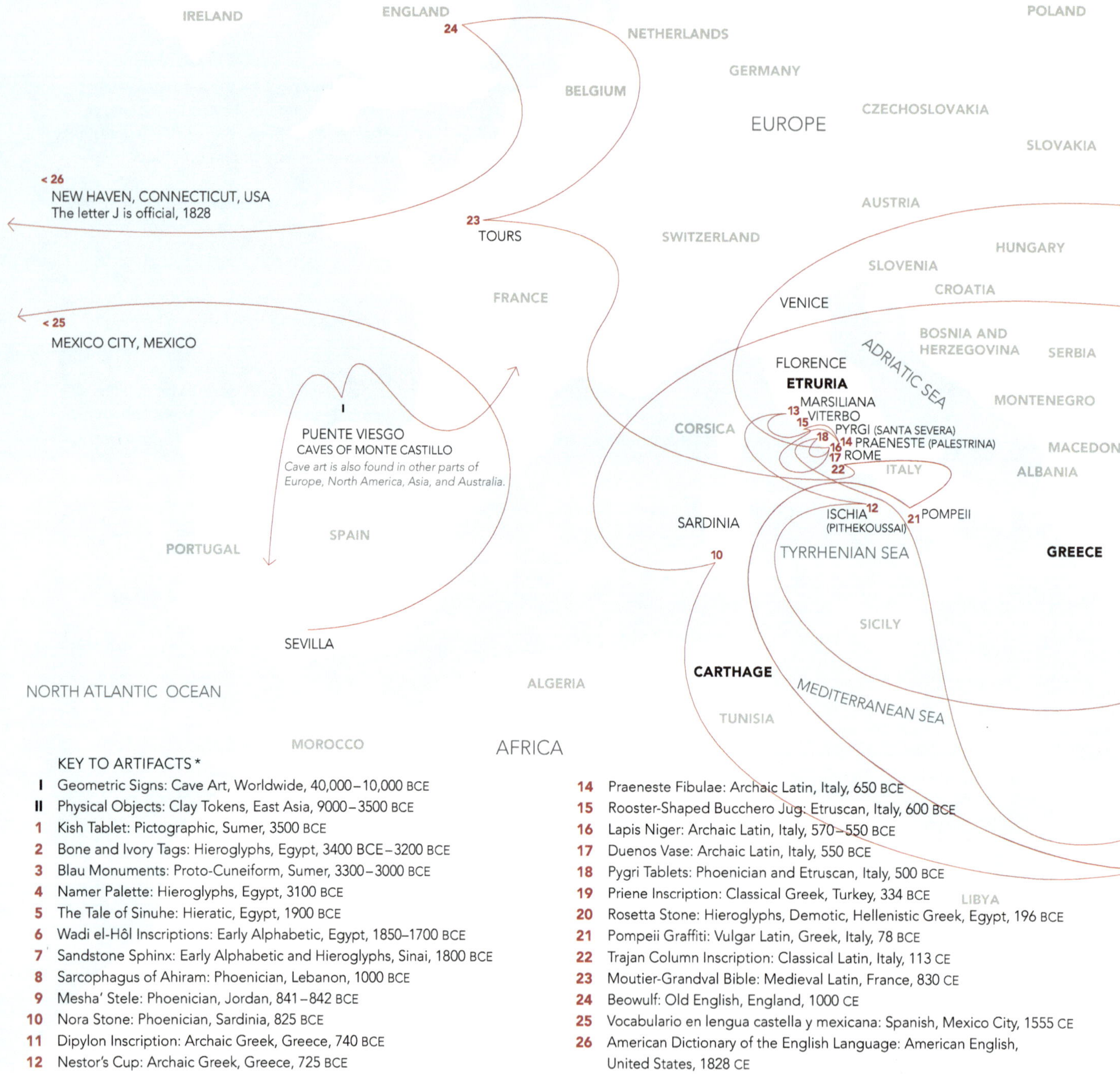

KEY TO ARTIFACTS *

- **I** Geometric Signs: Cave Art, Worldwide, 40,000–10,000 BCE
- **II** Physical Objects: Clay Tokens, East Asia, 9000–3500 BCE
- **1** Kish Tablet: Pictographic, Sumer, 3500 BCE
- **2** Bone and Ivory Tags: Hieroglyphs, Egypt, 3400 BCE–3200 BCE
- **3** Blau Monuments: Proto-Cuneiform, Sumer, 3300–3000 BCE
- **4** Namer Palette: Hieroglyphs, Egypt, 3100 BCE
- **5** The Tale of Sinuhe: Hieratic, Egypt, 1900 BCE
- **6** Wadi el-Hôl Inscriptions: Early Alphabetic, Egypt, 1850–1700 BCE
- **7** Sandstone Sphinx: Early Alphabetic and Hieroglyphs, Sinai, 1800 BCE
- **8** Sarcophagus of Ahiram: Phoenician, Lebanon, 1000 BCE
- **9** Mesha' Stele: Phoenician, Jordan, 841–842 BCE
- **10** Nora Stone: Phoenician, Sardinia, 825 BCE
- **11** Dipylon Inscription: Archaic Greek, Greece, 740 BCE
- **12** Nestor's Cup: Archaic Greek, Greece, 725 BCE
- **13** Marsiliana Tablet: Archaic Greek and Etruscan, Italy, 700 BCE
- **14** Praeneste Fibulae: Archaic Latin, Italy, 650 BCE
- **15** Rooster-Shaped Bucchero Jug: Etruscan, Italy, 600 BCE
- **16** Lapis Niger: Archaic Latin, Italy, 570–550 BCE
- **17** Duenos Vase: Archaic Latin, Italy, 550 BCE
- **18** Pygri Tablets: Phoenician and Etruscan, Italy, 500 BCE
- **19** Priene Inscription: Classical Greek, Turkey, 334 BCE
- **20** Rosetta Stone: Hieroglyphs, Demotic, Hellenistic Greek, Egypt, 196 BCE
- **21** Pompeii Graffiti: Vulgar Latin, Greek, Italy, 78 BCE
- **22** Trajan Column Inscription: Classical Latin, Italy, 113 CE
- **23** Moutier-Grandval Bible: Medieval Latin, France, 830 CE
- **24** Beowulf: Old English, England, 1000 CE
- **25** Vocabulario en lengua castella y mexicana: Spanish, Mexico City, 1555 CE
- **26** American Dictionary of the English Language: American English, United States, 1828 CE

* NOTE: Though this map follows one sequential circuitous route, the journey of the alphabet followed a thousand different paths.

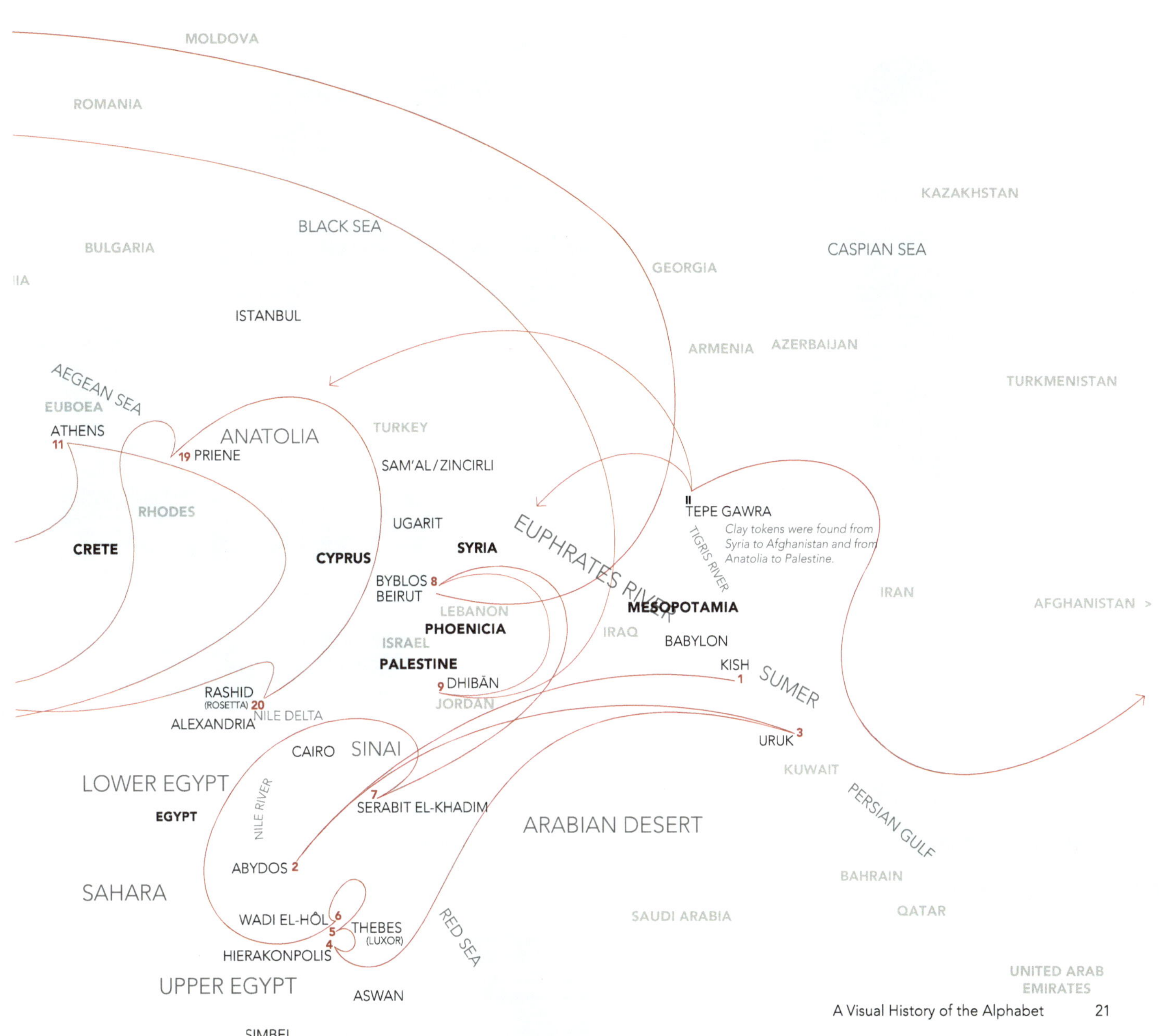
RUSSIA
UKRAINE
MOLDOVA
ROMANIA
BLACK SEA
BULGARIA
KAZAKHSTAN
CASPIAN SEA
GEORGIA
ISTANBUL
ARMENIA
AZERBAIJAN
TURKMENISTAN
AEGEAN SEA
EUBOEA
ATHENS
11
19 PRIENE
ANATOLIA
TURKEY
SAM'AL / ZINCIRLI
RHODES
UGARIT
II
TEPE GAWRA
TIGRIS RIVER
Clay tokens were found from Syria to Afghanistan and from Anatolia to Palestine.
CRETE
CYPRUS
SYRIA
EUPHRATES RIVER
BYBLOS 8
BEIRUT
LEBANON
PHOENICIA
ISRAEL
PALESTINE
MESOPOTAMIA
IRAQ
BABYLON
KISH
1
SUMER
IRAN
AFGHANISTAN >
9 DHIBĀN
JORDAN
RASHID
(ROSETTA) 20
ALEXANDRIA
NILE DELTA
CAIRO
SINAI
URUK
3
KUWAIT
LOWER EGYPT
EGYPT
NILE RIVER
7
SERABIT EL-KHADIM
ARABIAN DESERT
PERSIAN GULF
ABYDOS 2
SAHARA
BAHRAIN
QATAR
SAUDI ARABIA
WADI EL-HÔL 6
5
THEBES
(LUXOR)
4
HIERAKONPOLIS
RED SEA
UPPER EGYPT
ASWAN
UNITED ARAB EMIRATES
SIMBEL
OMAN

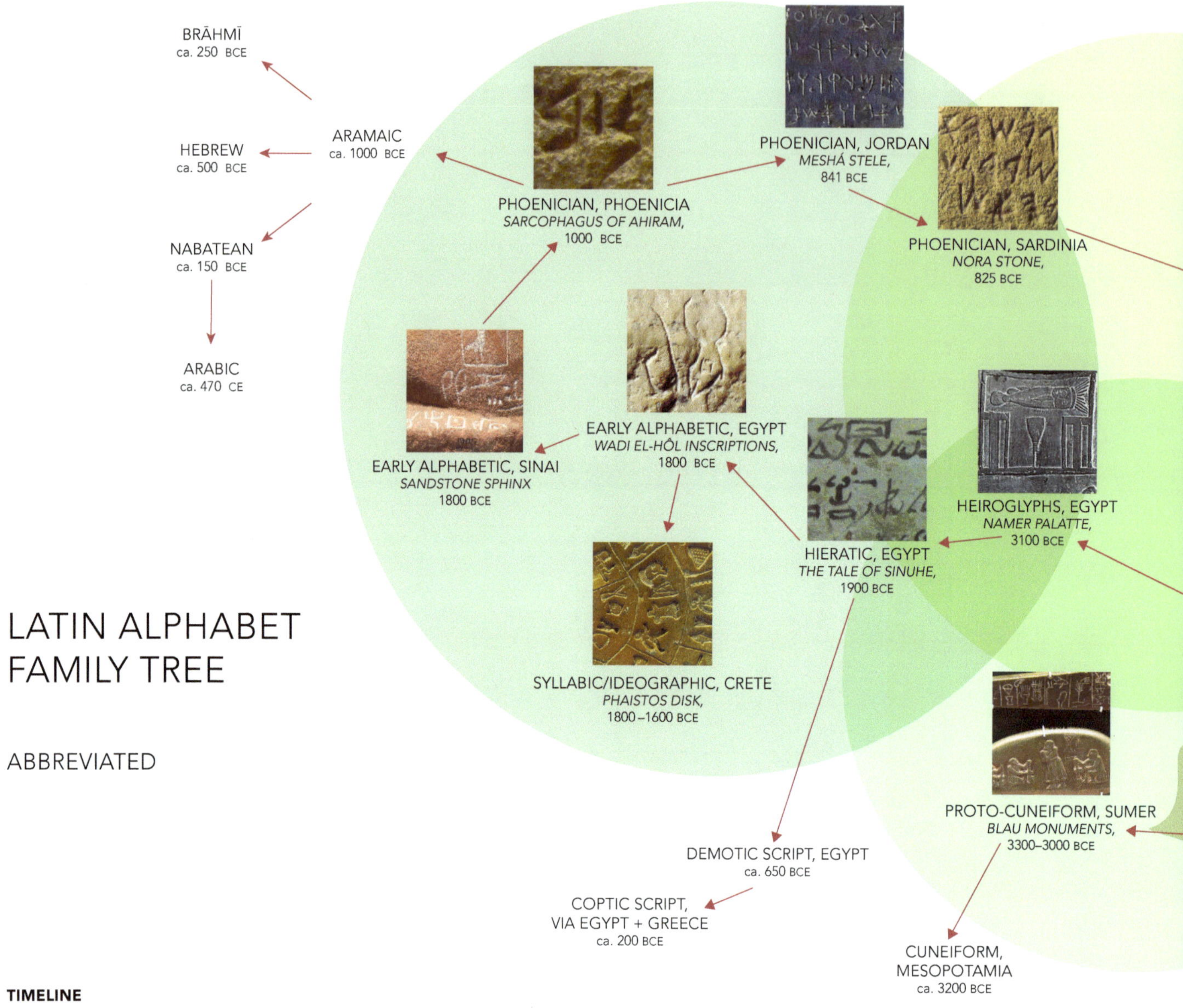

LATIN ALPHABET FAMILY TREE

ABBREVIATED

TIMELINE

EARLY ALPHABETIC
ca. 1800–1500 BCE

CANAANITE
before 1200 BCE
Historically, geographically, and culturally synonymous with Phoenician

PHOENICIAN
after 1200 BCE

ARCHAIC GREEK
ca. 800 BCE–479 BCE

ETRUSCAN
ca. 900 BCE– 27 BCE
after the Villanovan culture

ARCHAIC LATIN
ca. 750 BCE–75 BCE
Also known as Old Latin

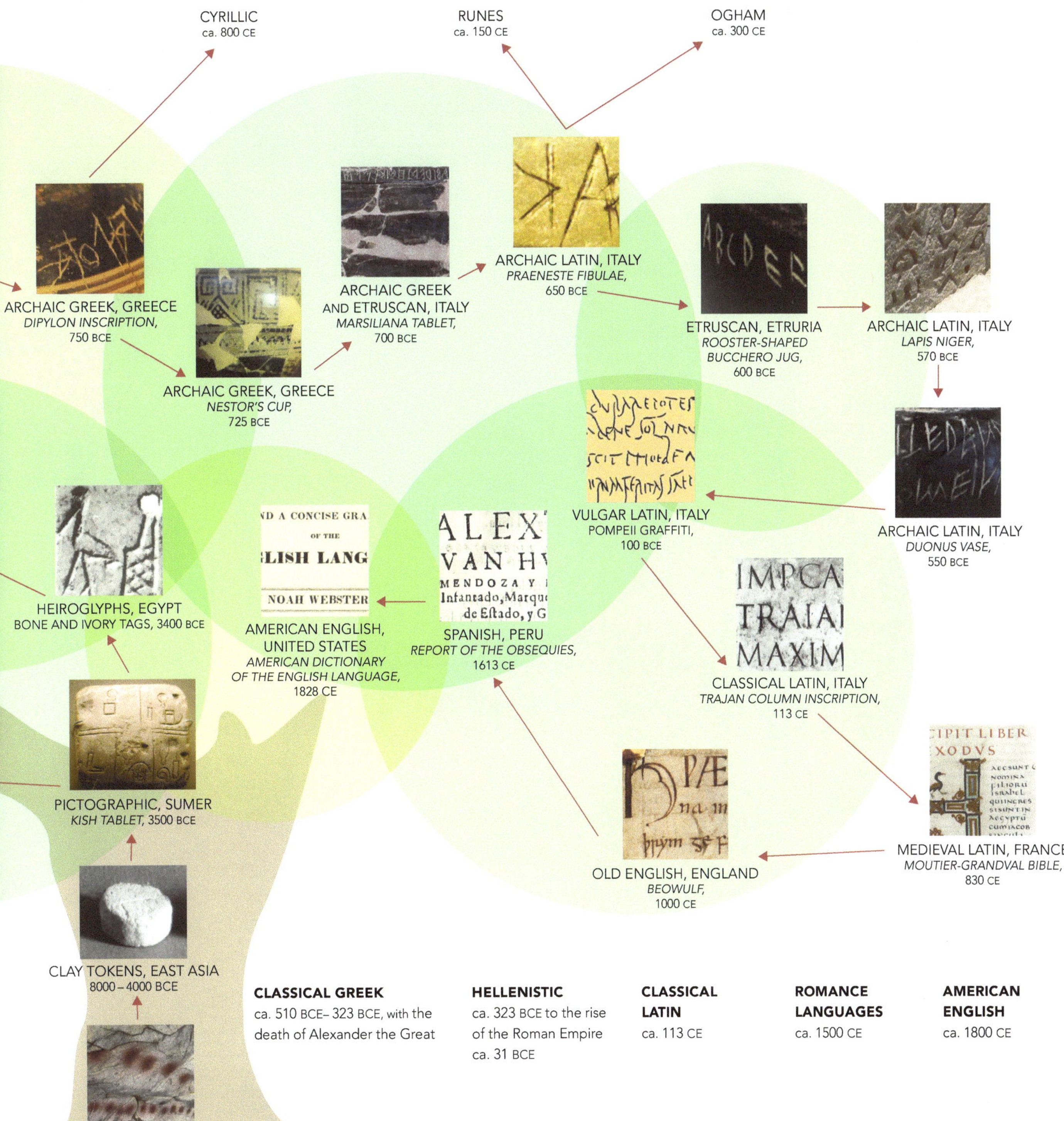
CYRILLIC
ca. 800 CE
RUNES
ca. 150 CE
OGHAM
ca. 300 CE
ARCHAIC GREEK, GREECE
DIPYLON INSCRIPTION,
750 BCE
ARCHAIC GREEK, GREECE
NESTOR'S CUP,
725 BCE
ARCHAIC GREEK
AND ETRUSCAN, ITALY
MARSILIANA TABLET,
700 BCE
ARCHAIC LATIN, ITALY
PRAENESTE FIBULAE,
650 BCE
ETRUSCAN, ETRURIA
ROOSTER-SHAPED
BUCCHERO JUG,
600 BCE
ARCHAIC LATIN, ITALY
LAPIS NIGER,
570 BCE
ARCHAIC LATIN, ITALY
DUONUS VASE,
550 BCE
VULGAR LATIN, ITALY
POMPEII GRAFFITI,
100 BCE
CLASSICAL LATIN, ITALY
TRAJAN COLUMN INSCRIPTION,
113 CE
MEDIEVAL LATIN, FRANCE
MOUTIER-GRANDVAL BIBLE,
830 CE
OLD ENGLISH, ENGLAND
BEOWULF,
1000 CE
SPANISH, PERU
REPORT OF THE OBSEQUIES,
1613 CE
AMERICAN ENGLISH,
UNITED STATES
AMERICAN DICTIONARY
OF THE ENGLISH LANGUAGE,
1828 CE
HEIROGLYPHS, EGYPT
BONE AND IVORY TAGS, 3400 BCE
PICTOGRAPHIC, SUMER
KISH TABLET, 3500 BCE
CLAY TOKENS, EAST ASIA
8000 – 4000 BCE
GEOMETRIC SIGNS, WORLDWIDE
40,000 BCE
CLASSICAL GREEK
ca. 510 BCE– 323 BCE, with the death of Alexander the Great
HELLENISTIC
ca. 323 BCE to the rise of the Roman Empire ca. 31 BCE
CLASSICAL LATIN
ca. 113 CE
ROMANCE LANGUAGES
ca. 1500 CE
AMERICAN ENGLISH
ca. 1800 CE

I

40,000–10,000 BCE

GEOMETRIC SIGNS

WORLDWIDE

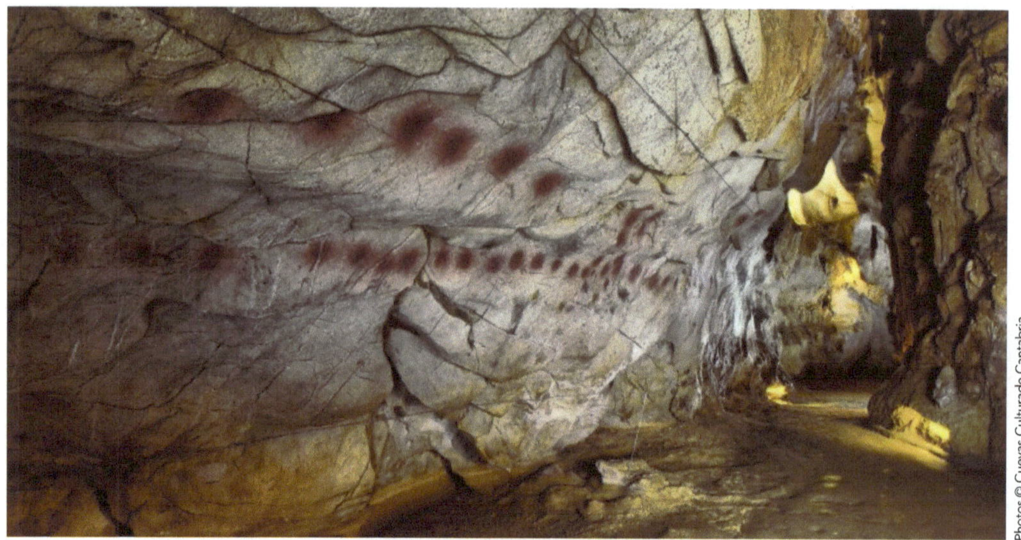
Photos © Cuevas Culturade Cantabria

El Castillo Cave Paintings, ca. 39,000 BCE, Spain. The world's oldest parietal art, or artwork done on cave walls or large stones, red-ochre disks and hand stencils. Discovered in 1908, the caves of Monte Castillo have the largest collection of rock art in the world, containing over five hundred paintings and engravings.

...there is a surprising degree of similarity in the earliest rock art found all the way from France and Spain to Indonesia and Australia. With many of the same signs appearing in such far-flung places, especially in that thirty to forty-thousand -year range, it's starting to seem increasingly likely that this invention actually traces back to a common point of origin in Africa.
—Genevieve von Petzinger, *Why Are These 32 Symbols Found in Caves All Over Europe* (2015)

THE HUMAN NEED TO CREATE, DOCUMENT, AND VISUALLY COMMUNICATE: IT BEGINS AS A VISUAL SYSTEM OF HUMAN IDEAS

There are three basic types of communication: verbal, nonverbal, and visual (graphic or written). Verbal communication is oral and includes storytelling. Nonverbal communication encompasses what is not said—such as facial expressions, body language, and appearance. Visual communication refers to the transmission of ideas through graphic symbols or written language, capable of reaching many people across time.

Historically, before the invention of technologies to record sound or movement, both verbal and nonverbal communication were entirely temporal; the exchange of ideas required the simultaneous presence of both parties. Visual communication, however, existed beyond the constraints of time. It allowed individuals to create enduring visual representations of ideas—messages that could be revisited and interpreted later. As Adrian Frutiger noted in *Signs and Symbols: Their Design and Meaning* (1989): "One of the most important aspects of human life and a basic condition for survival has always been the means of expression for mutual understanding between members of a tribal or social group."

Beginning in the Upper Paleolithic period, the oldest known prehistoric art—dating back over thirty-five thousand years—has been discovered around the world. This early art typically falls into three categories: petroglyphs (carvings), pictographs (paintings), and earth figures (large surface markings). In Europe alone, there are over 350 known rock art sites, with some of the oldest works found in the caves of Spain.

The purpose and creators of these works, and the reasons for their placement in deep, dark cave spaces, remain the subject of scholarly debate. Some researchers suggest they were linked to sacred rituals, perhaps intended to bring luck to hunting expeditions. Others propose they were created as part of coming-of-age ceremonies, or that they symbolized cosmic cycles, nature, and fertility. Scholar Genevieve von Petzinger studied fifty-two cave sites across France, Spain, Portugal, and Sicily. At seventy-five percent of these sites, she identified previously undocumented geometric signs. In most locations, these abstract symbols far outnumber depictions of animals or human figures. Remarkably, thirty-two specific signs appear repeatedly across a 30,000-year span throughout Europe—with few exceptions (see sidebar). Of these signs, sixty-five percent remained in continuous use during the entire period. Strikingly similar geometric signs appear worldwide from 40,000 to 30,000 years ago, pointing to their likely origins in Africa. The human impulse to express ideas, document experiences, and leave lasting marks—essentially to say, "we were here"—laid the groundwork for the invention of writing. As Christopher Woods writes in *Visible Language: The Earliest Writing Systems*: "Although writing is born of speech, it belongs to the realm of the visual rather than the oral and aural, and so has a different basis from speech."

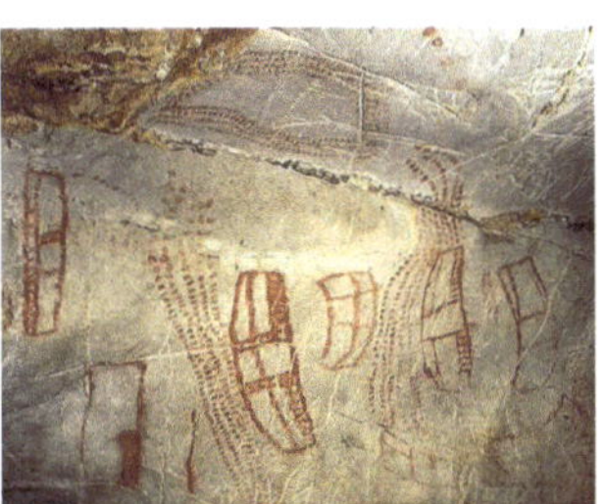

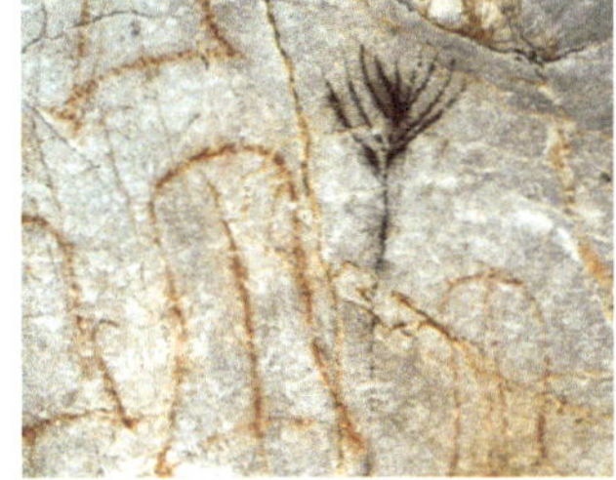

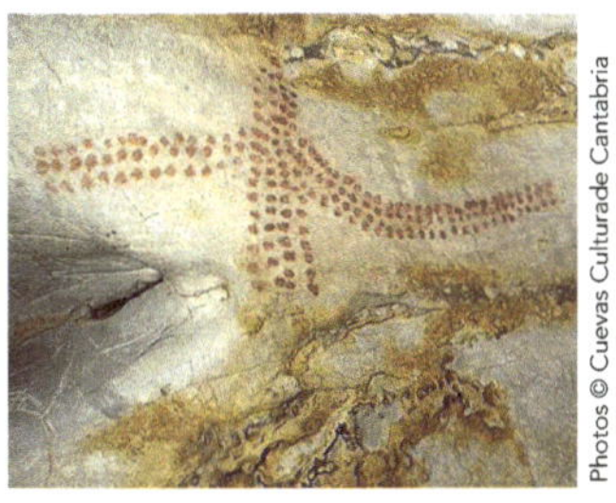

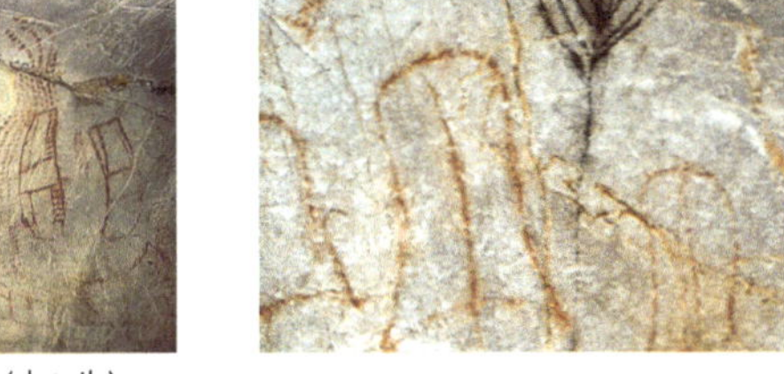

El Castillo Cave Paintings (details).

Photos © Cuevas Culturade Cantabria

GEOMETRIC SIGNS TODAY

A geometric sign is a fundamental unit of visual communication. It functions as an agreed-upon visual system for conveying human ideas—something that represents or stands in for something else. It may take the form of an emblem, token, letter, figure, mark, or a combination of these, used to designate or symbolize a concept or object.

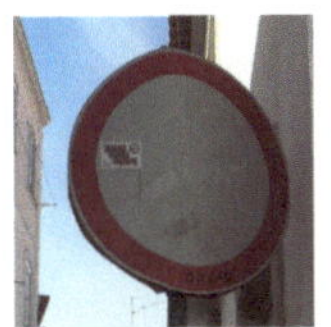

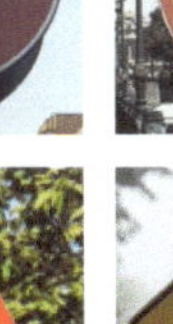

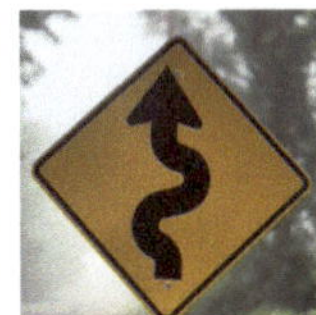

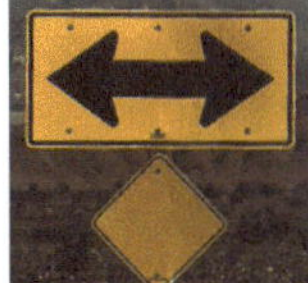

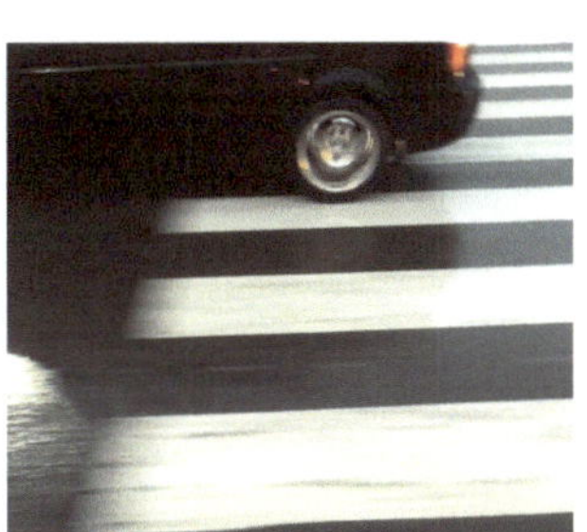

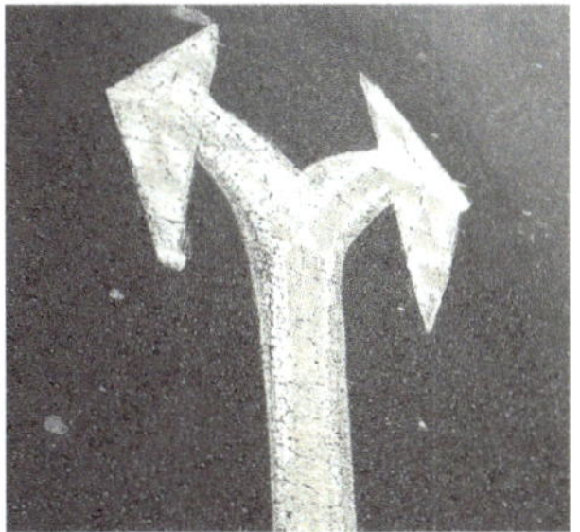

THIRTY-TWO PREHISTORY GEOMETRIC SIGNS

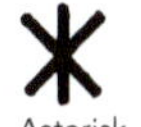
Asterisk

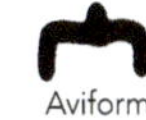
Aviform

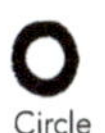
Circle

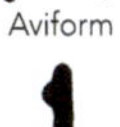
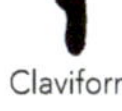
Claviform

Cordiform

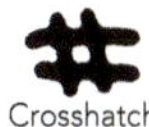
Crosshatch

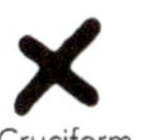
Cruciform

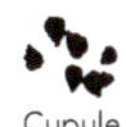
Cupule

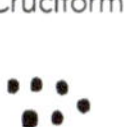
Dot

Finger Fluting

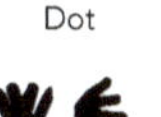
Flabelliform

Half-Circle

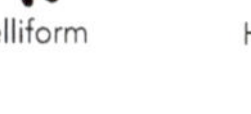
Line

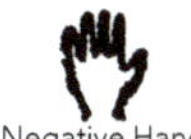
Negative Hand

Open-Angle

Oval

Pectiform

Penniform

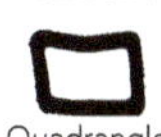
Positive Hand

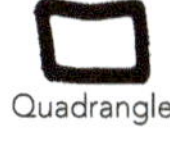
Quadrangle

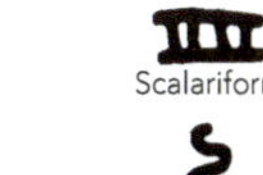
Reniform

Scalariform

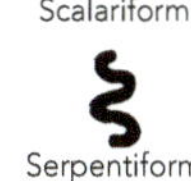
Segmented

Serpentiform

Spanish Tectiform

Spiral

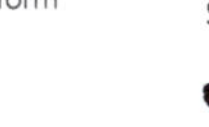
Tectiform

Triangle

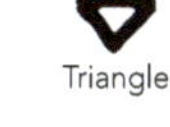
Unciform

W-Sign

Y-Sign

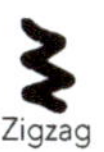
Zigzag

Illustrations by Genevieve von Petzinger.

I I

9000–3500 BCE

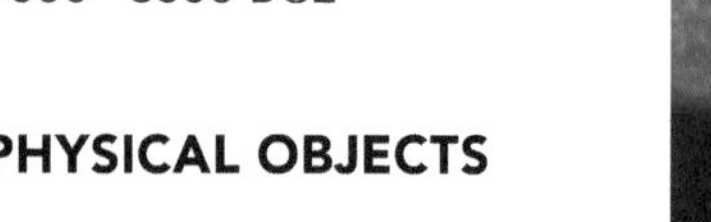

PHYSICAL OBJECTS

EAST ASIA

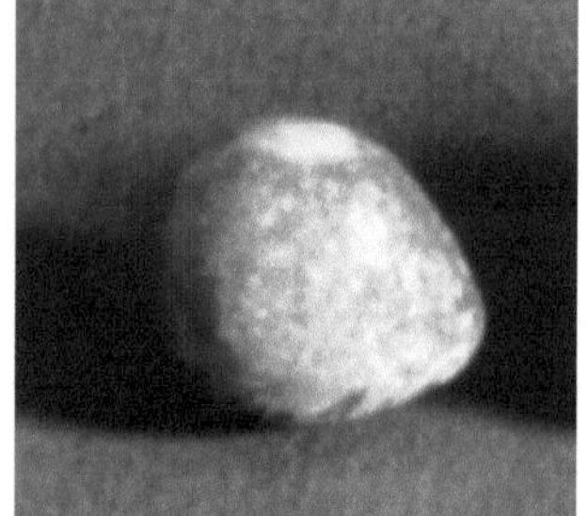
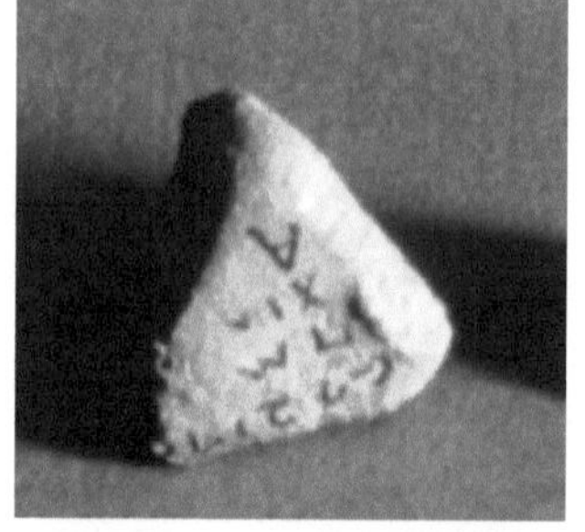
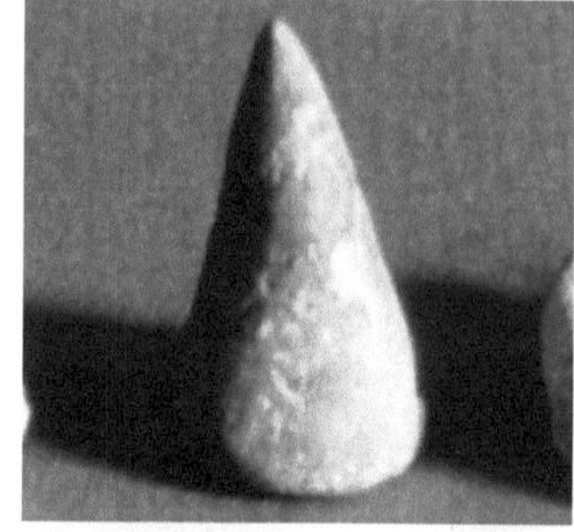
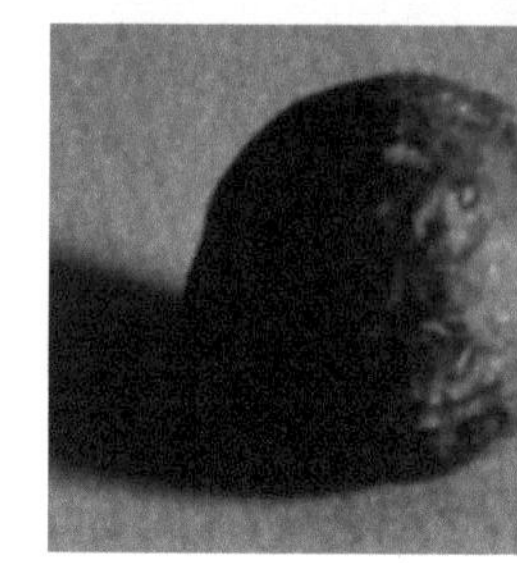
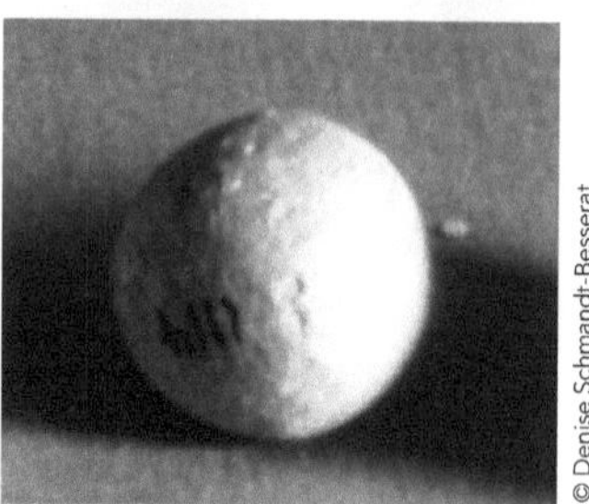

Plain tokens, ca. 4000 BCE, from Tepe Gawra, Iraq.

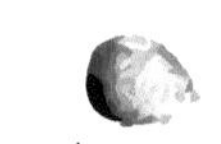
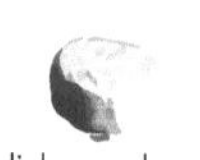

ovoid = a jar of oil disk = a sheep cone = small amount of barley sphere = large amount of barley

There can be no doubt that the simple clay tokens served well the Neolithic and Early Bronze communities since they were used consistently for five thousand years from Syria to Afghanistan and from Anatolia to Palestine.
—Denise Schmandt-Besserat, From Accounting to Writing (2015)

SOCIETIES PROSPER, TRADE GROWS, EXCHANGE IS DOCUMENTED

The region between the Euphrates and Tigris rivers—known as the Fertile Crescent or the Cradle of Civilization—is where trade first evolved. Its largest city was Uruk, which later became Al-Iraq, the Arabic name for Babylonia. By 3500 BCE, the estimated population of Uruk, a city along the Euphrates, had reached fifty thousand. As the population expanded, commerce became increasingly complex.

To manage trade, the Sumerians (4000–2000 BCE), a preliterate culture, developed a system for recording transactions. One method involved the use of clay tokens, either as individual units or sealed within clay envelopes. Each token represented a specific unit of a commodity—a three-dimensional form of an ideogram.

These tokens were made in six basic shapes and two sizes—typically one or three centimeters across—with identifying marks pressed into them. The marks indicated quantity and helped track goods, making the tokens an early form of record-keeping. The invention of clay tokens allowed the Sumerians to represent objects, amounts, or commodities in physical form—essentially, to record what needed to be remembered.

To eventually reach alphabetic writing, symbols had to evolve to represent sounds rather than just objects or quantities. Just as the name of the city Uruk evolved, so too did the systems for documenting trade.

AGREED-UPON SYMBOL AS IDEA OR QUANTITY

WESTERN ARABIC (INDIAN), EASTERN ARABIC, AND ROMAN NUMERAL SYSTEMS

1	١	I
2	٢	II
3	٣	III
4	٤	IV
5	٥	V
6	٦	VI
7	٧	VII
8	٨	VIII
9	٩	IX
0	٠	
10	١٠	X
50	٥٠	L
100	١٠٠	C
500	٥٠٠	D
1000	١٠٠٠	M

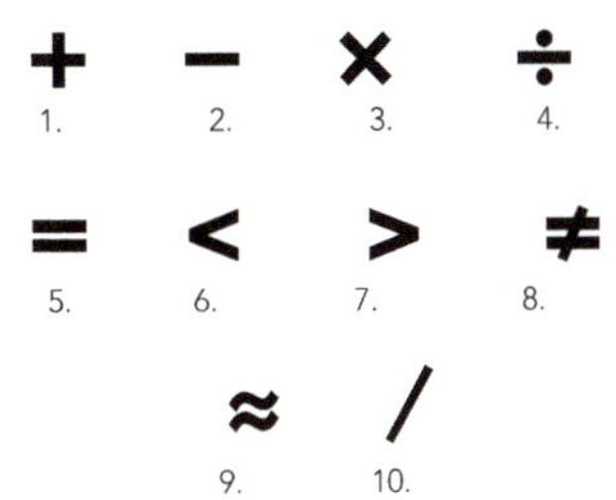

Mathematical symbols (partial list): 1. Add; 2. Subtract; 3. Multiply; 4. Divide; 5. Equals; 6. Less than; 7. Greater than; 8. Does not equal; 9. Approximately; 10. Divide

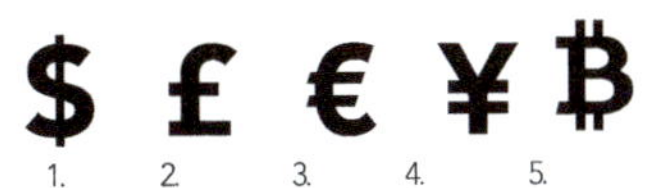

Currency symbols: 1. US Dollar; 2. British Pound Sterling; 3. EU Euro; 4. Chinese Yuan and Japanese Yen; 5. Cryptocurrency Bitcoin

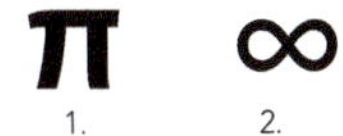

Algebraic symbols (partial list): 1. Pi, the numerical value of the ratio of the circumference of a circle to its diameter (approximately 3.14159); and the sixteenth letter of the Greek alphabet; 2. Infinity symbol

32°F 0°C

The degree symbol when used with an F or a C indicates temperature: either Fahrenheit, where thirty-two degrees is freezing or Celsius, where it is zero, or to express the arc in an angle, e.g. 180°.

Designer Adrian Frutiger wrote in *Signs and Symbols* (1989) that the ampersand "is neither a letter of the alphabet nor a pronunciation mark. It is a separate ideogram, derived from a ligature of the very commonly written junction et (and) [from Latin]..." (see page 37).

IDEOGRAM

An ideogram is a graphic symbol, image, or color that directly represents an idea or object, rather than a specific word or sound. It does not occur in nature and is not tied to any language. Some ideograms are abstract and may appear complex, especially to viewers unfamiliar with their established meanings. Examples include mathematical symbols, Arabic numerals, and wayfinding signage. "Danger," for instance, is an idea, not a physical object. Its symbol must be a commonly understood visual mark. Some ideograms resemble the objects they represent. When this resemblance is strong, they may also be called pictograms.

No symbol, or *Prohibited*, International Organization for Standardization, ISO 3864-1, first published in 1984, revised in 2002, and again in 2011.

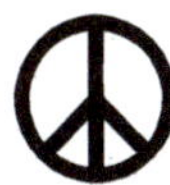

Peace, 1958, designed for the British nuclear disarmament movement.

Power Button, International Electrotechnical Commission (IEC), 2015. Originated from the on/off button; the circle and the line represent the binary 1, meaning "on," and 0, meaning "off."

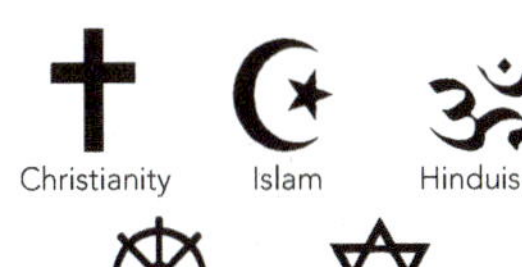

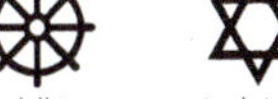

Symbols: most populous religions.

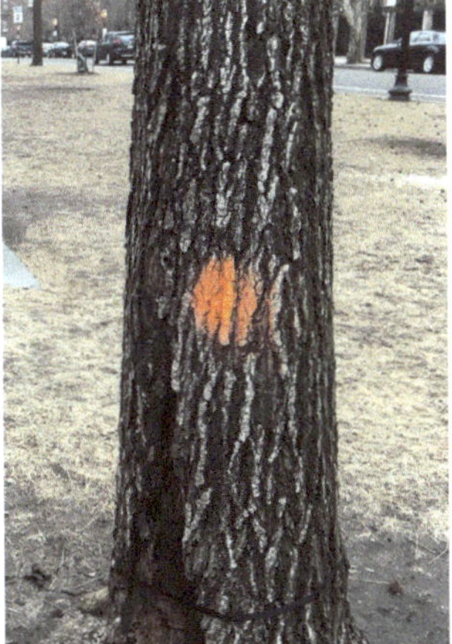

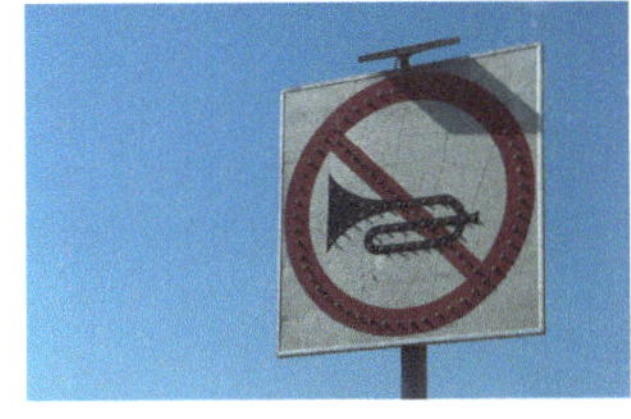

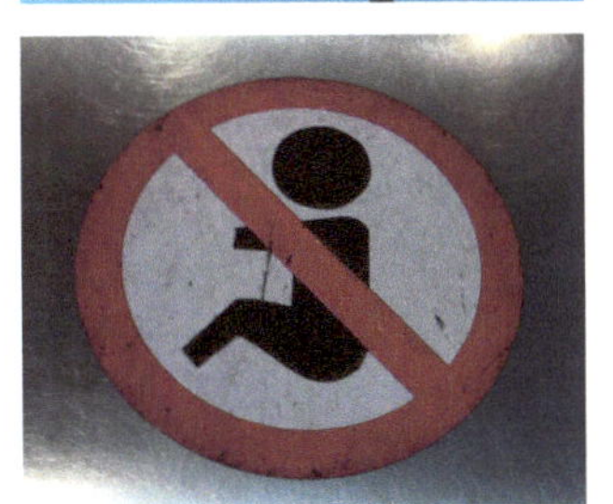

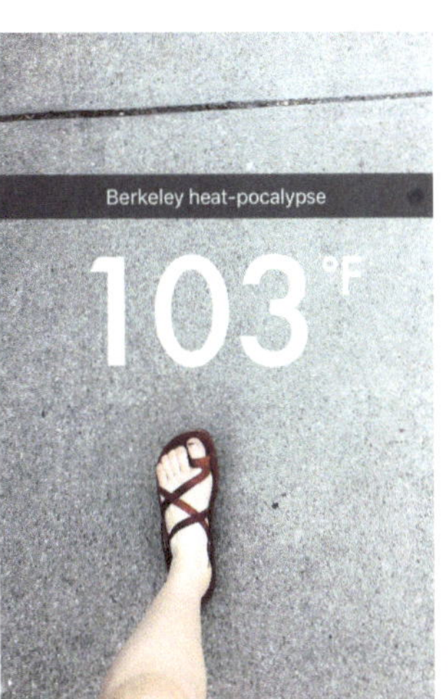

1

3500 BCE

PICTOGRAPHIC

SUMER
Syria, Iran, Iraq

Essential to the development of full writing... was the discovery of the rebus principle. This was the radical idea that a pictographic symbol could be used for its phonetic value.
— Andrew Robinson,
The Story of Writing: Alphabet, Hieroglyphs, and Pictograms (1999)

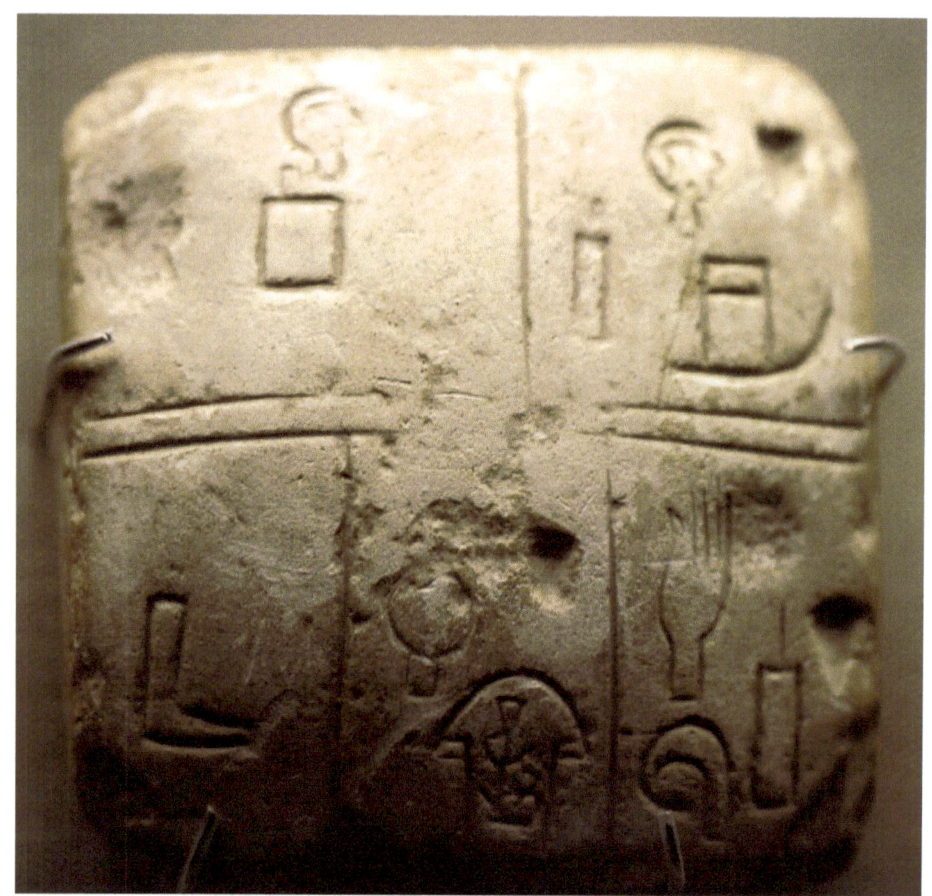

Kish Tablet, Uruk period (3500 BCE), limestone, with pictographic writing, from Kish, Iraq. British Museum, London.

A RADICAL IDEA: PICTURES REPRESENT SOUND

As societies flourished and trade became more complex, the Mesopotamian government required that economic activity be recorded. The clay token system used for accounting was evolving and needed to track more information—such as the names of people involved in trade, the commodities exchanged, the quantities, places of origin, and the taxes collected. To address these needs—especially the challenge of recording names and locations that couldn't easily be depicted with images—a form of phoneticism began to emerge. While pictograms and logograms were used to write nouns, verbs, and adjectives, new symbols were required to represent sounds (see page 30). As a result, homonyms and rebuses began appearing in early Mesopotamian writing. These are the earliest known records of names, goods, and quantities—inscribed on clay tablets, sealed clay envelopes, or carved into stone cylinder seals.

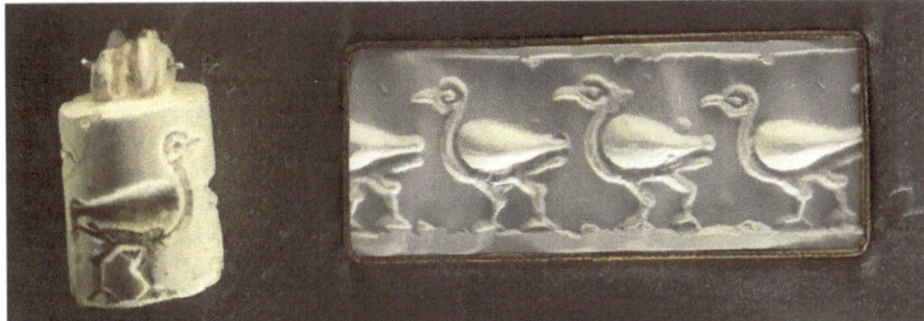
Cylinder Seal, Mesopotamia, ca. 3500 BCE.

It is unclear whether the rebus concept originated with the Sumerians or the Egyptians, as both appear to have developed it independently and for different purposes: the Sumerians generally for trade, and the Egyptians generally for religious expression. In the photo above, small carved cylinders served as a kind of "signature" for their owners. Often made from precious stones like hematite, some seals featured rebuses that phonetically represented the owner's name. For example, when bundles of goods were tied with string, a lump of soft clay was placed over the knot, and the cylinder seal was rolled across it, leaving an impression of ownership. With a hole through the center, the seal could be strung and worn as a necklace—always ready to "sign" a transaction. Like the names they represented, each seal was unique. However, it would take another two centuries for the rebus to play a more central role in the development of writing. And it would be nearly a thousand years before pictograms, logograms, and rebuses evolved into cuneiform (Latin for "wedge-shaped")—the Sumerian writing system that allowed seals to indicate not just identity, but eventually, occupation as well.

REBUS

The term "rebus" comes from the Latin *rebus non verbis*, meaning "by means of objects, not words." It represents a word or phrase using pictures or symbols suggesting the word, phrase, or its syllables. This is language-specific. A rebus can also be a heraldic emblem, where symbols play on the name of the person. Both ancient Mesopotamian and Egyptian cultures used this technique in their writing systems.

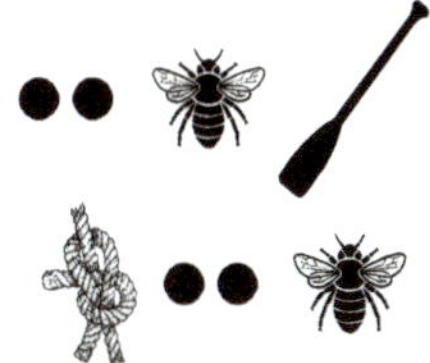
To be or not to be: symbols and pictures representing words.

IBM Rebus, poster, Paul Rand, designed in 1981, produced in 1982.

PICTURES AS WORDS, IDEAS, OR SOUNDS

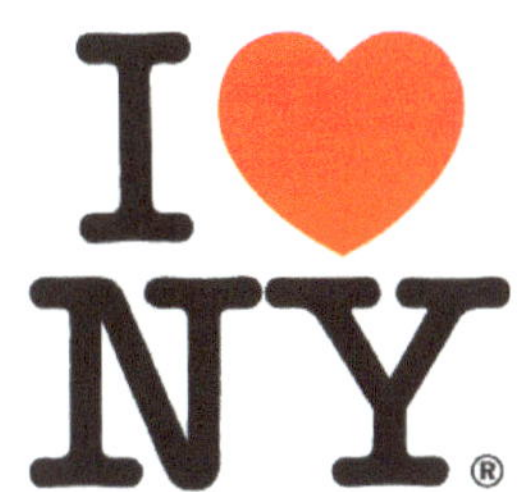

LEFT: *I [heart] New York*, logo, Milton Glaser. Designed in the back of a taxi in 1976; implemented in 1977. The original drawing is in the Museum of Modern Art New York.

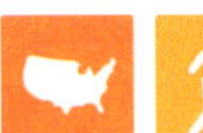

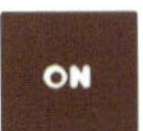

America Runs on Dunkin, Dunkin Donuts advertising campaign, Hill Holiday, 2006

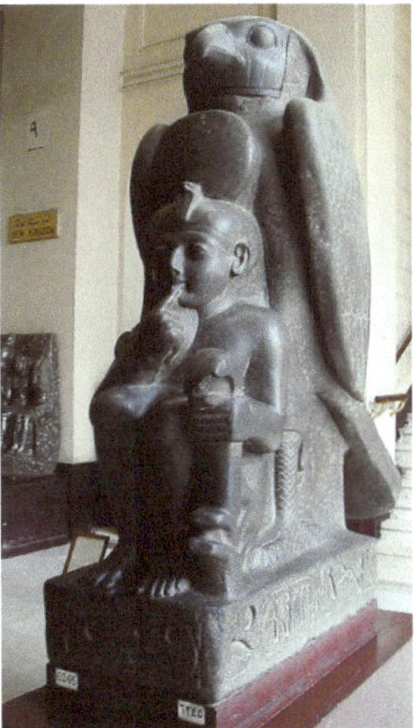
RIGHT: *Ramses and Horus*, ca. 1297–1213 BCE, Gray granite and limestone, Egyptian Museum, Cairo. Though not contemporary, this work is an early example of a three-dimensional rebus. It depicts Ramses II as a child holding a sedge plant, protected by Horus, the sun god, shown as a falcon. The name "Ramses" is represented through symbols: Ra ("sun disk") + mes ("child") + su ("plant").

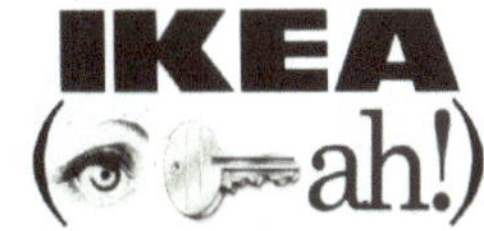

IKEA Advertisement, designer unknown,1985.

2

3400 BCE

HIEROGLYPHS

EGYPT

Abydos

Basically the Egyptians had invented what we could call alphabetic signs, but the sacred conventions governing the uses of hieroglyphs prevented official scribes from ever using the characters by themselves in an alphabetic way. However, informal use of the single- sound hieroglyphs around 2000 BC may be the way our alphabet came to be born.

—Lyn Davies, A is for Ox: A Short History of the Alphabet (2006)

REPRESENTS QUANTITY

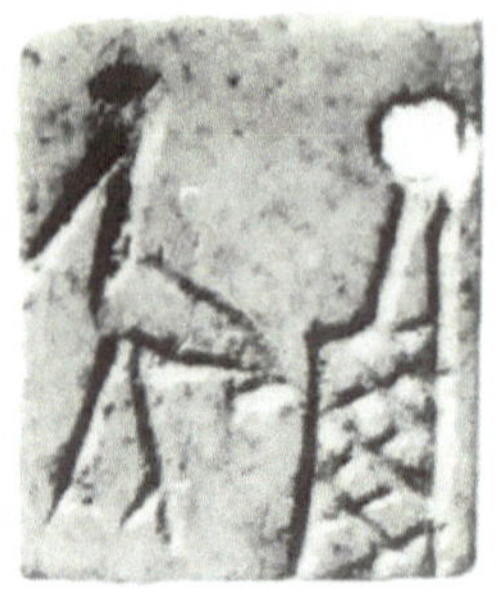

REPRESENTS PLACE OF PRODUCTION

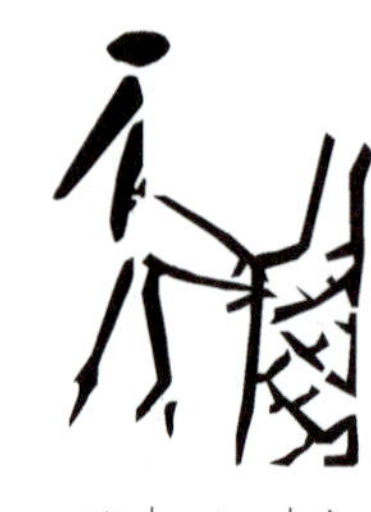

Bone and Ivory Tags, ca. 3400-3200 BCE, bone and ivory, found in tombs in Abydos, Egypt. Actual size between 1.5–2 cm. Oldest known examples of Egyptian writing with rebus principle applied. In Abydos, they were used as both phonetic signs and ideograms. In the above left tag, the incised notches represent quantity. In the above right tag, each symbol represents a sound. Given where they were found, they are thought to have been designed more for ceremony than for economic purposes.

In predynastic Egyptian the stork represented the sound "ba," while the chair, to its right, represented the sound "sta." Together they make "Basta," the name of a Nile Delta town in the Old Kingdom, the place of production.

PICTURE AS SOUND AND SYMBOL

Between 3400 and 3200 BCE, the Egyptians began applying the rebus principle to pictograms etched onto tags made from bone or ivory. These tags, an early form of product packaging design, were attached to commodities such as grain, olive oil, or fabric, identifying the product, its place of origin, and the individuals involved in the exchange. A small hole in the tag allowed it to be attached to jars or bundles. So far, 70% percent of predynastic hieroglyphs (before 3100 BCE) have been translated using the rebus system. Some scholars suggest that the Egyptians borrowed the idea of writing from the Sumerians, but not the form. Like later Egyptian hieroglyphs, these early writings were read in the direction the symbols faced—left to right in the example above (see page 35).

While early Mesopotamian writing was primarily focused on the economic administration of government, early Egyptian writing was used for religious ceremonies, both monumental and decorative. From the beginning, phoneticism played a more significant role in Egypt than in Mesopotamia. In ancient Egypt, where the Nile River was central to life, cosmology and belief in gods and goddesses were essential. The gods brought either order or chaos. Failing to practice religious rituals, including showing respect to the gods, could provoke their wrath. For example, it could result in the Nile's annual flooding being too excessive, destroying homes and farms, or too scarce, depriving the soil of the nutrients necessary for agriculture. Therefore, paying homage to the gods was critical. This belief system is reflected in early hieroglyphs, which began with images—or sets of images—that represented ideas. These images primarily depicted animals, birds, fish, or plants. The two earliest gods were Horus and Set. Horus, depicted as a falcon, was the god of order, the sky, and the patron god of all Egyptian kings. Set, his complement and competitor, was the god of chaos and the desert, taking various forms over time. The ibis and bull's head continued to be represented throughout the evolution of hieroglyphs. The ibis was associated with Thoth, the god of the moon and wisdom. The bull's head, *Ka*, symbolized power, and would eventually become the first letter of the alphabet (see page 39).

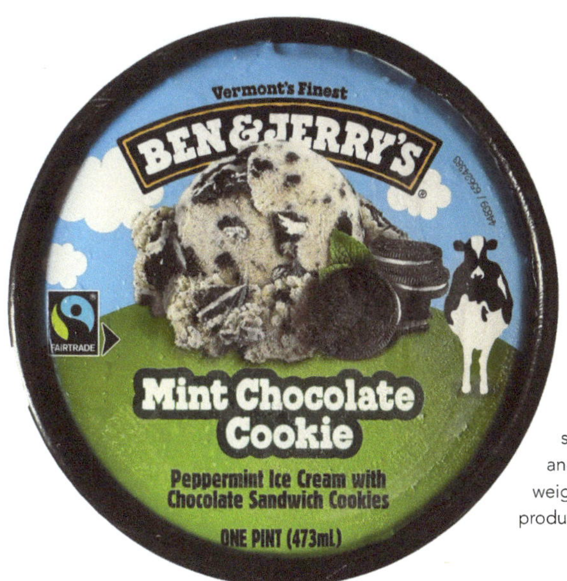

PACKAGING TODAY

Ice cream maker, *Ben & Jerry's*, apply the same information on their packaging as ancient Egyptians did on theirs: product weight, name of producer, ingredients, and product's origin.

PICTOGRAM

Pictograms are symbols that represent concrete objects, not ideas. They are the basis of hieroglyphic and cuneiform writing and relate to the senses—things you can see, touch, smell, hear, or taste. Today, pictograms appear in charts or graphs using symbols to represent people, cars, factories, and more.

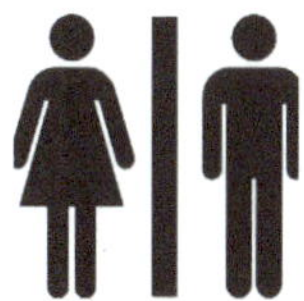

Women's and Men's Toilet, AIGA, 1974.

Wi-Fi, Interbrand, 1999, commissioned by the Wi-Fi Alliance, who needed a name and logo more interesting and memorable than *IEEE 802.11b*.

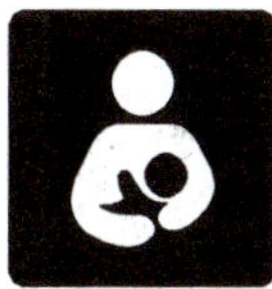

International Breastfeeding, Matt Daigle, 2006.

LOGOGRAM

According to Robert Bringhurst, a logogram is "a specific typographic form tied to a certain word. Example, the non-standard capitalizations in the names ee cummings, TrueType and WordPerfect," or Chinese characters.

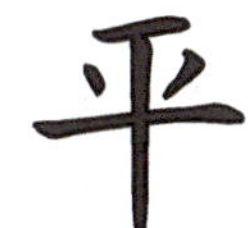

Chinese character for *peace*.

PICTOGRAMS TODAY

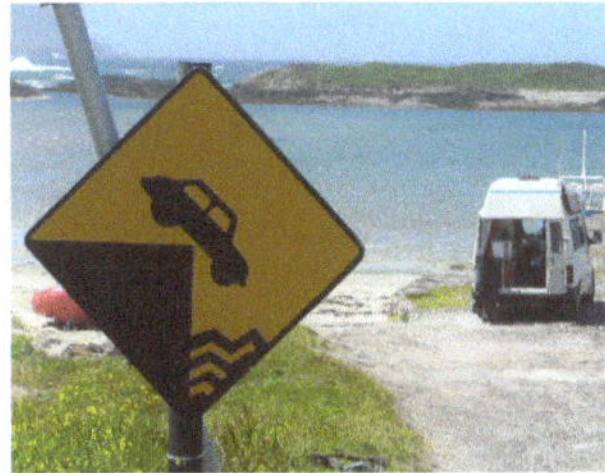

Derrynane, County Kerry, Ireland.

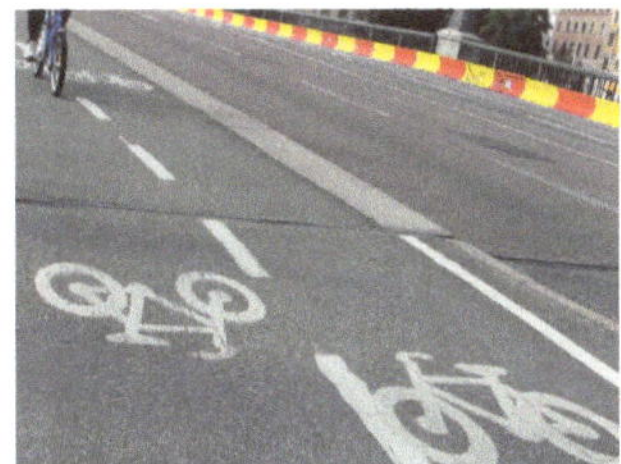

Stockholm, Sweden.

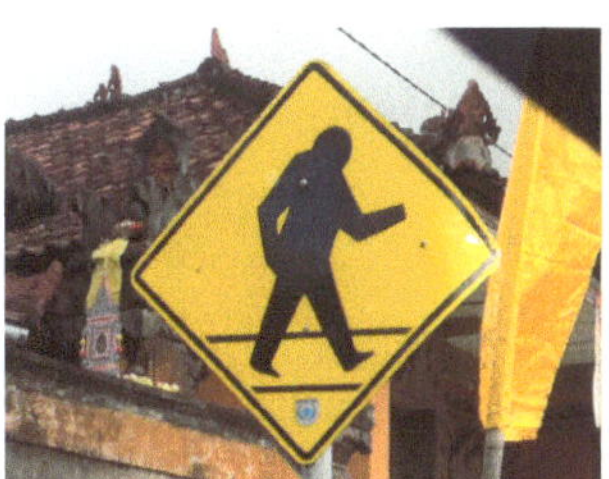

Bali, Indonesia.

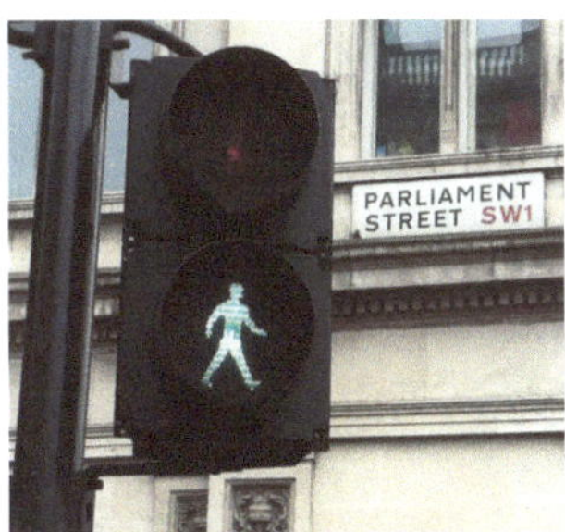

London, England.

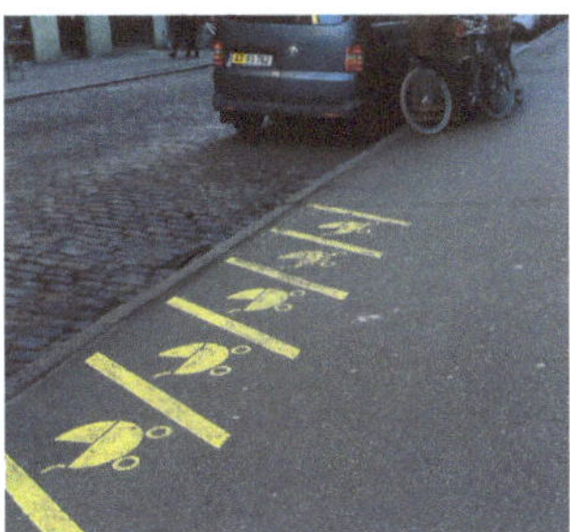

Copenhagen, Denmark.

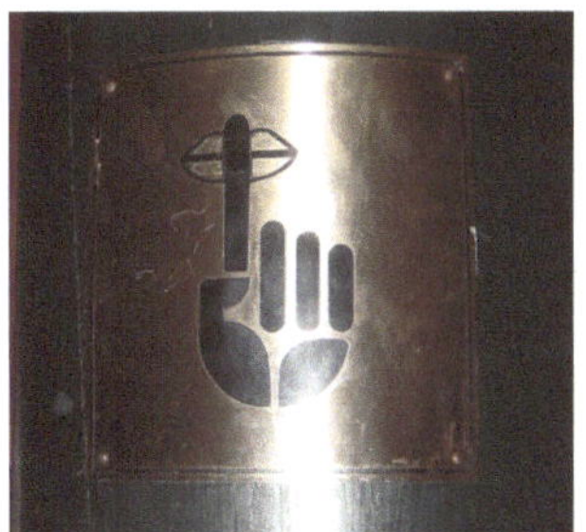

Basilique Notre-Dame de Montréal, Canada.

3

3300–3000 BCE

PROTO-CUNEIFORM

SUMER
Syria, Iran, Iraq

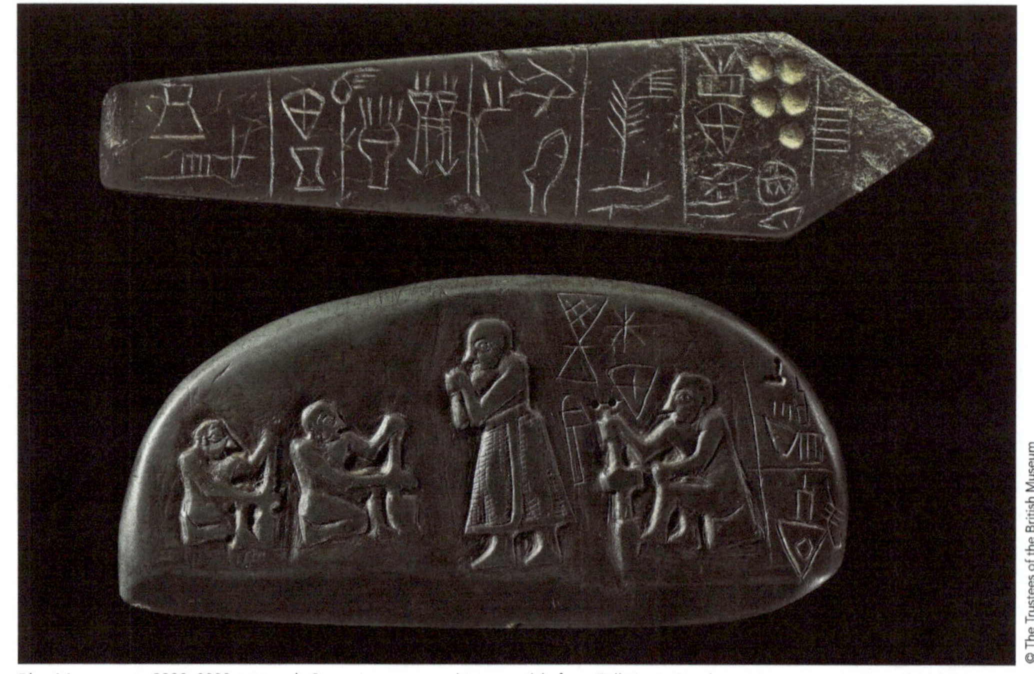

Blau Monuments, 3300–3000 BCE, early Sumerian, green schist, possibly from Tell Uqair, Southern Mesopotamia, Iraq, British Museum.

EARLIEST ARTIFACT COMBINING TEXT AND IMAGE

The *Blau Monuments* may be the world's earliest artifacts to combine both text and imagery. Although not fully understood, they are generally believed to be early *kudurrus*—boundary stones representing land exchange and ownership. The term *kudurru* comes from the Akkadian word for "frontier" or "boundary." Inscriptions on the monuments suggest a transaction involving land in exchange for goods such as goats, beer, wool, and silver. Their shapes resemble craftsman's tools: a chisel and a pottery scraper. Named in 1886 after their first recorded owner, German physician Dr. A. Blau, the monuments were acquired near Uruk, where he served in the Turkish medical service. The inscriptions reflect proto-cuneiform—a system still primarily pictographic, with features similar to Egyptian hieroglyphs. Egypt, like Mesopotamia, exerted a far-reaching influence across regions and cultures. The word *Mesopotamia* is a geographic term given by Greek historians during the time of Alexander the Great (356–323 BCE). It means "the land between two rivers," referring to the Tigris and Euphrates. The Sumerians lived in Sumer—later known as Babylonia—in what is now southern Iraq. By 2800 BCE, cuneiform had evolved into a semanto-phonetic writing system—symbols that convey both meaning and sound—including logograms, phonograms, and determinatives (similar to Egyptian writing).

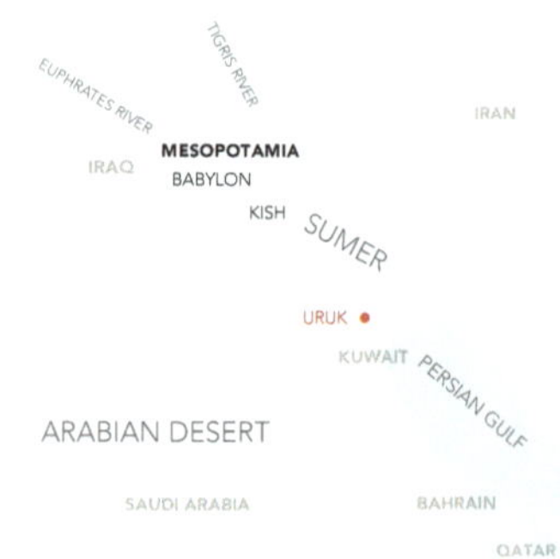

Writing allowed the bureaucracy to have an institutional memory that extended beyond the lifetime of any single priest or scribe. Writing continues to fill those exact same needs of the state, five thousand years later.
—Gil J. Stein,
Visible Language (2015)

Over the next two centuries, the Sumerians developed signs for vowels and syllables, reducing the total number of symbols from around 1,000 to 600. Though the Sumerian language died out around 1700 BCE, cuneiform remained in use until roughly 100 BCE, when alphabetic writing systems began to dominate. The student exercise tablet below reflects more than a thousand years of evolution—from the pictorial forms on the Blau Monuments to the more abstract script of classical cuneiform. These clay tablets were used to train scribes in writing Sumerian and Akkadian. On one side, the teacher wrote the word or symbol; on the other, the student repeated it. In this example, the word *Urash* (a goddess of the earth) is written six times. Like today's smartphones, these tablets were compact enough to fit in the palm of a hand. Although the Sumerians developed cuneiform, it was adopted and adapted by the Akkadians, Babylonians, Hittites, and Assyrians. Ultimately, cuneiform was used to write over fifteen languages.

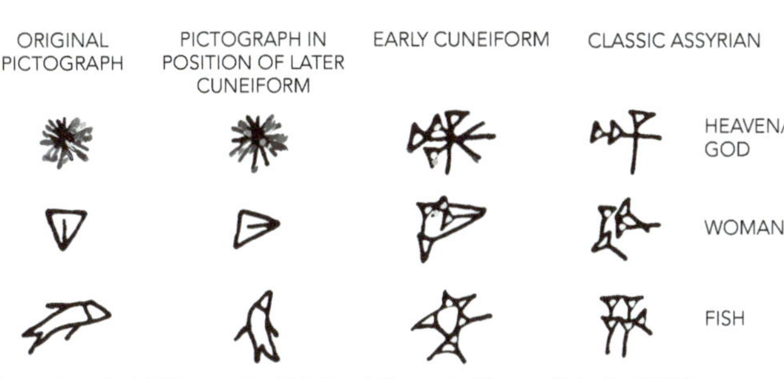

Illustrations: David Diringer, *The Alphabet: A Key to the History of Mankind* (1948).

Student Exercise Tablet, cuneiform, clay, Sumerian, ca. 2000-1500 BCE.

COMBINING PICTOGRAMS AND IDEOGRAMS

Today, the most common use of pictograms and ideograms involves a combination of object images and geometric symbols. While the two terms are often used interchangeably, they have distinct meanings. A familiar example is a "no dogs" sign, which shows an image of a dog crossed out with a red line (see below). The red line—the universal symbol for "no"—modifies the meaning of the image, much like determinatives (see page 35) in cuneiform and Egyptian hieroglyphs, which silently altered the meaning of the surrounding symbols.

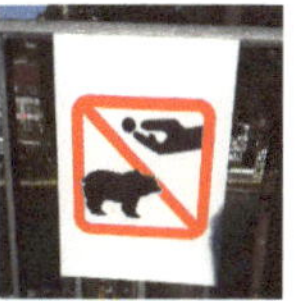

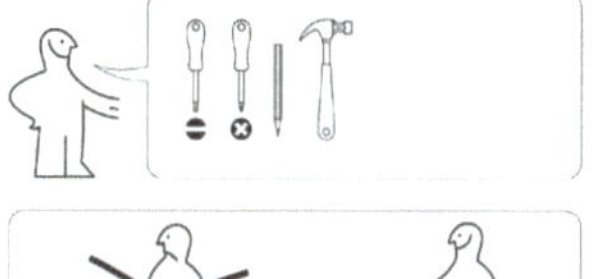
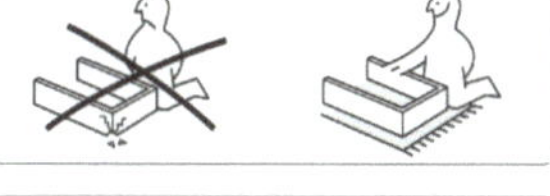
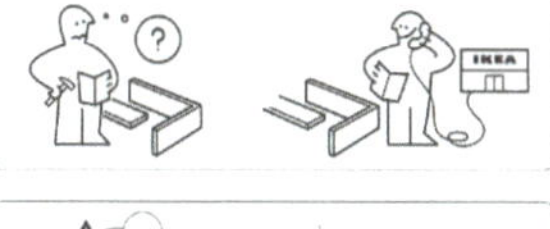
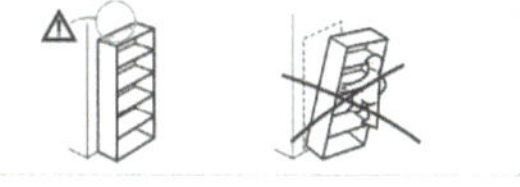

IKEA Directions, with pictograms, ideograms (question mark and exclamation point), and a word, IKEA.

TEXT AND IMAGE

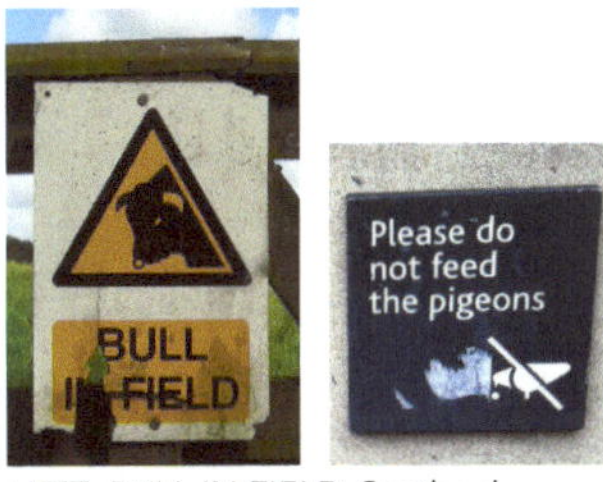

LEFT: *BULL IN FIELD*, Scotland; RIGHT: *Please do not feed the pigeons*, London.

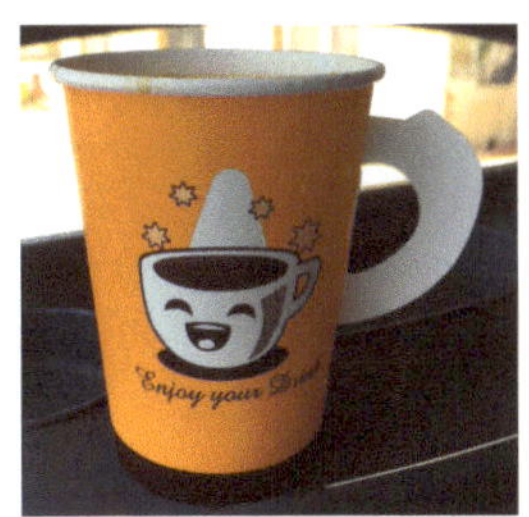

Weather app, screenshot, shows city, local time, temperature, and sky conditions.

LEFT: *Enjoy your Drink*, disposable coffee cup, Cairo.

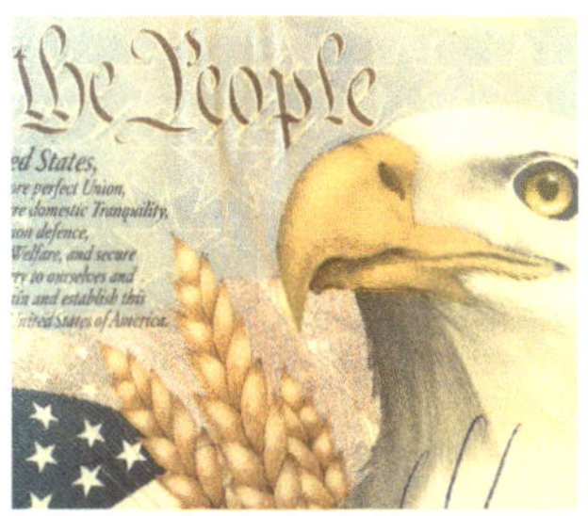

TOP: Utilities cover, Madrid. ABOVE: Inside page, United States passport..

4

3100 BCE

HIEROGLYPHS

HIERAKONPOLIS
Egypt

It takes time to create change. New ideas are always opposed. Humans like normality, we like our comfort-zone, they don't like change that is drastic. But enlightenment is not selective. Some people keep dreaming. Dreaming of a better future. We hope to grow the circle of dreamers. Society is not driven by people that are pragmatic and realistic. It's only driven by the crazy ones, the dreamers.

— Bahia Shehab, *Art As a Tool for Change* (2014)

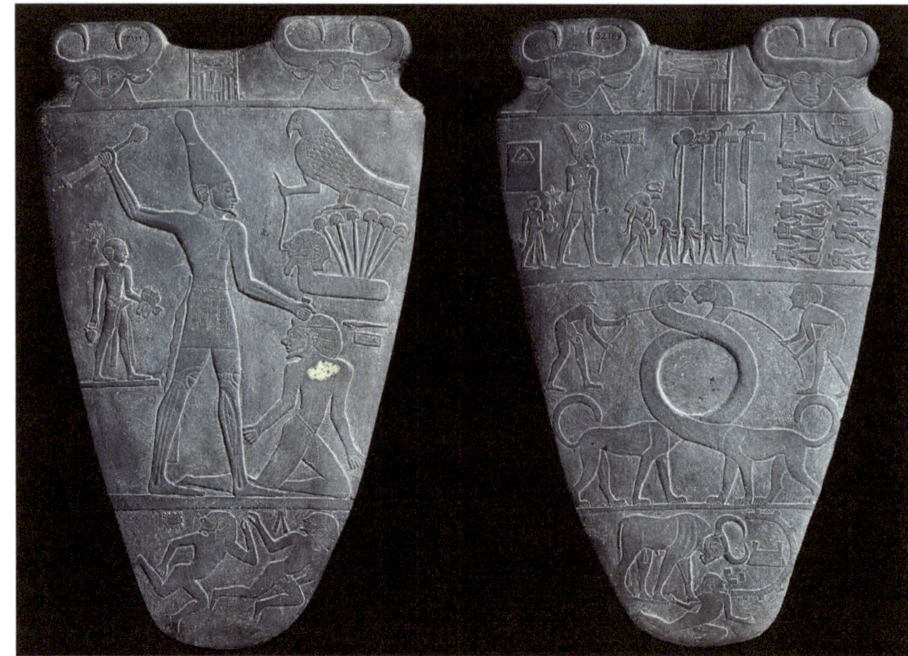

Narmer Palette, ca. 3100 BCE, slate, Hierakonpolis, Egypt, Egyptian Museum, Cairo.

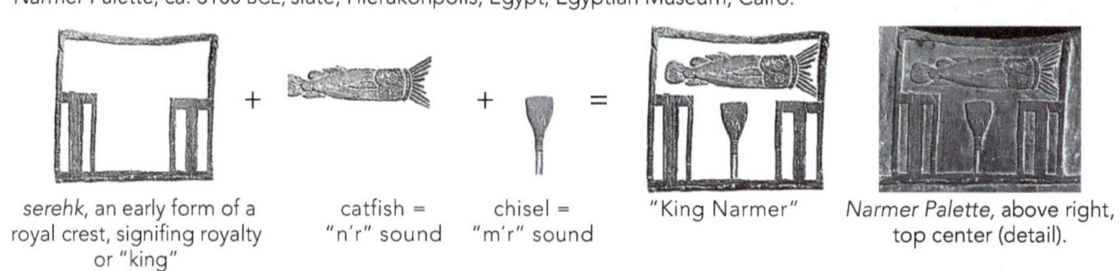

HIEROGLYPHIC FORM AS SOUND

Like the Mesopotamians, the ancient Egyptians used pictures to represent sounds—especially for things that could not easily be depicted, such as names. The *Narmer Palette*, which symbolizes the unification of Upper (southern) and Lower (northern) Egypt, features some of the earliest hieroglyphic forms used phonetically. The name of King Narmer is shown using two phonetic symbols at the top center of the palette, on both sides. The sound "nār" is represented by a catfish, and "mer" by a chisel. These two symbols are enclosed within a rectangular frame symbolizing the façade of the king's palace. This form is called a *serekh*, a precursor to the cartouche. Like the cartouche, the serekh encloses royal names or titles. Egyptian hieroglyphs were distinctive in their versatility. They could be used in four main ways: 1) Phonograms, representing individual sounds; 2) Logograms, representing entire words; 3) Determinatives, clarifying meaning; and 4) Pronunciation aids, reinforcing how a word should be spoken. Over time, the Egyptians developed twenty-four symbols representing consonant sounds. However, they did not write vowels.

EGYPTIAN HIEROGLYPHS ARE UNDERSTOOD IN FOUR WAYS:

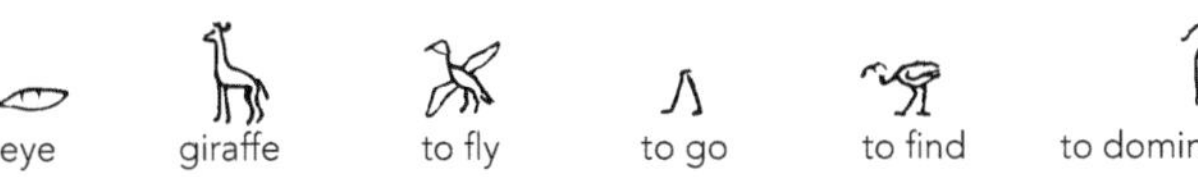

eye | giraffe | to fly | to go | to find | to dominate/govern

1) *Logograms:* signs that represent a single word, which could be a thing, an action, or an abstract idea

f | *kh* | *m–n* | *m–s* | *kh–n* | *n-k-h*

2) *Phonograms*: signs that represent a single, or uni-consonantal, bi-consonantal, or tri-consonantal sound

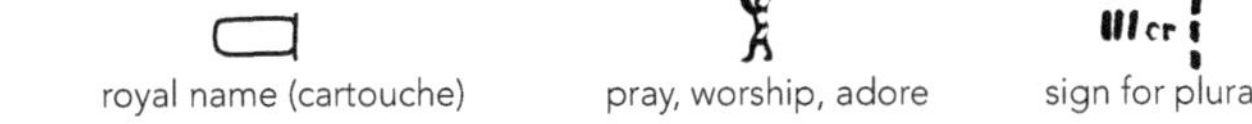

royal name (cartouche) | pray, worship, adore | sign for plural

3) *Determinatives*: signs placed around, or at the end of, a picture or collection of pictures to clarify meaning, as many signs could be used as both a logogram and phonogram. They are not pronounced.

4) *Phonetic Complements:* signs added to emphasis pronunciation

READ LIKE AN EGYPTIAN Egyptian hieroglyphs are read according to the direction of the symbols. When hieroglyphs are enclosed within a cartouche, ▭, it signifies royalty. In ancient Egypt, only about one in a hundred people could read.

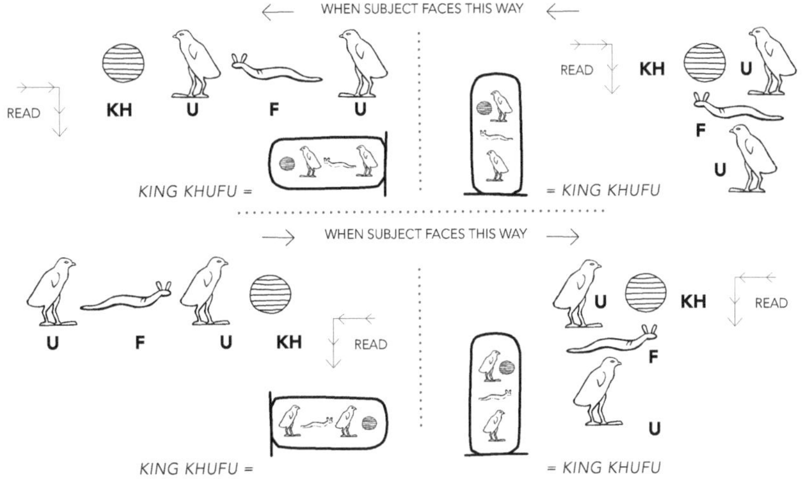

TYPES OF ROYAL CARTOUCHE AND CRESTS

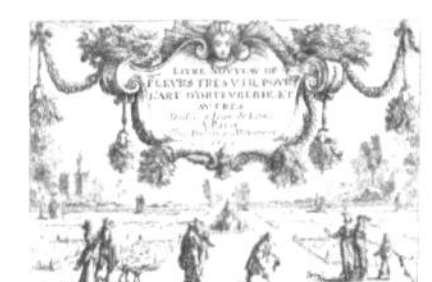

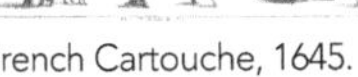

French Cartouche, 1645.

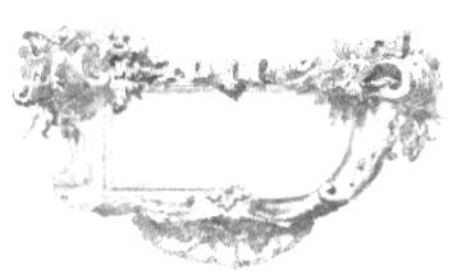

Italian Cartouche, ca. 1700s.

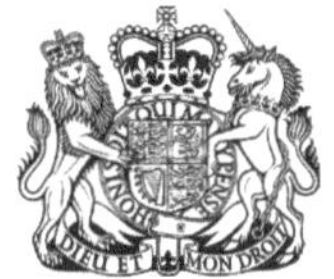

British Coat of Arms, 1837.

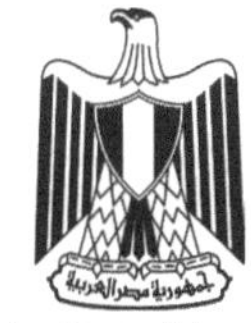

Egyptian Coat of Arms, 1984.

ANIMALS AS CONCEPTS

As early as 3000 BCE, ancient Egyptians used animals to symbolize for their gods and goddesses. For example, Horus, the god of the sky, was represented as a falcon; Hathor, the goddess of the sky, was depicted as a cow (as seen at the top of the *Narmer Palette*); her son, Apis, was symbolized by a bull; referred to as a bull; and Sobek, the god of strength and power, was portrayed as a crocodile.

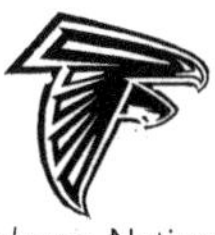

Atlanta Falcons, National Football League, USA.

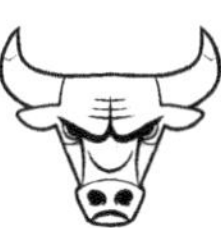

Chicago Bulls, National Basketball Association, USA.

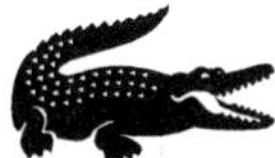

Lacoste, clothing company, France.

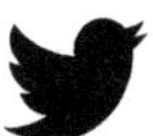

Twitter (now *X*), microblogging and social networking company, USA.

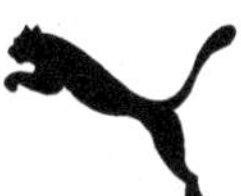

PUMA, Inc., athletic apparel and footwear company, Germany.

Penguin Books, book publisher, UK/USA.

5

1900 BCE

HIERATIC SCRIPT

THEBES (LUXOR)
Egypt

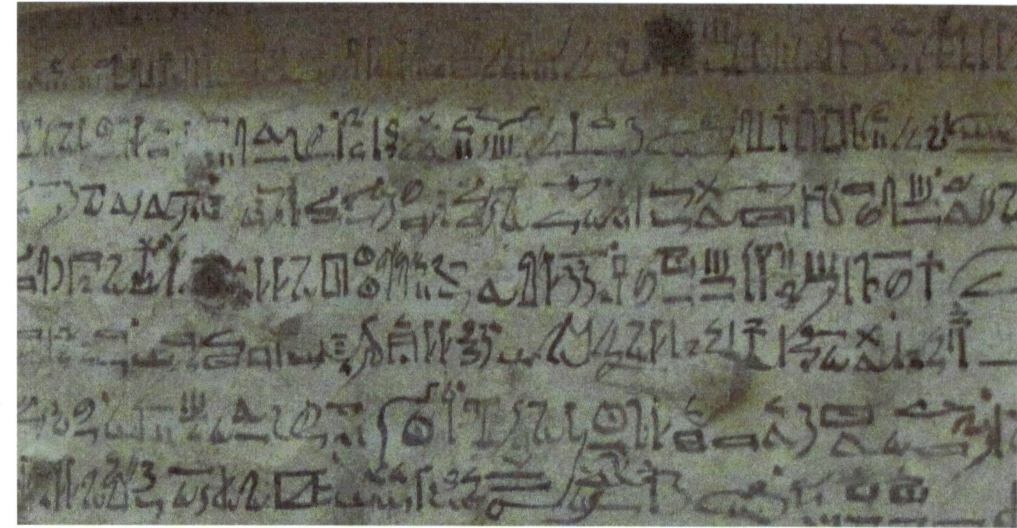

The Tale of Sinuhe, ca.1991–1786 BCE, ostracon fragment, ink on limestone, hieratic, Egyptian Museum, Cairo. Found in 1886 in the tomb of Sennedjem, Deir el-Medina, west bank of the Nile, Luxor (ancient Thebes), Egypt. Largest known ostracon containing the beginning of the story composed during the Twelfth Dynasty of the Middle Kingdom.

Over time, because hieroglyphs wer ideally suited for stone and not for pen and papyrus, two new varieties of writing developed based directly on the hieroglyphs. These are called hieratic ("religios" or "priestly" script) and Demotic ("the people's" script).
— Ahmad Abdel-Hamid Youssef, *From the Pharaoh's Lips: Ancient Egyptian Language in the Arabic of Today* (2003)

STORYTELLING WITH AN ABSTRACTED SCRIPT

Hieratic was a cursive form of hieroglyphic writing, created using a reed brush. Though developed alongside hieroglyphic writing, it evolved to serve a different purpose. It was needed for everyday tasks, such as administrative, legal, personal, educational, and literary work. Writing with a reed brush and ink on papyrus or stone was much faster than using a hammer and chisel for hieroglyphic inscriptions. As a result, the signs became more abstract, but they retained their connection to hieroglyphs. These signs still indicated sound, combined to form ligatures, and used diacritics help with meaning (similar to how diacritics help with pronunciation today). Unlike hieroglyphs, which could be read left to right or right to left, hieratic was written exclusively right to left. One of the most well-known works written in hieratic is *The Tale of Sinuhe* (also known as "Son of the Sycamore"), authored by an anonymous writer and often compared to Shakespeare. According to R.B. Parkinson, the translator, the story is "an adventure in foreign lands," but it also prompts reflection on Egyptian life, especially the relationship between individuals and the king. Its themes—such as foreign wars, a king's assassination, and a David-and-Goliath-like duel—mirror those found in Biblical texts.

In ancient Egypt, *ostraca*—pieces of broken limestone or pottery—were used like scrap paper. They were cheap and plentiful, making them ideal for students to practice writing or sketching, and for managers to keep notes. The term "ostracon" comes from the Greek word *ostrakon*, meaning "a shard of pottery." Interestingly, the word *ostracism* originated from ancient Athens (circa 450 BCE). During annual voting, citizens could banish a person from the city for ten years, typically targeting corrupt politicians. The highly literate electorate would write the name of the person they wished to banish on an ostracon, which served as a ballot. If enough votes were cast, the individual would be exiled from the city.

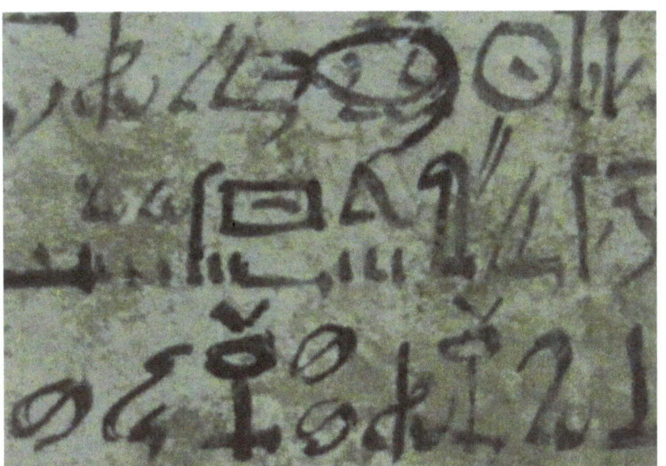

The Tale of Sinuhe (detail, from left).

EXCERPT: *THE TALE OF SINUHE*, ca.1985–1795 BCE LINES 129-141

At night-time I strung my bow, and tried my arrows. I drew out my dagger, and polished my weapons. Day dawned and Retenu was already come; it had stirred up its tribes and had assembled the countries of a half of it, it had planned this fight. Forth he came against me where I stood, and I posted myself near him. Every heart burned for me. Women and men jabbered. Every heart was sore for me, saying: Is there another mighty man who can fight against him? Then his shield, his battle-ax and his armful of javelins fell, when I had escaped from his weapons and had caused his arrows to pass by me, uselessly sped; while one approached the other. I shot him, my arrow sticking in his neck. He cried aloud, and fell on his nose.

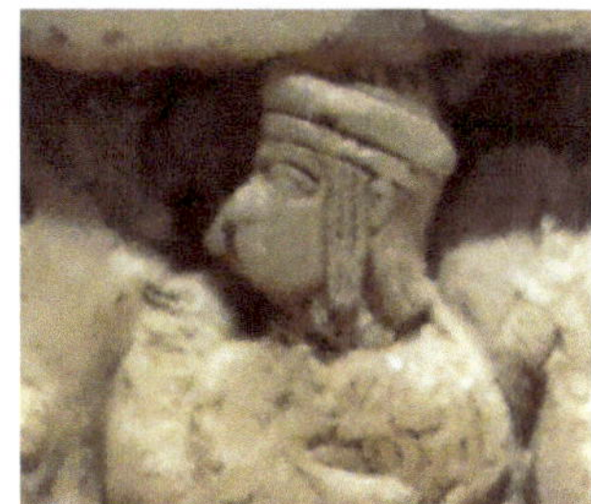

***I, ENHEDUANNA*: PRIESTESS, POET, ca. 2285–2250 BCE**

Enheduanna, poet, high priestess, princess, and wife of Nanna (the Sumerian moon god), was the daughter of King Sargon of Akkad. She is considered the world's first author of historical record, with works written in cuneiform. To help her father expand his empire, she married the moon god, Innana. Through this union and her writings, her role was to unite the gods of the northern Akkadians with those of the southern Sumerians. She composed hymns for the forty-two major temples across Sumer and Akkad, called the "Sumerian Temple Hymns," and is credited with writing the first anti-war poem.

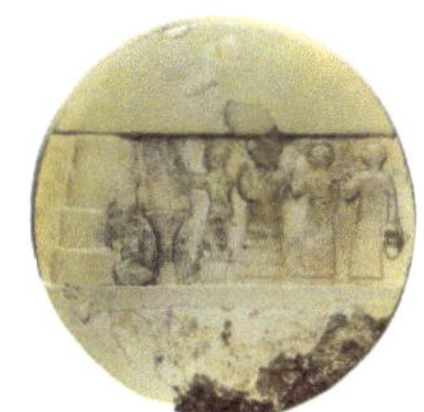

Disc of Enheduanna, ca. 2300 BCE, limestone, Penn Museum, Philadelphia.

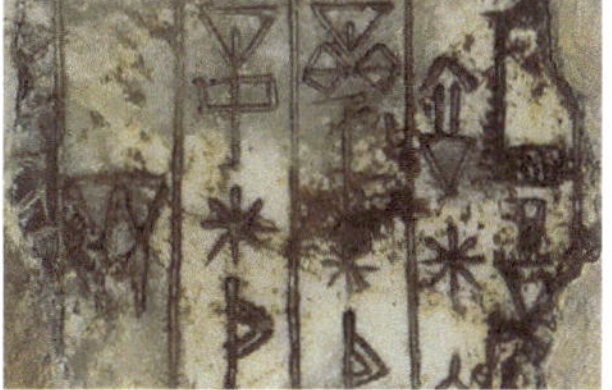

Disk of Enheduanna, back, cuneiform inscription (detail).

COMBINING AND ADDING TO LETTERFORMS TODAY

LIGATURES

From the Latin ligātus, meaning "bound" (from ligāre, "to bind"), ligatures occur when two or more letters connect to form a new glyph. A typical Latin text font contains ten to twelve ligatures, though not all fonts include ligatures or diacritics. The ampersand (&), one of the oldest alphabetic abbreviations, comes from the Latin word et, meaning "and" (see page 27). It can be particularly ornate in italic fonts.

et > & > *&*

TYPES OF LIGATURES

æ œ Æ Œ ß	fi fl ffi ffl fj ffj	Th ct st
Lexical with characters	Typographic with glyphs	Decorative glyphs

DIACRITICS

From the ancient Greek word diakritikos, meaning "distinguishing," a diacritic is a symbol added to a letter. It can appear above, below, between two letters, or combined with another accent. Its primary function is to indicate pronunciation, helping preserve the unique sounds of a language—otherwise, all languages would look the same. Marks like the comma, period, horizontal bar, and apostrophe can also serve as diacritical marks. English is the only language using the Latin alphabet that does not regularly use diacritics, except in borrowed words.

À à Á á Â â Ã ã Ä ä Å å Ç ç Č č
Ĕ ĕ Ġ ġ Į į Ķ ķ Ľ ľ Ō ō Ű ű

Partial list of diacritics in the Latin alphabet across multiple languages.

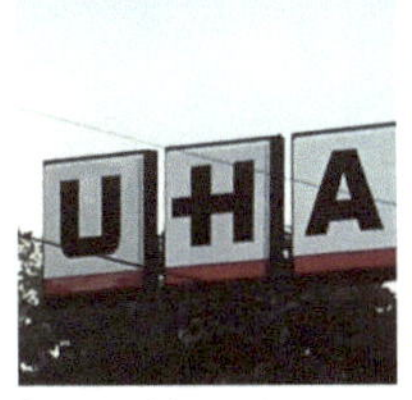

Boston, Massachusetts.

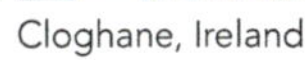

Cloghane, Ireland.

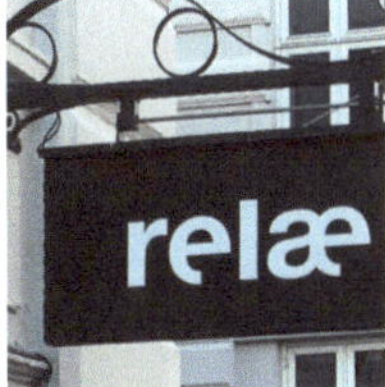

Copenhagen, Denmark.

Istanbul, Turkey.

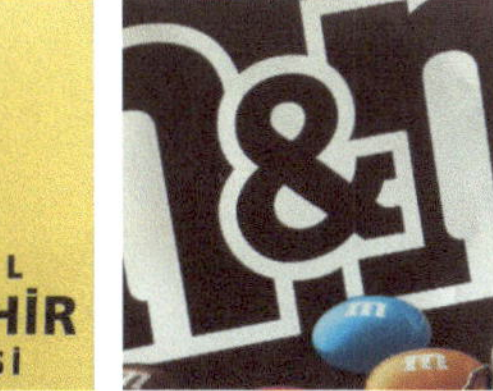

Everywhere.

6

1800 BCE

EARLY ALPHABETIC

WADI EL–HÔL
Egypt

The importance of these two short inscriptions [right] *for understanding the origins of alphabetic writing cannot be overstated.*
—John Colman Darnell,
Two Early Alphabetic Inscriptions from the Wadi el-Hôl (2005)

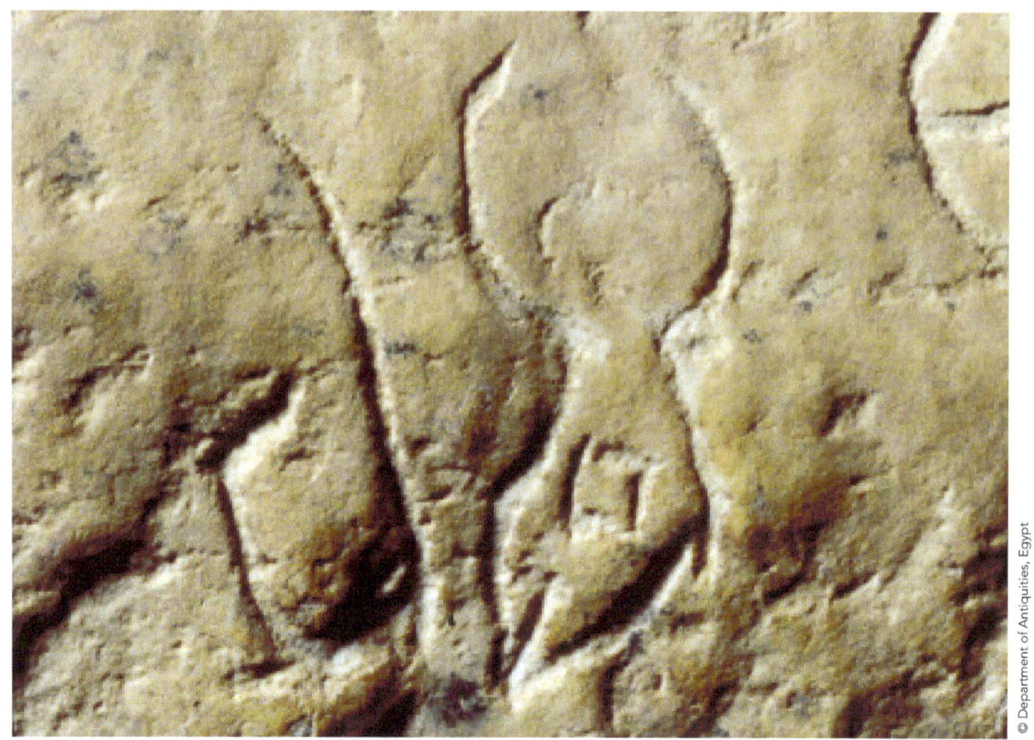

DETAIL: *Wadi el-Hôl Alphabetic Inscription 2* (Vertical Inscription), ca. 1850–1700 BCE, incised in limestone, Wadi el-Hôl, Egypt.

SIMPLIFIED SOUND-BASED CHARACTERS

During the 1993–94 Theban Desert Road Survey, two rock inscriptions were discovered in Wadi el-Hôl that fundamentally changed scholars' understanding of the alphabet's origins. According to Egyptologist John Darnell, the discovery provides "99.9 percent certainty" that early alphabetic writing emerged in Egypt. He further explains that it occurred "initially in a plurality of cultural contexts." Whether they were working with Semitic-speaking mercenaries in Wadi el-Hôl, laborers in the turquoise mines of Serâbît el-Khâdim, or merchants trading along the Nile River, polyglot Egyptian scribes needed a practical way to communicate and document their interactions with foreigners. Hieroglyphs were numerous and complex, so there was a growing need for a more accessible system. The two short alphabetic inscriptions found at Wadi el-Hôl, though not definitively deciphered, most likely read from right to left. Inscriptions 1 and 2 contain sixteen and twelve characters, respectively. Both inscriptions include forms that appear to derive from hieroglyphic and hieratic scripts. These forms are more distinct than those found

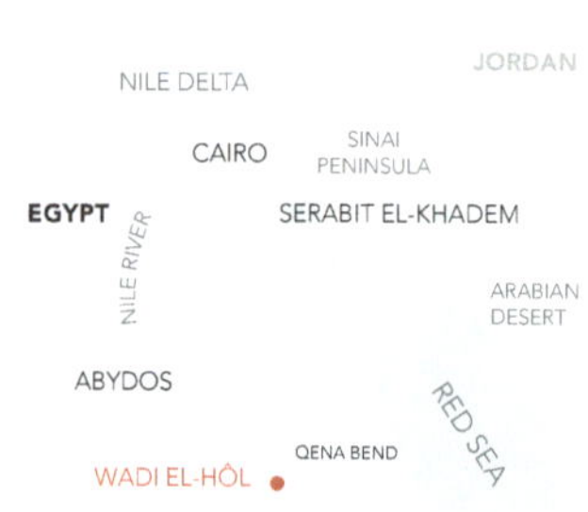

in the Serâbît texts from Serâbît el-Khâdim in Sinai (see page 36) or in other early alphabetic inscriptions discovered in Palestine. Darnell notes that "only a mixture of both types of Egyptian writing [hieroglyphic and hieratic] can comprehensively and compellingly account for the range and complexity of attested alphabetic forms." These two inscriptions represent a new way of conveying information—through a simplified, sound-based (alphabetic) adaptation of hieroglyphic and hieratic signs. Several of these signs would eventually evolve into letters such as A, B, C, E, K, M, N, O, and R.

Wadi el-Hôl, located in the Qena Bend of the Nile, was a key area for trade, religious practices, and military operations. It was also known as the Valley of Terror—a crucial juncture for travelers entering the harsh Western Desert. Numerous inscriptions have been found in this region, including a writer's name and title, the name of a deity, a prayer for safe passage across the desert, references to religious celebrations, and literary texts. Most of these inscriptions are written in hieratic script.

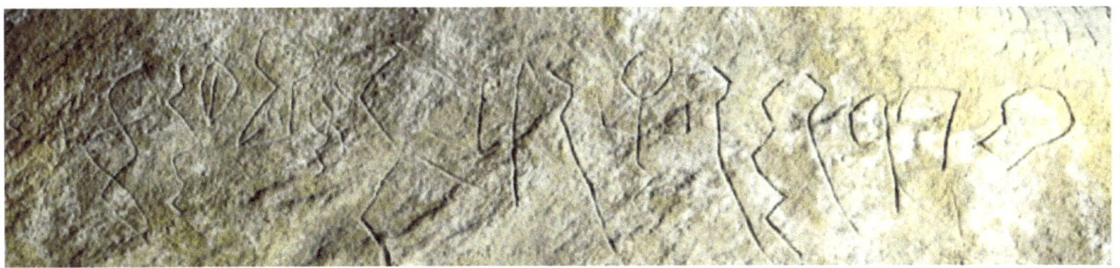

Wadi el-Hôl Early Alphabetic Text No. 1 (Horizontal Inscription), ca. 1850–1700 BCE, incised in limestone, approximately 20 cm. long, Wadi el-Hôl, Egypt.

EGYPTIAN HIEROGLYPHS on left (see right sidebar) and **HIERATIC** on right.
ca.1900 BCE

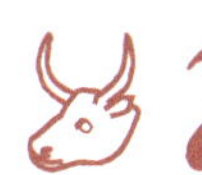
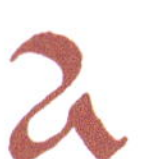
Ox head = *aleph*

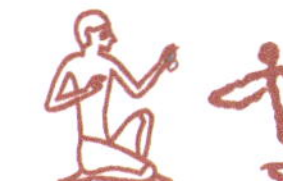
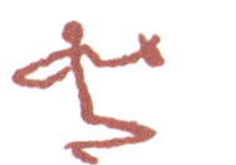
Seated man with raised arms = *he*

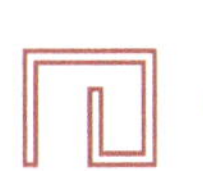
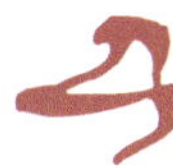
House = *beth*

EARLY ALPHABETIC, WADI EL-HÔL (from above Text No. 1, Horizontal Inscription)
ca.1800 BCE

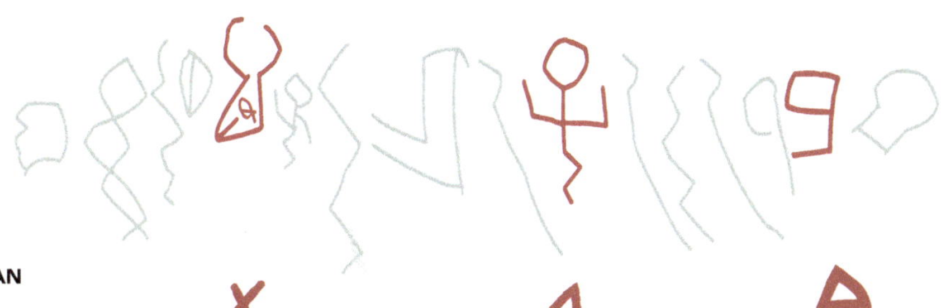

PHOENICIAN
ca.1000 BCE

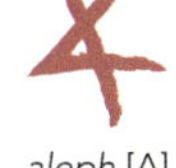
aleph [A]

he [E]

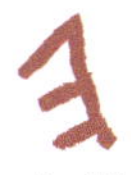
beth [B]

The illustrations are based on the research of John Colman Darnell et al. 2005.

EVOLUTION OF NINE LETTERS

Beginning with Sir Alan Gardiner's *Sign List of Egyptian Hieroglyphs* (1957): his symbols, naming and numbering convention; the Phoenician name of the letter; the hieratic and today's Roman letter.

HIEROGLYPH	HIERATIC	ROMAN
Ox head (F1), *aleph*		A
House (O4), *beth*		B
Throw stick (T14), *gimel*		C
Man with raised arms (A28), *he*		E
Hand (D46), *kaph [drt]*		K
Water (N35), *mem*		M
Cobra sign (I10), *nun*		N
Eye (D4), *ayin*		O
Human head (D1), *resh*		R

7

1800 BCE

EARLY ALPHABETIC and HIEROGLYPHS

SERÂBÎT EL-KHÂDIM
Sinai Peninsula, Egypt

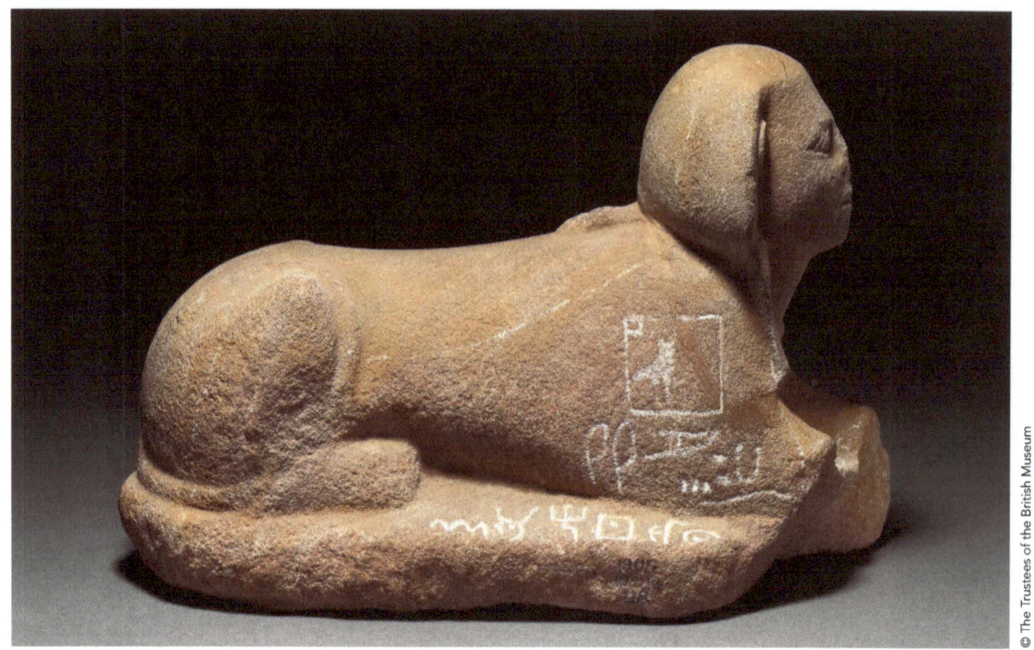

Sandstone Sphinx, ca.1800–1700 BCE, right side, possibly a votive offering to the goddess Hathor, found at the Hathor Temple Complex, Serâbît el-Khâdim, Sinai, Egypt. Bilingual inscription: Egyptian hieroglyphs and Early Alphabetic (Proto-Sinaitic).

Egypt's geographic location played a critical role in its social, cultural, and economic development, as well as in its interaction with other areas of the ancient world, and contributed to its diverse history and heterogeneous population. Of all the ancient cultures, Egypt is perhaps unique in having maintained roughly the same boundaries throughout its history.
—Salima Ikram, *Ancient Egypt: An Introduction* (2009)

USING THE SOUND OF ONE SCRIPT TO DECIPHER ANOTHER

The *Sandstone Sphinx* may be referred to as a type of "Rosetta Stone." Like the Rosetta Stone (see page 66), it contains more than one language and script, albeit in a brief single phrase. It was enough for Egyptologist Sir Alan Gardiner (1879–1963) to decipher it. According to Gardiner, the inscription in Egyptian hieroglyphs on the sphinx's right shoulder reads: "Beloved of Hathor, Lady of Turquoise." Based on the sounds of the characters written on the left and right base in early alphabetic script the Semitic word for *Hathor* was identified: "Beloved of Ba'alat [Lady]" (see page 43, on the excavation of the Temple of Ba'alat in Byblos, Lebanon). It is a rare example of the development of the alphabet at this stage and in this region. By applying the sound-based characters of Egyptian hieroglyphs, one sound for one sign, an alphabetic system slowly began to emerge. Other inscriptions known as Proto-Canaanite (1700–1550 BCE) were found outside the Sinai Peninsula in the ancient cities of Gezer and Lachish (present-day Israel) and in the ancient city of Shechem (Palestine). After the *Sandstone Sphinx* there is little surviving evidence of the formation of the alphabet until about 1550 BCE.

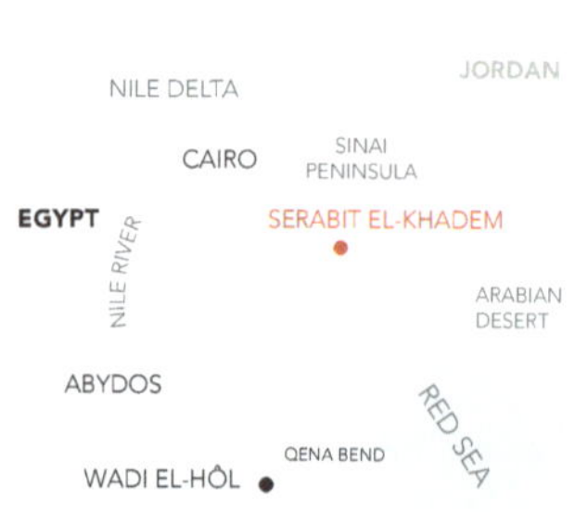

The exchange between the Semitic-speaking miners and the Egyptian managers in the turquoise mines of Serâbît el-Khâdim reflected the greater economic, cultural, religious, and linguistic exchange throughout the region. With different languages, dialects, and writing systems, people needed to find a common way to communicate. By 1400 BCE in the coastal city of Ugarit, Syria, a city at the crossroads of major cultural and economic exchange, the alphabet was used in a cuneiform style. It was a cuneiform *abjad*, a consonantal alphabet. It had the same sequence as the Phoenician alphabet, though read from left to right, using twenty-nine to thirty characters. By 1100 BCE, as the forms evolved from early alphabetic to Phoenician, the direction of writing and the number of letters stabilized.

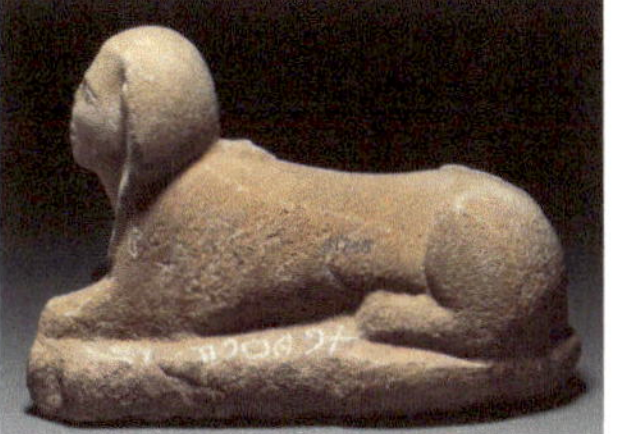

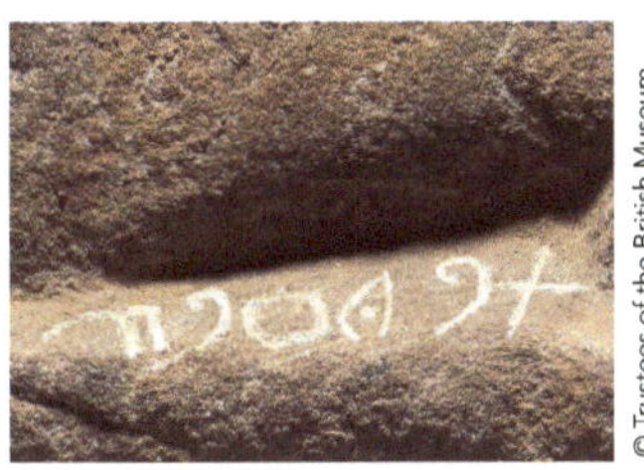

Sandstone Sphinx, ca.1800–1700 BCE, left side, reading from left to right in Early Alphabetic (Proto-Sinaitic), "l b'l t," or "b'alat," meaning "to the Lady" or "for Ba'alat." DETAIL on right.

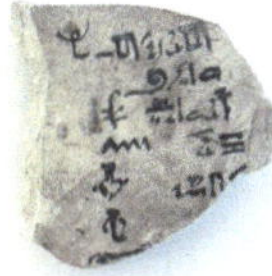

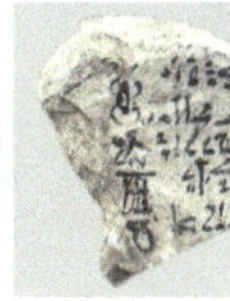

Double-sided limestone ostracon, ca. 1400 BCE, 10 x 10 cm, written in hieroglyphs and hieratic. Found in the Tomb of Senneferi, Luxor. Researchers conclude it is part of an *abecedary*—perhaps the first written evidence of letter order, in not one, but two forms of early alphabets. It may have been used as a mnemonic device by Egyptian scribes, or, given that it is a partial abecedary, a practice sketch. Both sides include: *aleph* [A], *beth* [B], and *gimel* [C].

MEANWHILE, ON THE ISLAND OF CRETE

A syllabic script called Linear B (ca. 1340–1190 BCE) was used by the Mycenaeans to write Mycenaean Greek. It evolved from an earlier Minoan script known as Linear A (ca. 1400–1500 BCE). Although Linear B predates the Greek alphabet, it is unrelated to it. The script included 87 syllabic signs and over 100 ideographic symbols. It was written left to right. It appears to have been used exclusively for administrative purposes.

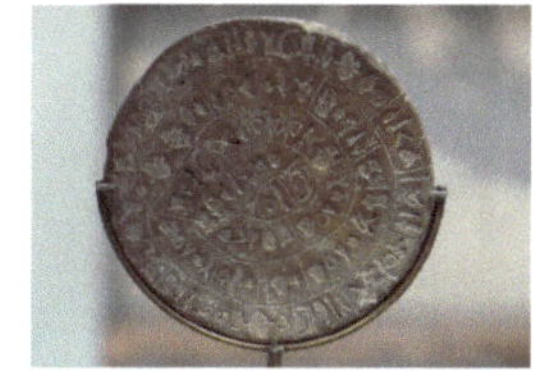

Phaistos Disk, Side B, ca. 1800-1600 BCE, terracotta, 6–7 inches across, five coils, double sided, Archaeological Museum of Heraklion, Phaistos, Crete. Scholars suggest it may be a Minoan prayer to a mother goddess. The disk has both pictographs and what appears to be alphabetic forms stamped into both sides, suggesting movable signs.

GIVING THANKS—
USING THE SOUND OR SHAPE OF ONE ALPHABET TO WRITE ANOTHER

Dōmo

Latin letters to spell *domo*, which on its own in Japanese means "very much," but here means a casual form of "thank you." Dōmo is a Japanese restaurant in Denver, Colorado.

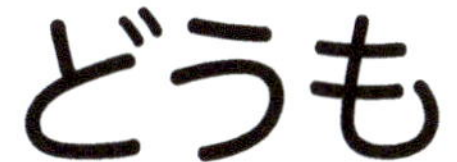

The casual form of *thank you* in Japanese is pronounced "dough-mo."

Shukran

Arabic and Latin letters used to spell *shukran*, "thank you" in Arabic. The four Arabic letters, *kaaf* (ك), *yaa'*(ي), *i'een* (ع), and *meem* (م), resemble the shapes (not sounds) of the Latin letters S, U, R, and A, and like Arabic, are written with the letters connected. Shukran is a Lebanese restaurant in Guatemala City, Guatemala.

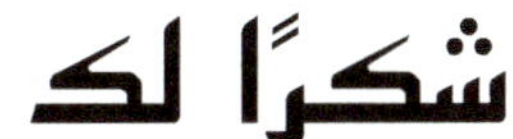

Thank you in Arabic is pronounced "shukran." It reads from right to left.

Xie Xie

Latin letters to spell *xie xie*, which is "thank you" in Mandarin. Xie Xie is a sushi restaurant in Limassol, Cyprus.

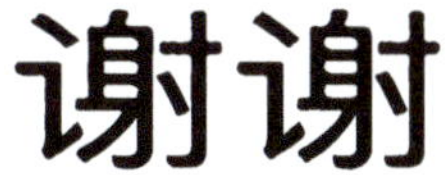

The word *thank you* in Mandarin is pronounced "shay-shay."

HYKSOS PERIOD: ca. 1730–1580 BCE

The Hyksos period marked the colonization of the northeast Nile Delta by Asian peoples. They founded the settlement Avaris, which became a central hub for business. The Egyptian term for Hyksos was *heqa-khase*, meaning "rulers of foreign lands." They came from various regions, including Mesopotamia, Crete, Cyprus, Anatolia, Greece, and the Levant. The Hyksos introduced new technologies and ideas, including the horse and chariot, and the compound bow. There is no doubt that this convergence of diverse peoples with different languages and scripts contributed to the development of a common form of communication.

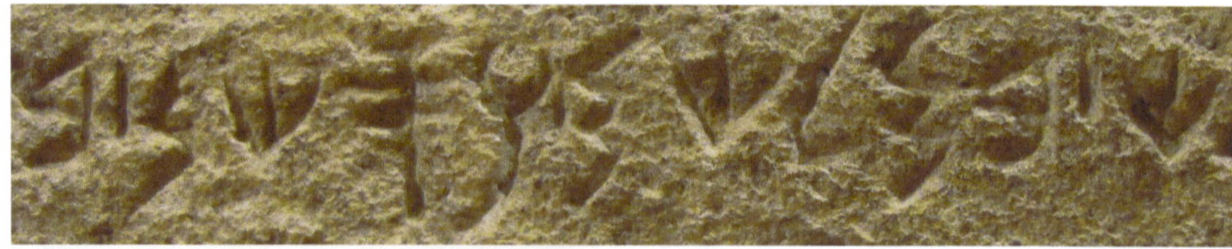

8

1000 BCE

PHOENICIAN

PHOENICIA
Lebanon

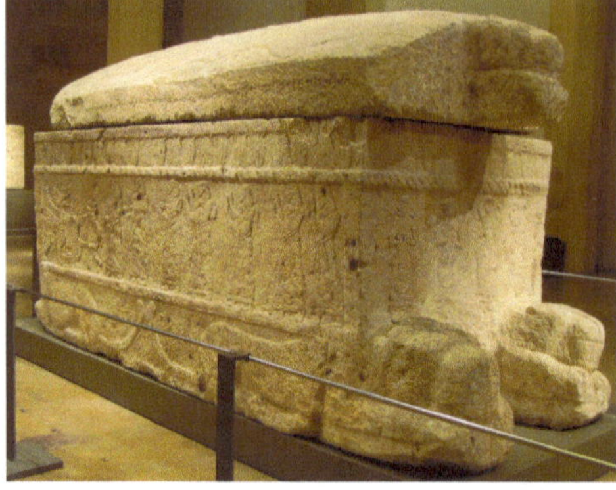

ABOVE, DETAIL: *Sarcophagus of Ahiram Inscription*, average height of inscription is approximately 26 mm. See facing page for entire inscription.

LEFT: *Sarcophagus of Ahiram, King of Byblos*, ca. 1000 BCE, limestone, Phoenician, National Museum of Beirut.

It reflects how a small nation adopted the cultural practices of a more powerful one—applying a curse to a king's sarcophagus, as was done on royal Egyptian tombs.

A TWENTY-TWO LETTER ALPHABET EMERGES

The importance of the Phoenician script for the history of writing cannot be overestimated.
—David Diringer,
The Alphabet: A Key to the History of Mankind (1948)

Over seven hundred Egyptian hieroglyphs primarily represented word-signs, phonograms, and determinatives. In contrast, the twenty-two letter Phoenician alphabet represented individual syllables and consonants. Vowels would be introduced later, with the Greeks. The discovery of the *Sarcophagus of Ahiram* (also spelled *Ahirom*, 𐤀𐤇𐤓𐤌 in Phoenician, reads from right to left) was a major contribution to understanding the history of the alphabet, as it reflects the gradual evolution towards abstraction and simplification.

The sarcophagus was found after a landslide on a hillside in Byblos, north of Beirut, Lebanon, in 1923. The thirty-eight word inscription is incised around the top rim of its cover. Although the writing is small and in the old Phoenician dialect, it conveys a dire warning to anyone who attempts to disturb it. Using nineteen of the twenty-two characters, it is sophisticated in context and form. It stands as one of the earliest known examples of the Phoenician alphabet. Phoenician inscriptions dating from 1000 BCE to 200 BCE have been found throughout the coastal Mediterranean. These inscriptions reflect a culture with not only sailing and trading skills, but with a significant idea: a one-sign, one sound alphabet. Discovery sites include Cyprus, Greece, coastal North Africa, Egypt, Malta, Sicily, Sardinia, Marseilles, and Spain (see map on page 47 for Phoenician colonization). However, Byblos, Lebanon, with its long history of continuous settlement, remains unique. As Maurice Dunand, a mid-20th-century French archeologist, wrote: "Few places in the world convey such a sense of remote history as Byblos offers."

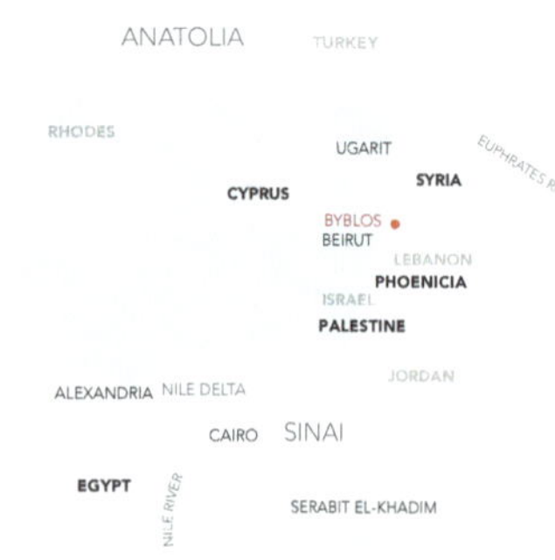

TRANSLATION: REINHARD G. LEHMANN (2005)

Sarcophagus of Ahiram Inscription (top), its translation (above), and the highlighted part of the text from the facing page.

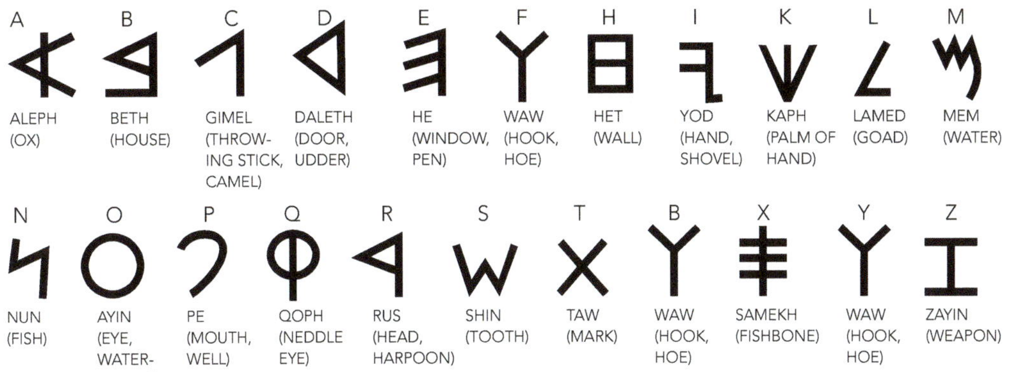

Phoenician alphabet, circa 1000 BCE, twenty-two letters (less G, J, U, W).

TEMPLE OF BA'ALAT GEBAL (2800 BCE), ANTIQUITIES COMPLEX, BYBLOS, LEBANON

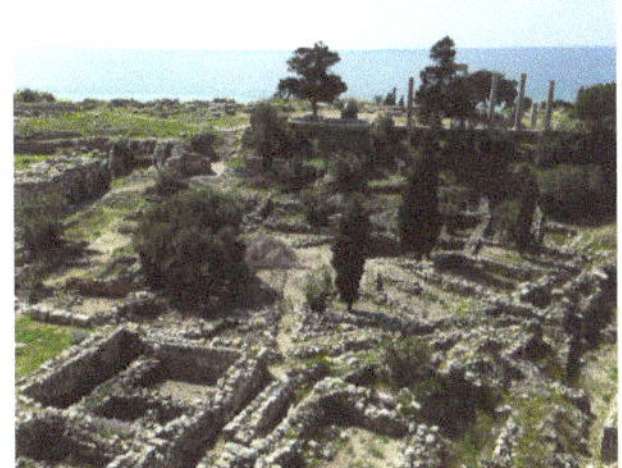

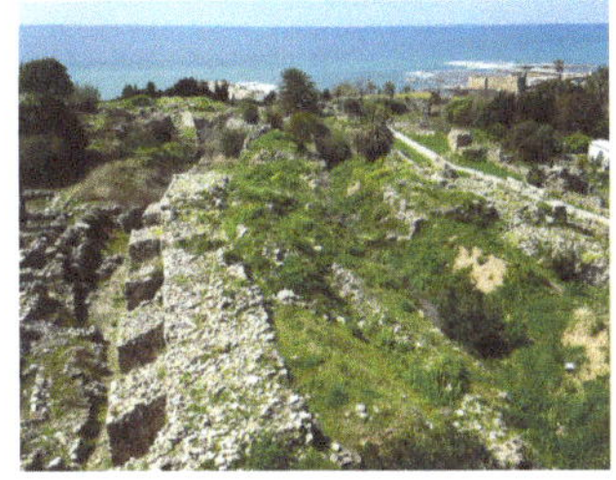

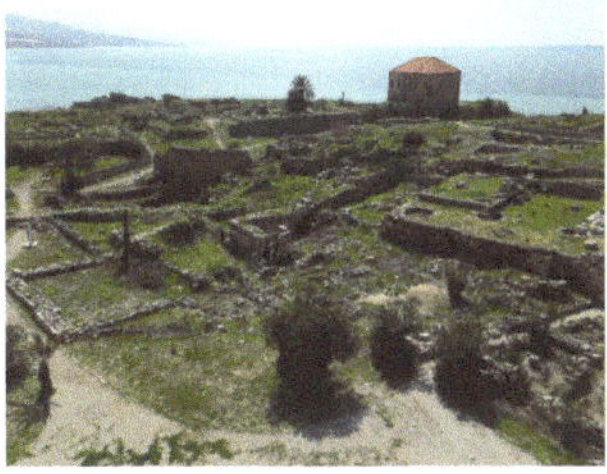

The ancient village of Byblos, Lebanon, first settled between 8800–7000 BCE, is the oldest continuously inhabited port in the world. Its many names reflect the diverse peoples who lived and traded there. By 2600 BCE, the ancient Egyptians were exchanging both goods and religious ideas with the region, referring to Byblos as *Kebny*. The Canaanites, or pre-Phoenicians, called it *Gubla*, meaning "mountain." The ancient Greeks named it *Byblos*, after the Egyptian papyrus they purchased there. In Greek, *biblia* means "books;" and *biblion* means "book," "paper," or "scroll." The word *Bible* ultimately derives from *Byblos*. Today, the village is known as *Jbeil*, the Arabic word for "mountain," which reflect the landscape that surrounds it. Byblos is also considered the birthplace of the alphabet.

A NEW TECHNOLOGY: PAPER

Over four thousand years ago, with the invention of papyrus as a writing surface, Egypt became the Silicon Valley of the ancient world. Papyrus was one of the most important technologies traded, helping to democratize knowledge across the region.

The word paper comes from the Latin *papyrum*, meaning "paper plant" or "paper made from it," which comes from the Greek *papyros*, referring to any plant of the papyrus genus. However, its roots lie in the ancient Egyptian word *pa-per-aa* or *p'p'r*, meaning "that of the Pharaoh" or "Pharaoh's own," suggesting a royal monopoly on papyrus production. The word entered English through the French *papire* during the Norman Conquest of 1066 CE.

The oldest known inscribed papyrus (see below) was discovered in 2013 at the Red Sea port of Wadi al-Jarf, Egypt. Dating from the reign of King Khufu (2566 BCE), it is a logbook written by the inspector Merer, who supervised the construction of the Great Pyramid. The document contains two columns of information: one detailing materials being transported and consumed, the other describing Merer's activities and those of his 200 workers. Written in both hieroglyphic and hieratic script, some scholars have referred to Merer's scroll as the world's first spreadsheet.

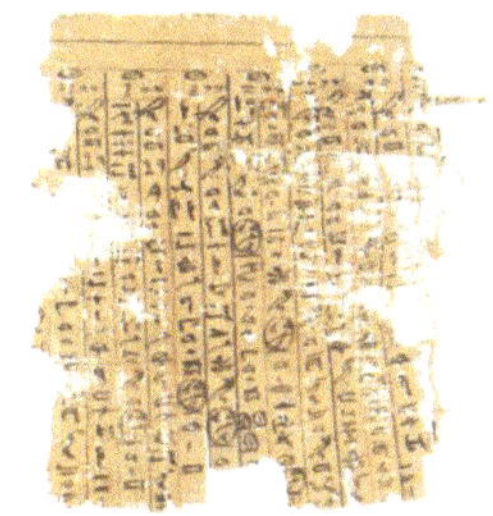

9

850 BCE

PHOENICIAN in ARCHAIC GREEK LETTERS

DHIBĀN
Jordan

Mesha' Stele (Moabite Stone), 841 or 842 BCE, basalt, 3 feet 10 inches tall x 2 feet wide, Phoenician, The Louvre Museum, Paris.

It is like an old patriarch of the tribe, who under his shaggy brow and copious beard bears strong lineaments of resemblance to the smooth-faced, smiling infant that lies unconscious in his arms.
—W. Pakenham Walsh, on comparing the Phoenician letters with Roman letters, *The Moabite Stone: The Substance of Two Lectures*, 5th Edition, George Herbert, Publisher, Dublin (1872)

DIFFERENT LANGUAGE, SAME LETTERS

The *Moabite Stele* contains a 34-line inscription in the Moabite language—closely related to Hebrew and Aramaic—written in the Phoenician alphabet. It tells a story of geography and history in the language of the Bible. Discovered in 1868 by French missionary F. A. Klein in Dhibān (present-day Jordan), the ancient capital of the Moabite kingdom, the stele is a first-person "self-glorification" by King Mesha of Moab.

The text is divided into three parts: the first recounts his wars with Omri, King of Israel, and his successors; the second highlights his leadership and public works; the third details his victory over Horonen, a region southeast of the Dead Sea. Mesha attributes his success to Chemosh, the Moabite god.

In 1870, M. de Vogüé wrote, "I venture to say that there does not exist in the domain of Hebrew antiquities a document which can be compared with it." E. Deutsch of the British Museum added in 1869 that "nearly the whole of the Greek alphabet is found here, not merely similar to the 'Phoenician' shape, but as identical with it as can wellbe." Unfortunately, the last five lines of the inscription are broken and illegible. The content of the stele supports events described in the Hebrew Bible.

As the Phoenician script evolved, it split into two branches: the homeland (Phoenician) branch, used from 1000–300 BCE, and the colonial branch. The colonial branch included three major scripts: Cypro-Phoenician (1000–200 BCE), Sardinian (seen on the *Nora Stone*, ca. 825 BCE), and the Carthaginian script, which developed into the Punic alphabet. Punic, a more cursive form, was used until ca. 300 CE—about 500 years longer than Phoenician.

The Phoenician script was adopted by Aramaic- and Greek-speaking cultures. Aramaic eventually split into Hebrew, ca. 500 BCE, and Nabataean, ca. 150 BCE, the latter evolving into Arabic, ca. 470 CE. The Greek alphabet was later adopted by the Etruscans, ca. 150 BCE.

DIFFERENT LANGUAGE, SAME LETTERS TODAY

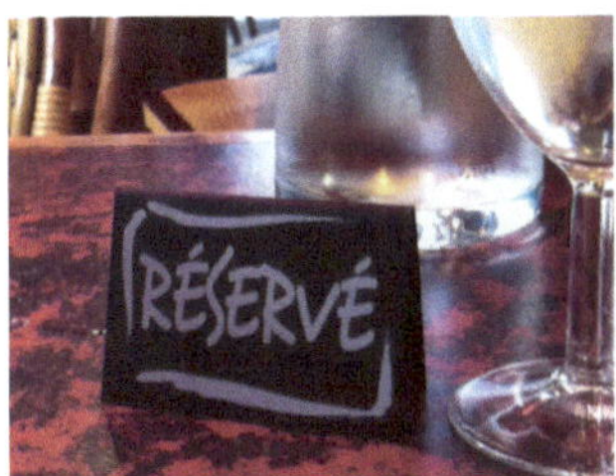

French, restaurant signage, Paris, France.

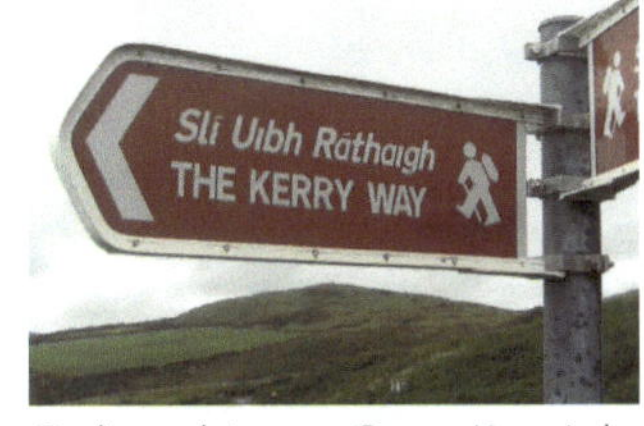

Gaelic, rural signage, County Kerry, Ireland.

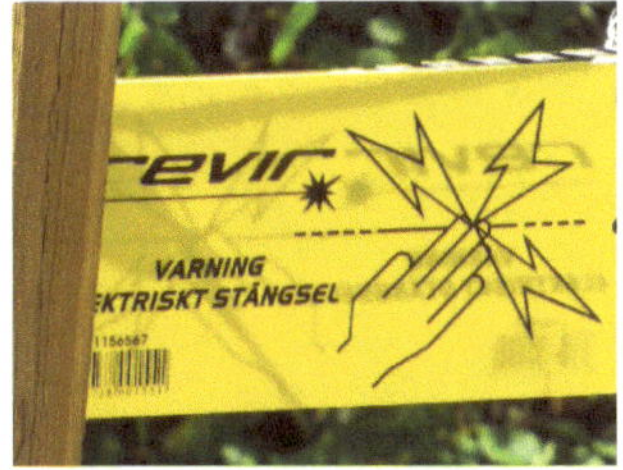

Swedish, park signage, Stockholm, Sweden.

Turkish, airline seat signage, Turkey.

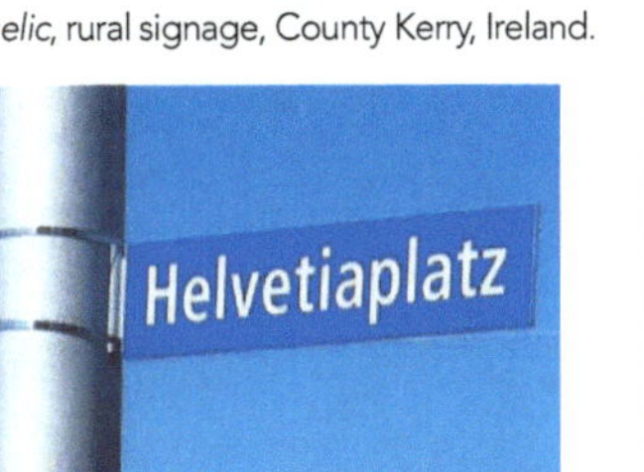

German, street signage, Bern, Switzerland.

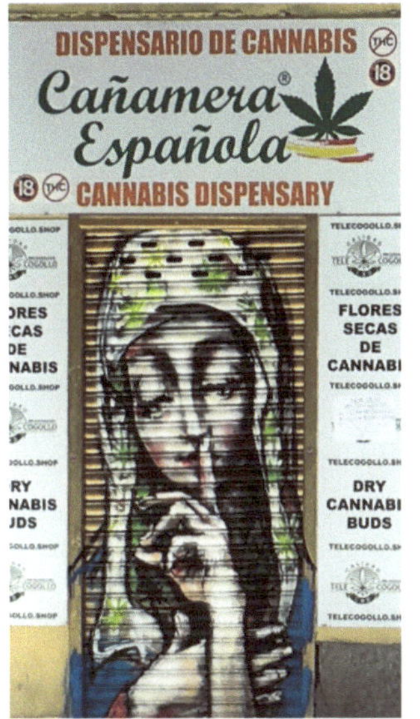

Spanish, street signage, Madrid, Spain.

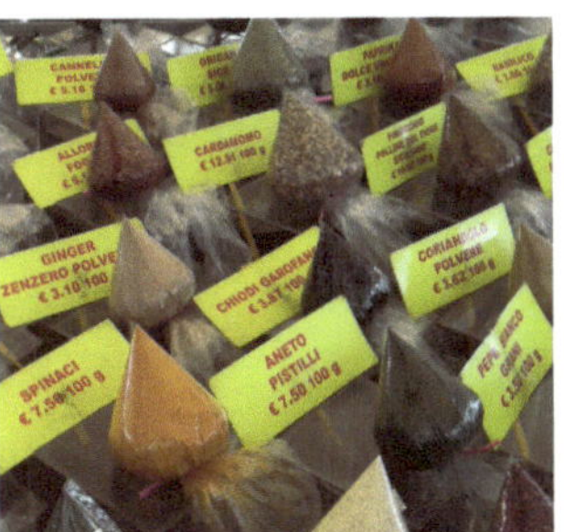

Italian, spice packaging, Rome, Italy.

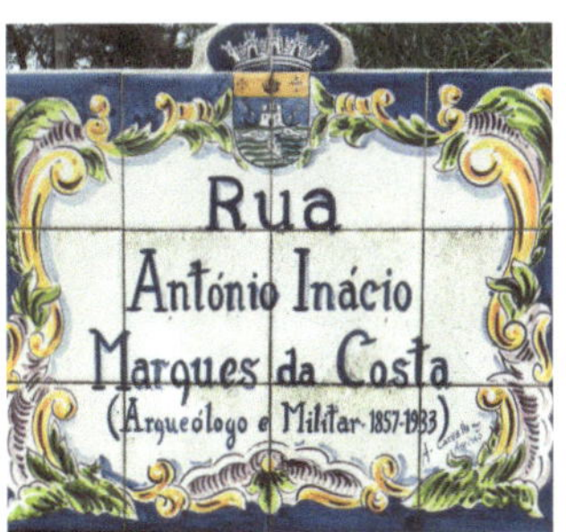

Portuguese, property signage, Setúbal, Portugal.

DIFFERENT | SAME

Though we all have common needs, the way we visually communicate them is based on culture, customs, and language.

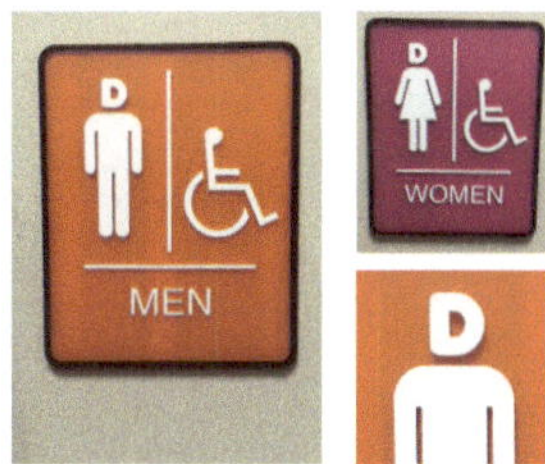

Boston, Massachusetts, USA.
Note that the D and the colors come from the Dunkin' Donuts identity.

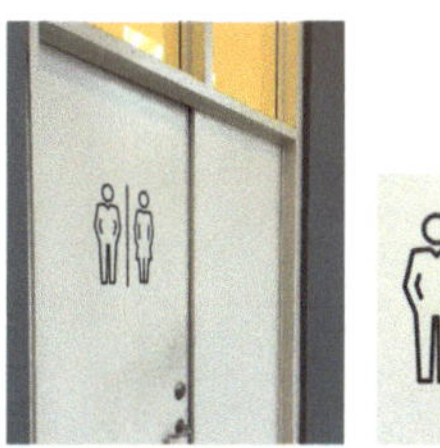

Copenhagen, Denmark.

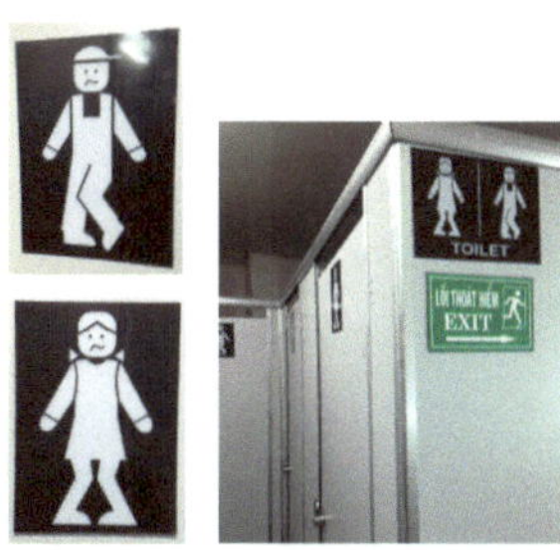

Ho Chi Min City, Vietnam.

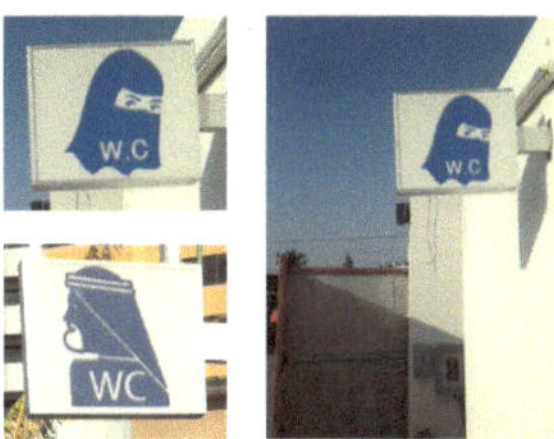

Jeddah, Saudi Arabia.

10

825 BCE

PHOENICIAN

SARDINIA
Italy

If culture is, as many scholars think, "a communicable intelligence," and if writing is, as it is, one of the most important means of communication—the only one indeed which can defy time and space—it is not an exaggeration to say that writing is the main currency of man's civilization.
—David Diringer,
The Alphabet: A Key to the History of Mankind (1948)

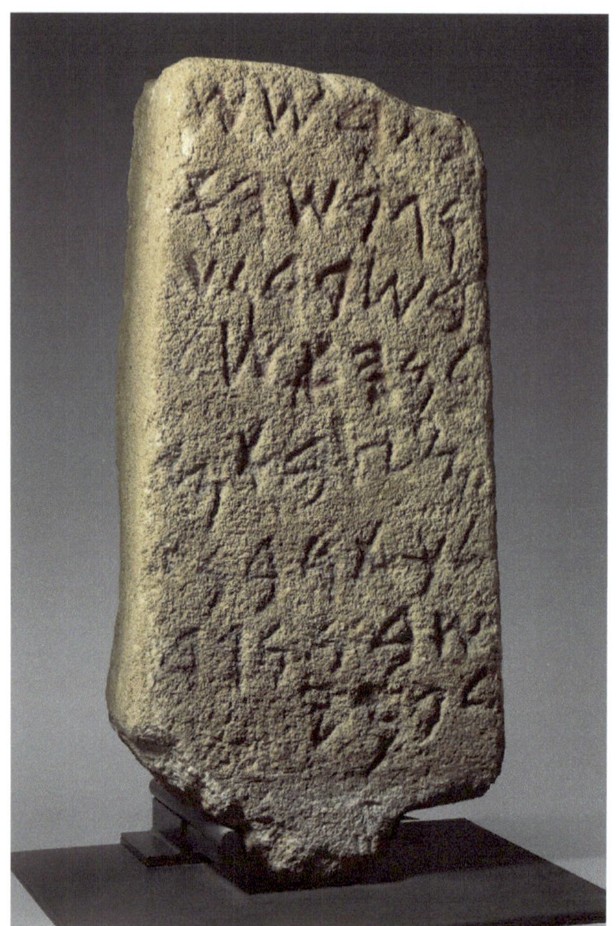

Nora Stone, ca. 825 BCE, Sardinia, Phoenician, Museo Archeologico Nazionale, Cagliari. It is considered the oldest example of Phoenician found outside of Phoenicia.

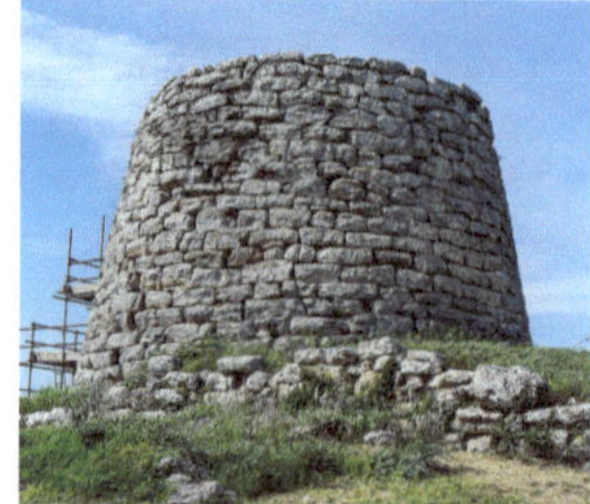

Example of a central Nuraghe tower, Nuraghe Is Paras, Isili, Sardinia, Italy, ca. 1500 BCE. Nuraghi towers were built as single family defensive structures. In certain areas of Sardinia they were built together as collective defensive complexes. The name Nuragic comes from the Nuraghe, the stone fortresses found throughout Sardinia, of which seven thousand have been identified.

A house he beat down
And he drove out.
In Sardinia,
he is at peace;
his army is at peace.
Milkyton, son of
Shubon, the Commander.
For [the god] Pummay.

TRANSLATION: NATHAN PILKINGTON (2012)

TRADE, COLONIZATION, AND WAR: LETTERS ON THE MOVE

The Nora Stone is named after the now-abandoned port city of Nora, located on the southwest coast of the island of Sardinia, where it was discovered in 1773. The exact location of the stone's discovery has since been lost, leading scholars to debate the completeness of its inscription. Some theorize that it is a religious text discussing the foundation of a temple, while others suggest it is a military document. What is clear, however, is that the Nora Stone reflects the Phoenician colonization of Sardinia, which began in the ninth century BCE. The stone was found in a region once part of the Nuragic civilization, which began around 1900 BCE and lasted until the arrival of the Romans in 238 BCE. There are several different translations of the Nora Stone's text. According to scholar Nathan Pilkington, the inscription suggests that Tyre—a coastal city in present-day

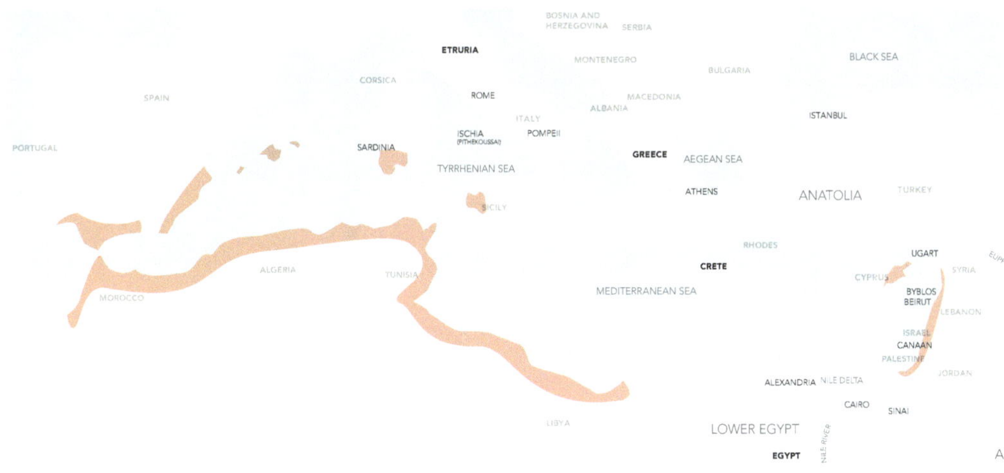

southern Lebanon and home to the Tyrian King Pygmalion—sent an army to Sardinia to protect its mining interests. Pilkington concludes that the stone commemorates a Phoenician conquest over the Nuragic people. By 814 BCE, as the Phoenicians were settling Carthage, the Greeks had adopted nineteen of the twenty-two Phoenician letters. They preserved the original order, names, and shapes with only minor changes and began writing—even though Greek was as different from Phoenician as English is from Arabic. Initially, the Greeks wrote the left-facing letters from right to left, and later adopted the boustrophedon style (see page 59). Within two hundred years, three distinct versions of the Phoenician script had emerged, reflecting the diverse developments in Phoenicia and beyond. As different groups of people—speaking different languages—adopted and adapted the alphabet, they reimagined old characters, created new ones, and added diacritics to reflect their specific linguistic needs.

LETTERS COLONIZE

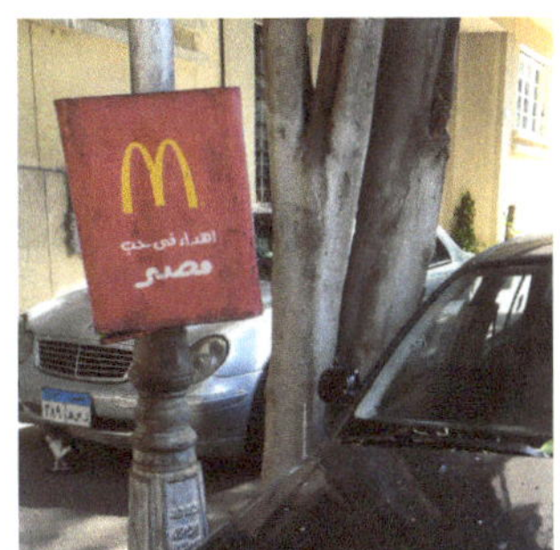

In 1994, McDonald's opened its first two restaurants in Cairo, Egypt, and in 1995, opened a third in Alexandria.

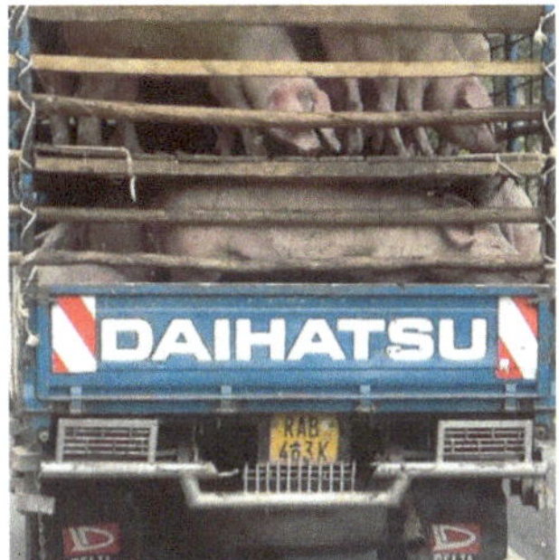

In 1977, SAR Motors became the sole importer and distributor of Diahatsu, a Japanese car company, in Kigali, Rwanda.

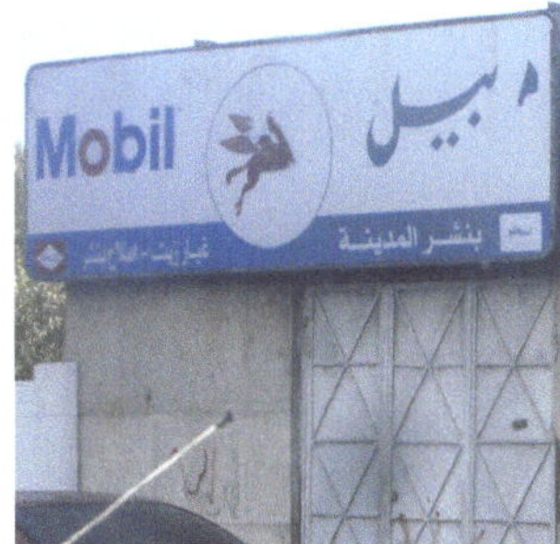

In 1927, Socony, later Mobil, began marketing products in western Saudi Arabia, including this location in Jeddah.

PHOENICIA AND THE PHOENICIANS

Phoenicia was a region of city-states ruled by kings, located in what is now coastal Lebanon, Jordan, Syria, Israel, and Palestine. The region was originally settled by the Canaanites, a Bronze Age people who lived before 1100 BCE people, from whom the Phoenicians partly originated (3000 BCE). The Phoenicians were renowned for their boat-building and seafaring skills, which enabled them to expand their empire and establish trading posts throughout the Mediterranean. They were situated at the crossroads of two great civilizations: Egypt and Mesopotamia. The name "Phoenician" was given to them by the ancient Greeks. They referred to them as *Phoínikes*, which means "purple people," reflecting a major export of the Phoenicians: purple-dyed wool from the murex shell. Dutch historian Robert S. P. Beekes (1937–2017) suggested that a pre-Greek, Mycenaean name, *po-ni-ki-jo, po-ni-ki,* may have been borrowed from the ancient Egyptian *fnh ̮ w*, meaning "carpenters" or "woodcutters," possibly in reference to the famed Lebanon cedars. Today, Lebanon is still known for its cedar trees (it's on their national flag), although it is less recognized for its purple-dyed wool.

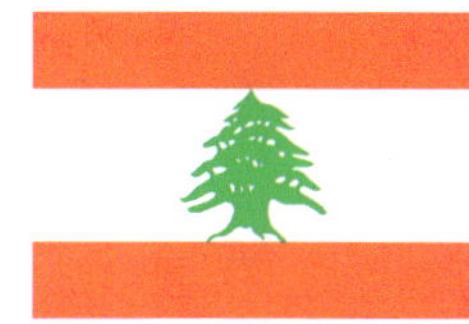

Flag of Lebanon, 1943, designed by Henri Philippe Pharaoun. The green cedar tree represents holiness, eternity, and peace. The cedar is mentioned seventy-seven times in the Bible. The white background represents the purity and peace of snow; the red stripes represent the blood lost in defending the country from invaders.

11

750 BCE

ARCHAIC GREEK

DIPYLON
Greece

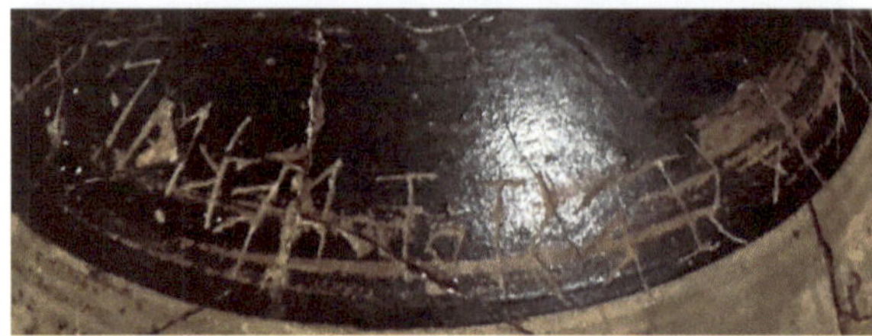

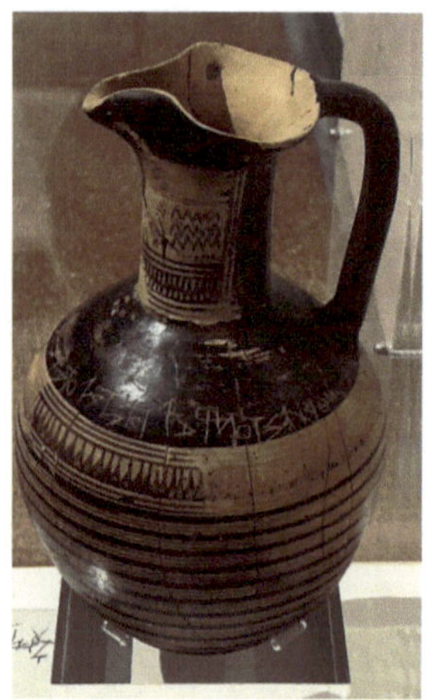

RIGHT: *Dipylon Inscription*, Greece, ca. 740 BCE, National Archaeological Museum of Athens. The oldest known example of Greek with letterforms similar to Phoenicians. Named after the cemetery where it was found in 1871. DETAILS LEFT.

INSCRIPTION

47 46 45 44 43 42 41 40 39 38 37 36 35 34 33 32 31 30 29 28 27 26 25 24 23 22 21 20 19 1
FIGURES

this thing [the jug] belongs to him, whoever of all the dancers now frolics most delicately

TRANSLATION: BARRY POWELL (1988)

While we are surrounded by the sight of letters, 8th-century Greeks were surrounded by the linear shapes of their Geometric decoration.
— Natasha M. Binek, *The Dipylon Oinochoe Graffito: Text or Decoration?* (2017)

THE GREEKS ADOPT THE PHOENICIAN ALPHABET

The Dipylon Inscription is the earliest surviving example of Greek writing in its infancy. It consists of forty-seven characters incised along the top of a clay wine jug, or oinochoe, marking it as a prize in a dance contest. Dating from the Late Geometric Period (750–700 BCE), the text reads from right to left. It retains many characteristics of the Phoenician alphabet's characteristics, such as the sideways alphas, ≯ (see above FIGURES 31, 29, and 27), and a crooked iota, ≀ (see FIGURE 32). These forms are precursors to our letters A and I (from I, J would later emerge). Despite these similarities, it is the first alphabet where some letters serve as vowels. Scholars generally agree on the translation of the first thirty-five letters, which form a perfect hexameter: "Whoever of all the dancers now frolics most delicately," and the next six letters (figures 36–41), which reads: "This thing [the jug] belongs to him"). Some scholars suggest there were two writers: one literate, who wrote the hexameter, and a second, perhaps his student, who, in FIGURES 42–47, might have been practicing his ABCs, starting with the letter kappa, K, ꓘ, figure 42. However, Classical Studies scholar Natasha M. Binek suggests that from our "deeply literate perspective," we expect to read words. Given figures 43, 44, and 46 are illegible and unusual, especially when viewed from a preliterate perspective, Binek posits that these last six figures may have been decorative. They combine features of letterforms and geometric patterns, reflecting the symmetry and repetition of the Late Geometric Period. Additionally, the Greek verb, **γράφειν**, graphein, means "to write or draw."

According to both Italian and Greek tradition, several mythological figures were credited with inventing or expanding the Greek alphabet. One such figure, Cadmus of Thebes, who lived for many years in Phoenicia, is said to have returned to Greece in 1313 BCE with sixteen letters. During the Trojan War (ca. 1183 BCE), Palamedes is believed to have added letters Θ, Ξ, Φ, Χ. Scholars debate the exact dates of these events, with some suggesting 1400 BCE and others placing them between 600-800 BCE. Eventually, the Greek alphabet evolved into an independent script with twenty-four letters, beginning with A, alpha, and ending with Ω, omega. This alphabet enabled the transciption of Homer's *Iliad* and *Odyssey* (ca. 750 BCE). Herodotus referred to these letters as both *Kadméia grámmata* ("Cadmean letter") and *Phoinikéia grammata* ("Phoenician letters"). Today, about thirty percent of English words are derived from classical Greek, while Greek letters are widely used in science and mathematics.

The twenty-two letter Phoenician alphabet was entirely consonantal, representing only sounds. The Greeks adopted and adapted Phoenician consonants to create seven vowels A, E, I, O, Ω, Y, H: 1) A (alpha) from 𐤀, aleph; 2) E (epsilon) from 𐤄, *he*; 3) I (iota) from 𐤉, *yodh*; 4) O (omicron) from O, *ayin*; 5) Ω (omega) was created as a variant of omicron; 6) Y (upsilon) was derived from *waw*, Y, which appears three times in the Phoenician alphabet; 7) H (eta) was created to represent the long "E" sound. This marks the first alphabetic script to have vowels.

𐤀 𐤁 𐤂 𐤃 𐤄 𐤅 𐤇 𐤉 𐤊 𐤋 𐤌 𐤍 𐤏 𐤐 𐤒 𐤓 𐤔 𐤕 𐤅 𐤎 𐤅 𐤆

Phoenician alphabet, ca. 1000 BCE, twenty-two letters (less G, J, U, W; see page 39).

Α Β Γ Δ Ε Ζ Η Θ Ι Κ Λ Μ Ν Ξ Ο Π Ρ Σ Τ Υ Φ Χ Ψ Ω

Archaic Greek alphabet, ca. 800-500 BCE, twenty-four letters.

Α Β Γ Δ Ε Ζ Η Θ Ι Κ Λ Μ Ν Ξ Ο Π Ρ Σ Τ Υ Φ Χ Ψ Ω

Ionic Greek alphabet, ca. 400 BCE–present, Twenty-four letters, vowels derived from Phoenician in red; vowels derived from Greek in green.

LETTERS AS THINGS, THINGS AS LETTERS

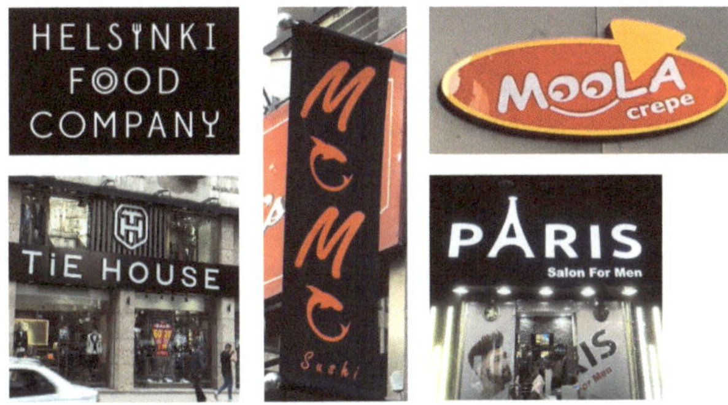

TOP LEFT: Helsinki Food Company, logo, Helsinki; CENTER: MoMo Sushi, logo, New York, NY; TOP RIGHT: Moola crepe, logo, Cairo; BOTTOM LEFT: Tie House, logo, Cairo; BOTTOM RIGHT: Paris Salon For Men, logo, Cairo.

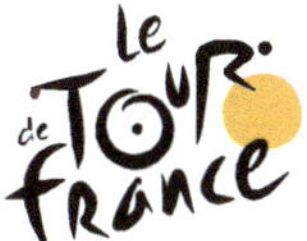

Tour de France, identity, Joel Guenoun, designer, 2002.

١٥٧٤٠

In Arabic, the Latin numbers 15740 translate to the characters ١٥٧٤٠ (see page 23), the English word, "love." It is also the phone number in Egypt to donate to a charity during Ramadan (2021).

PRINCIPLES OF DESIGN are stylistic elements within an artwork that creates a visual vocabulary, enabling both artists and viewers to analyse and discuss art. The examples below apply design characteristics from Greece's Late Geometric Period to a contemporary design lexicon.

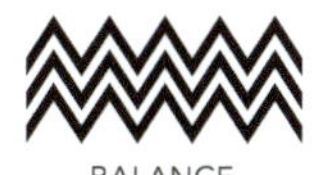

BALANCE

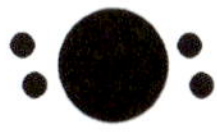

EMPHASIS

MOVEMENT

PATTERN

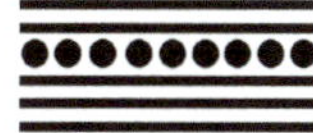

REPETITION

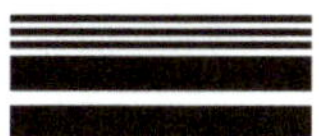

PROPORTION

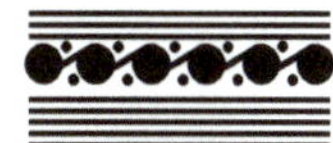

RHYTHM

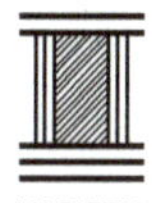

VARIETY

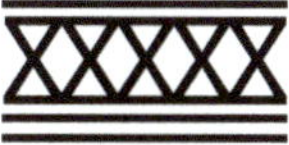

UNITY

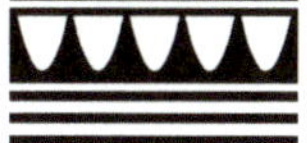

NEGATIVE SPACE

12

725 BCE

ARCHAIC GREEK

ISCHIA

Italy

When the audience, whether the assembly, the law court, the theatre, the symposium, or the temple, was replaced by a reading public, then the Greek mind ceased to create, and began to draw its inspiration, not from Nature and the life around it, but from books.

—Frank Byron Jevons, *A History of Greek Literature from the Earliest Period to the Death of Demosthenes* (1892)

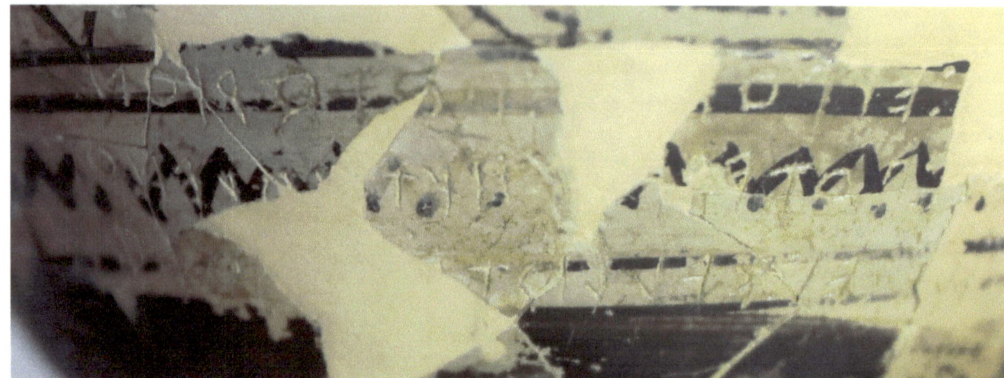

DETAIL: *Nestor's Cup.*

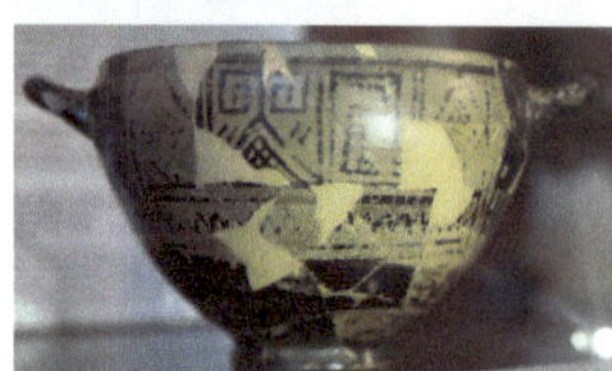

Nestor's Cup, ca. 725 BCE, clay, ancient Greek, Late Geometric Period, The Archaeological Museum of Pithecusa, Ischia.

ADDING CLARITY THROUGH ABSTRACT MARKS, WHILE HAVING A SENSE OF HUMOR

In the late eighth century BCE, the Greeks—like the Phoenicians before them— set sail for brighter shores. They arrived on the island of Pithekoussai, now known as Ischia, off the coast of Naples, Italy, and established a trading post, where, at the time, no writing system existed. It was one of the earliest Greek colonies in the West, offering close proximity to trade with the Etruscans, the dominant people of the region. *Nestor's Cup*, a Rhodian kotyle (ceramic drinking cup), embodies both the extraordinary and the everyday. It contains one of the oldest surviving examples of the Phoenician-inspired Greek alphabet in its earliest form: the Euboean script. As in earlier examples, the three-line verse reads from right to left.

Though the cup was made in Greece, it was discovered in 1954 in the grave of a young boy in an early Pithekoussai cemetery. The three-line inscription, scratched onto the side of the cup after it was made, has missing pieces and appears to use colon-like marks as word spacers. Due to the fragmentary first line—which is not hexametric, unlike lines 2 and 3—scholars differ in their interpretations. The general consensus is that the first line, "I am the cup of Nestor," is a reference to Book 11 in Homer's *Iliad* (written ca. 775 BCE), where the Greek king and hero of the Trojan War, Nestor, owned a large beautifully crafted gold goblet:

> ...and beside them a beauteous cup, that the old man had brought from home, studded with bosses of gold; four were the handles thereof, and about each [line 635] twain doves were feeding, while below were two supports. Another man could scarce have availed to lift that cup from the table, when it was full, but old Nestor would raise it right easily.

The second and third lines likely refer to a drinking game and to wine as an aphrodisiac—suggesting that the more one drinks, the more charming one's company becomes. The name Aphrodite implies sensual pleasure. The inscription is thought to be humorous and ironic, given the cup's humble form. Now, with a written alphabet, the eighth-century Greeks could transcribe their epic poems.

INSCRIPTION

ΝΕΣΤΟΡΟΣ:...:ΕΥΠΟΤΟΝ:ΠΟΤΕΡΙΟΝ
ΗΟΣΔΑΤΟΔΕΠΙΕΣΙ:ΠΟΤΕΡΙ..:ΗΥΤΙΚΑΚΕΝΟΝ
ΗΙΜΕΡΟΣΗΑΙΡΕΣΕΙ:ΚΑΛΛΙΣΤΕΦΑΝΟ:ΑΦΡΟΔΙΤΕΣ

I am the cup of Nestor good for drinking.
Whoever drinks from this cup, desire for beautifully
crowned Aphrodite [sex] will seize him instantly.

TRANSLATION: CHRISTOPHER A. FARAONE (1996)

Although dots had been used to separate words and phrases as early as the *Mesha' Stele* (ca. 840 BCE, see page 44), clarity in writing took time to evolve. By the sixth century BCE, it became standard to separate words by one or two dots. However it wasn't until the third century BCE that significant change occurred. Aristophanes of Byzantium (ca. 257 BCE–180 BCE), a Greek scholar, researcher, and head librarian of the Library of Alexandria in Egypt (appointed 195 BCE), was also an innovator. Perhaps frustrated by reading continuous lines of text thathadnowordorletterspacing (i.e., no kerning or tracking), he is credited with introducing Greek punctuation marks. He was the first to designate the final line of Homer's *Odyssey* at Book 23, line 296. As classical scholar Martin West wrote (2017): "He gave thought to the correct articulation of the text, using accents and other lectional signs to guide the reader." The Romans also experimented with word separation using dots as early as the *Praeneste Fibula* (650 BCE; see page 54). The *Trajan Column Inscription* (113 CE) also used separating dots (see page 70). However, like the Greeks, the Romans valued public speaking more than writing. Eloquence, articulation, and persuasive speech were much more important than the written word or clarifying dots. Latin was primarily a spoken language more than a written one. It would take another 1,400 years—and an Italian named Aldus Manutius (see page 77), to help standardize punctuation, including the comma and semicolon.

SMALL MARKS, BIG INFLUENCE IN AN OPENING LINE

But, you may say, we asked you to speak about women and fiction – what has that got to do with a room of one's own? I

—Virginia Woolf, *A Room of One's Own* (1928).

It was a marvelous night, the sort of night one only experiences when one is young. The sky was so

—Fyodor Dostoyevsky, *White Nights* (1848).

The door opened to reveal an infinitely spacious room: a whole world of meanings and motivations, not just a limited space buried in a mass of detail. Those who entered it.

—Naguib Mahfouz, *Respected Sir* (1975).

I had the story, bit by bit, from various people, and, as generally happens in such cases, each time it was a different story.

—Edith Wharton, *Ethan Frome* (1911).

IT is a truth universally acknowledged, that a single man in possession of a good fortune must be in want of a wife.

—Jane Austen, *Pride and Prejudice* (1813).

A WORD ABOUT ALL-CAPS

Today, using all-caps—or capital letters— SENDS A CLEAR MESSAGE. It has a distinct voice. Whether conveying volume, urgency, importance, or simply creating contrast with surrounding text, all-caps communicates something specific.

So, why not use them all the time?

According to type designer Jonathan Hoefler: "A typeface is designed to be used with capital and lowercase letters. That's because, from a physiological standpoint, lowercase letters are easier to read. They're more distinguishable, they have ascenders and descenders, they have modulated widths, and all this creates a texture that's easier and more pleasing to the eye. Capital letters don't have that."

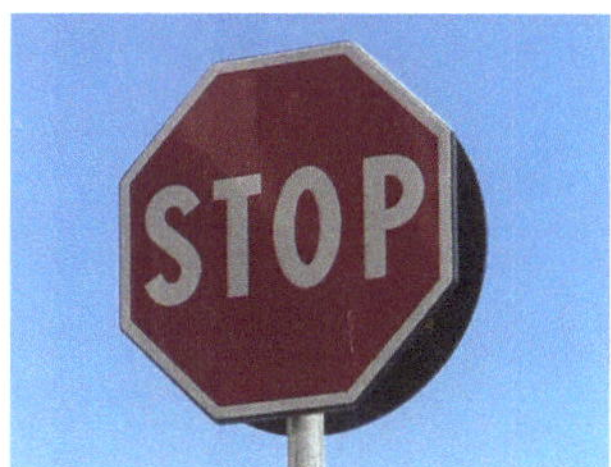

Rome, Italy.

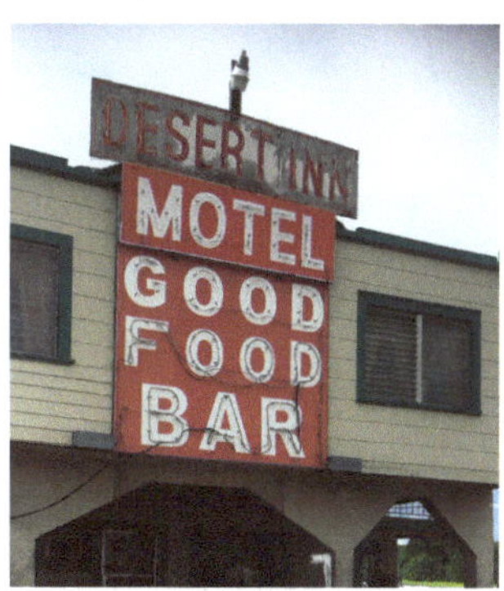

Yeehaw Junction, Florida.

13

700 BCE

ARCHAIC GREEK and ETRUSCAN

MARSILIANA
Italy

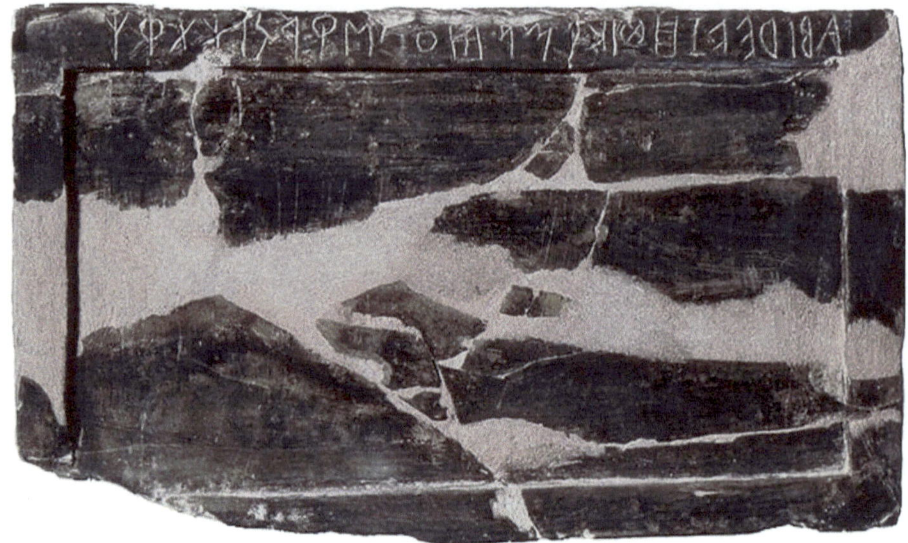

Marsiliana Tablet, Greek/Etruscan, ca. 700 BCE, ivory writing tablet, 8.8 cm. x 5 cm., National Archaeological Museum, Florence. The oldest Etruscan and Greek abcedarium, found in Marsiliana d'Albegna, Italy. It contains twenty-six letters.

After the Greeks copied the Phoenicians, around 750 BCE the Etruscans began using the Greek alphabet. Again, Etruscan was as different from Greek as Greek was from Phoenician, and the letters made the leap.
—David Sacks, *Letter Perfect: The Marvelous History of Our Alphabet from A to Z* (2003)

THE ALPHABET DIVIDES: GREEK AND ETRUSCAN

The Etruscans inherited the alphabet from the colonizing Greeks who came from Euboea—the second-largest Greek island after Crete, located off eastern Greece. It is at this point that the alphabet split into two distinct paths. The Greeks refined the alphabet and its many local variants into the Ionic Greek alphabet around 400 BCE (see page 60), which would eventually evolve into the modern Greek alphabet. Meanwhile, the Etruscans, and later the Romans, adapted the alphabet into the form you are reading today.

The *Marsiliana Tablet* was once believed to be a teaching tool. However, Etruscologist Massimo Pallottino theorized that, given its material (ivory) and compact size, it might have also served as a piece of jewelry worn around the neck—or perhaps it functioned as both. The tablet's center is hollowed out to hold melted wax, which, once cooled, could be inscribed with a stylus to practice writing. Along the top edge is the full Etruscan alphabet: twenty-six letters, including five vowels. These letters include twenty-two Greek characters in their Phoenician form and four additional letters from the Greek alphabet. Although the Etruscans preserved this twenty-six-letter model, they did not use the letters B, G, D, or O.

The Etruscan civilization reached its height between 750–500 BCE in a region north of Rome that stretched to the Po Valley near the Alps and eastward to the Adriatic Sea. This area, known as Etruria, shared a common language, religion, and culture.

Approximate scale

At the time, the Etruscans were the dominant power on the Italian peninsula. The Romans referred to them as *Etrusci* or *Tusci*, from which the name *Tuscany* is derived. The Greeks called them *Tyrsenoi* or *Tyrrhenoi*, giving the Tyrrhenian Sea its name. While the Etruscans profoundly influenced Roman culture, their lack of a centralized government ultimately allowed Rome to surpass them.

Etruscan is a non-Indo-European language with no known parent language, no descendants, and no surviving historical texts or literature. What remains are more than ten thousand inscriptions found across Etruria (modern-day Tuscany), northern Italy, Sicily, Sardinia, and even as far as Alexandria and Carthage. Most inscriptions include only names, dates, and places of death. As Andrew Robinson writes in *The Story of Writing* (2007): "Decipherment of the Etruscan language is like trying to learn English by reading nothing but gravestones."

One remarkable exception is the *Liber Linteus Zagrabiensis* (Latin for "Linen Book of Zagreb"; see sidebar on page 63), the longest known Etruscan text. Despite this and other findings, very little is known about the language. What has survived suggests a strong cultural focus on the afterlife.

FROM GREEK TO LATIN: LETTERS C, D, AND F

Letters C D
Ionian Greek, ca. 800–500 BCE

Letters C D
Euboean Greek, ca. 750 BCE

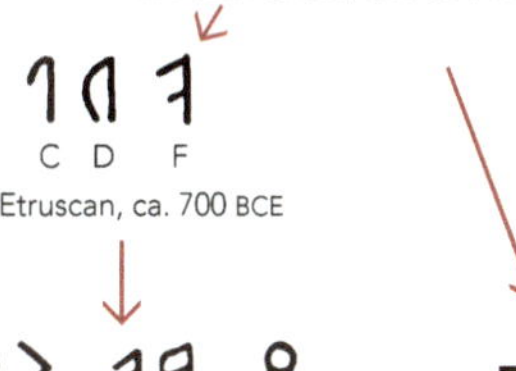

C D F
Etruscan, ca. 700 BCE

C D F F
Etruscan, ca. 400 BCE

C D F
Latin, ca. 100 CE
The third, fourth, and sixth letters of the Latin alphabet. Twenty-three letter alphabet.

Γ Δ
Classical Greek, ca. 400 BCE
From this period forward, the third and fourth letters are gamma and delta; there are no letters C, D, or F. Twenty-four letter alphabet.

SOCIETAL ADVANCEMENTS LEARNED FROM THE ETRUSCANS

In addition to adopting the Etruscan alphabet, the Romans also absorbed various engineering technologies. These included the construction of aqueducts, arched gates, the Tuscan column, and villas with central atriums. Such innovations greatly improved Roman daily life and supported the expansion of their cities. (During this same period, the Assyrians were using a similar water irrigation system known as *qanats*.) Beyond engineering, the Romans also adopted Etruscan practices such as gladiatorial combat and learned techniques for casting sculptures in bronze.

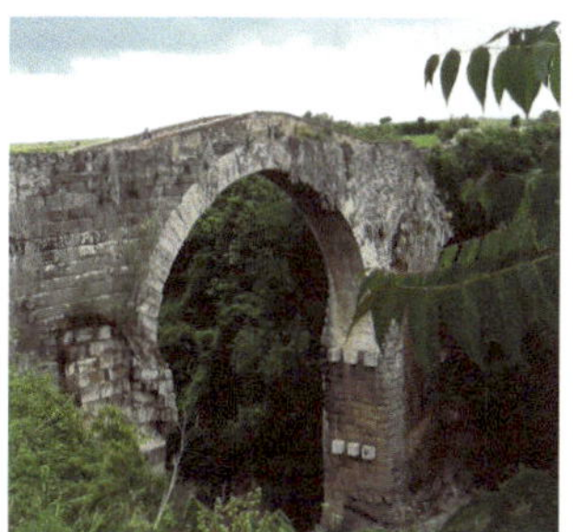

Ponte Di Badia Vulci, an Etruscan bridge, at Vulci, Viterbo, Italy.

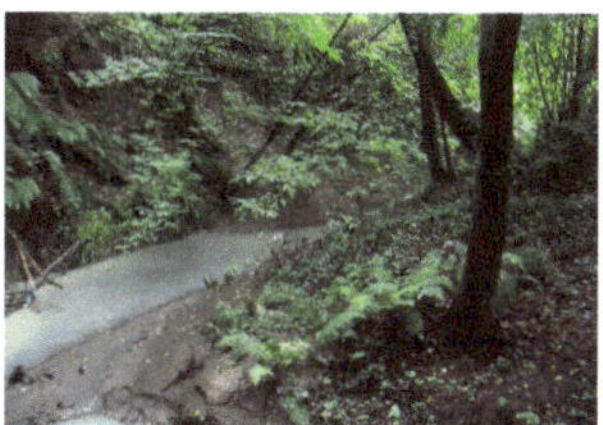

A *cuniculus* (plural *cuniculi*) is a water channel developed and used by the Etruscans. *Cuniculi* could be as simple as a system of trenches or could involve a complex system of tunnels. Today the word also means rabbit or burrow, deriving its meaning from the Latin, *cuniculus*.

ALPHABETS AS KEYBOARDS: PAST AND PRESENT

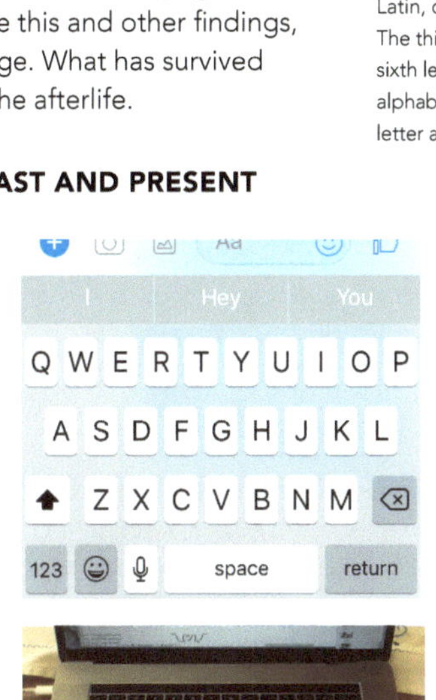

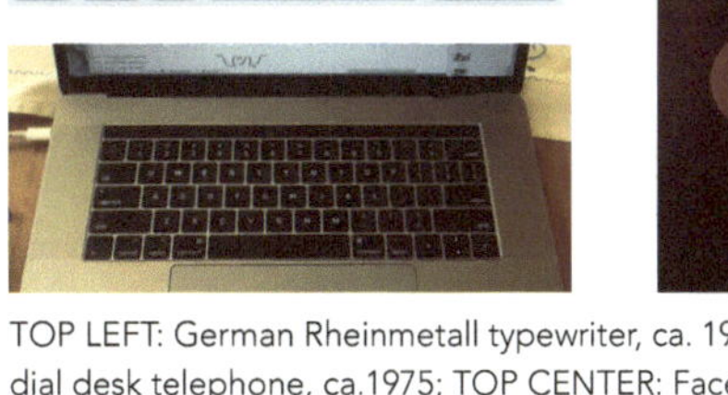

TOP LEFT: German Rheinmetall typewriter, ca. 1957; BOTTOM LEFT: AT+T Rotary dial desk telephone, ca.1975; TOP CENTER: Facebook Messenger app keyboard, 2022; BOTTOM CENTER: MacBook Pro keyboard, 2017; RIGHT: iPhone passcode keyboard, 2022.

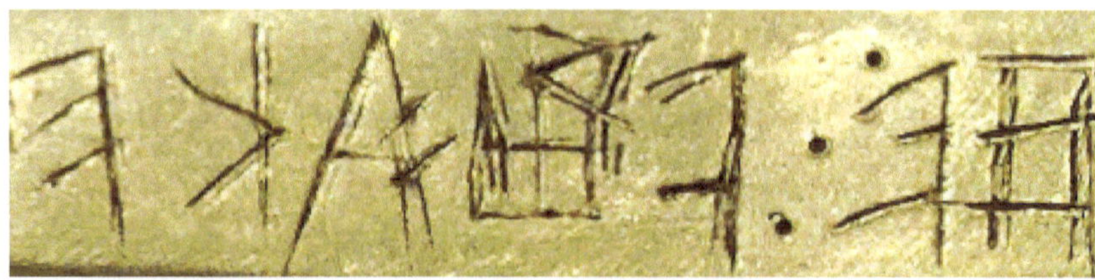

14

650 BCE

ARCHAIC LATIN

PRAENESTE
Italy

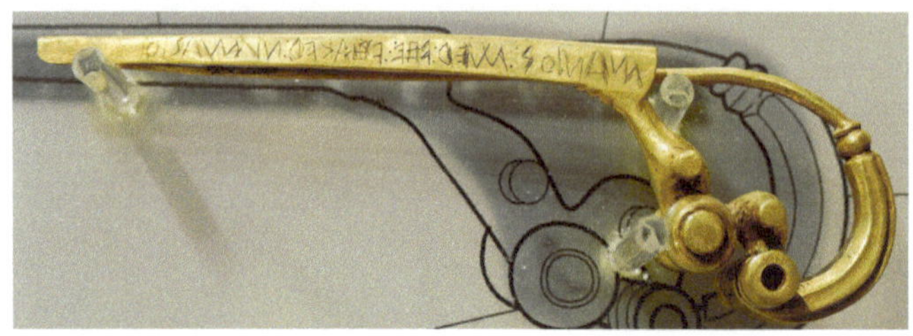

Praeneste Fibula, "the brooch of Palestrina," ca. 650 BCE, Roman, gold, 10.7 cm. long, Museo Preistorico Etnografico Luigi Pigorini (National Museum of Prehistory and Ethnography "Luigi Pigorini"), Rome (detail, top).

In BC 600 the art of writing was so well established in Greece that in a detachment of mercenaries a caertain number could write. There is, however, another point to notice: the names of these soldiers show that they came from different parts of Greece, some being Ionians, others Dorians; but all used the same Ionic alphabet.
—Frank B. Jevons, *A History of Greek Literature: From the Earliest Period to the Death of Demosthenus* (1886)

THE MAKER'S, AND RECEIVER'S, NAME ON A PRODUCT

Discovered in 1871 in a tomb in Praeneste, the Praeneste Fibula contains one of the oldest known examples of written archaic Latin. Etched into its clasp is a twenty-six-letter inscription written from right to left in boustrophedon style (see page 59). What makes this coat pin particularly remarkable is that it includes the first known instance of the letters F and H used together to represent the "eff" sound—a common sound in both Latin and Etruscan, but not in Greek (as previously discussed). This digraph (letter combination) originated in Etruscan, though soon the letter F would come to appear on its own. To revisit an earlier analogy: just as Greek differs from Phoenician as much as English does from Arabic, archaic Latin was equally distinct from Etruscan.

Due to the phonetic characteristics of archaic Latin, the Romans initially adopted only twenty-one of the twenty-six letters in the Etruscan alphabet: A, B, C, D, E, F, G, H, I, K, L, M, N, O, P, Q, R, S, T, U, X. They later borrowed letters Y and Z to write Greek words. Three Greek (and Etruscan) letters—Θ (theta), Φ (phi), and X (chi)—were excluded because Latin had no corresponding sounds. However, these and two others—Ψ (psi) and Δ (delta)—were retained for numerical purposes.

GREEK LETTER	LATIN EQUIVALENT	NUMERIC VALUE
X (chi)	X	10 (X was later reintegrated into the Latin alphabet)
Ψ (psi)	L	50
Θ (theta)	C	100 (*centum*)
Δ (delta)	D	500
Φ (phi)	M	1000 (*mille*)

ARCHAIC LATIN IOIS AMVИ:ᗡƎKABƎꟻ:ƎBƎꟻ:ᗡƎM:SOIИAM

CLASSICAL LATIN MANIUS ME FECIT NUMASIO

Manios (has) made me for Numasios

In its earliest form, the Latin alphabet included the following letters: **A**, **B**, **C** (pronounced with a "ka" sound), **D**, **E**, **F** (Greek *zeta*), **H**, **I**, **K**, **L**, **M**, **N**, **O**, **P**, **Q**, **P** (the original shape of **R**), **S**, **T**, **V**, **X**. This version clearly bore the DNA of its ancestors: Phoenician, Greek, and Etruscan—with shapes and sounds adapted but still recognizable. It could be called the Phoenician-Greek-Etruscan Alphabet. For example, the Phoenician daleth (◁) became the Greek delta (Δ), then the Latin dee (**D**); the Greek sigma (Σ) became the Latin ss (**S**), and the Latin R (**P**) developed from Greek rho (**P**). Later, the seventh Greek letter, zeta, was dropped from the Latin sequence, and **G** was introduced. By the first century BCE, as Rome expanded and conquered Greece, Y and Z were reintroduced at the end of the alphabet to accommodate Greek words, bringing the total to twenty-three letters. Over the next seven hundred years, the alphabet evolved, shaped by trade, religion, and war, refining its forms to meet practical communication needs. While the Romans were standardizing their alphabet, Greek graffiti was being etched into the colossal sandstone leg of Ramses in southern Egypt (see right sidebar).

Archaic Latin alphabet, ca. 600 BCE, twenty-one (in red) of the twenty-six Etruscan letters adapted in boustrophodon style.

Archaic Latin alphabet, ca. 300 BCE, twenty letters: A B C D E F H I K L M N O P Q R S T V X.

NAME AS MAKER

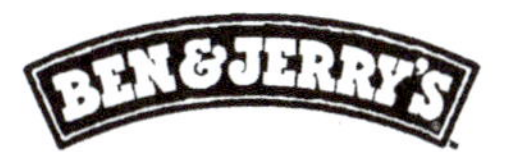

Ben Cohen & Jerry Greenfield, ice cream

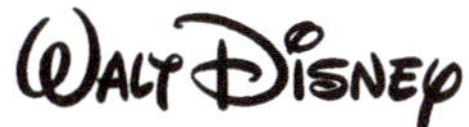

Walt Disney, entertainment

L.L.Bean

Leon Leonwood Bean, outdoor clothing and boots

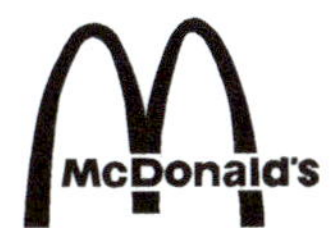

Richard & Maurice McDonald, fast food restaurant

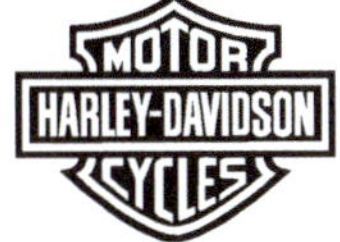

William Harley & Arthur Davidson, motorcycles

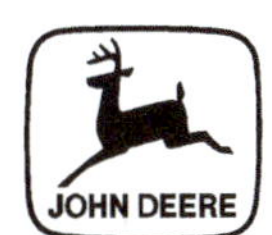

John Deere, farm equipment

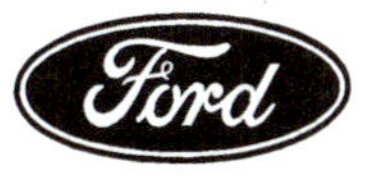

Henry Ford, automobiles

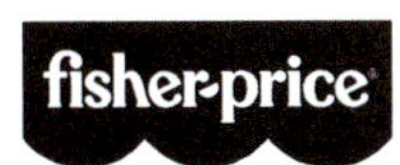

Herman Fisher and Irving Price, toys

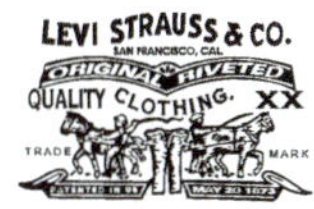

Levi Strauss, denim jeans and clothing

MEANWHILE, IN SOUTHERN EGYPT, GREEK GRAFFITI IS WRITTEN

In 591 BCE, during a military expedition into Ethiopia, Greek soldiers serving under Egyptian Pharaoh Psammetichos II (594–589 BCE) carved their names into the colossal leg of a statue of Ramses II. These inscriptions are among the oldest known examples of Greek writing. Most of the graffiti includes the soldier's name and their father's—such as "Python, son of Amoibichos." This naming reflects their linguistic and cultural identity: Dorian, Ionian, or Egyptian-born Greeks, all using the same Ionic alphabet. One inscription stands out. It is the longest and uniquely describes the soldier's military experience. Scholar Matthew P. J. Dillon suggests it contains a Homeric pun: "There are no known examples of *Pelekos* as a name, nor of *Oudamos*—these are likely not names." *Pelekos* means "axe" or "short blade," and *Oudamos* means "none" or "nobody." Dillon proposes the inscription may be read as: "Archon, son of Amoibichos, wrote us and Axe, son of Nobody." The joke, then, is that *Pelekos, son of Oudamos* literally means "hand axe, son of nobody."

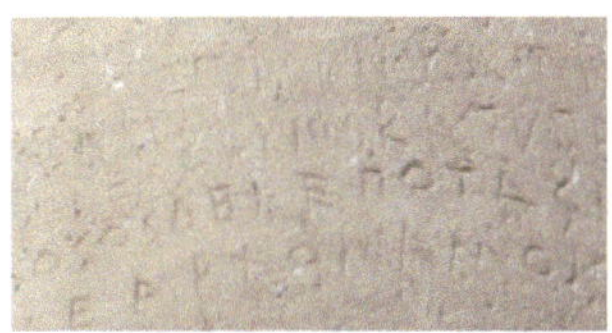

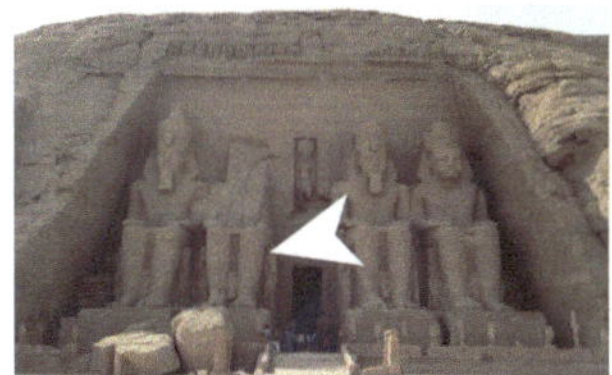

Temple of Ramses II, Greek Graffiti, incised into the massive limestone left leg of the second colossus funerary monument of Ramses II, 593 BCE, Abu Simbel, Egypt (detail, top).

15

600 BCE

ETRUSCAN

ETRURIA
Italy

As a prestigious sign of the new Orientalising style and as a status symbol, the alphabet decorates a number of Etruscan objects placed in rich tombs of the seventh century BC. These "model" alphabets, taken directly from the Greek alphabet as brought west by the Euboeans, bear witness to the speed with which this new development was adopted.
—Larissa Bonfante, *Reading the Past: Ancient Writing from Cuneiform to the Alphabet* (1990)

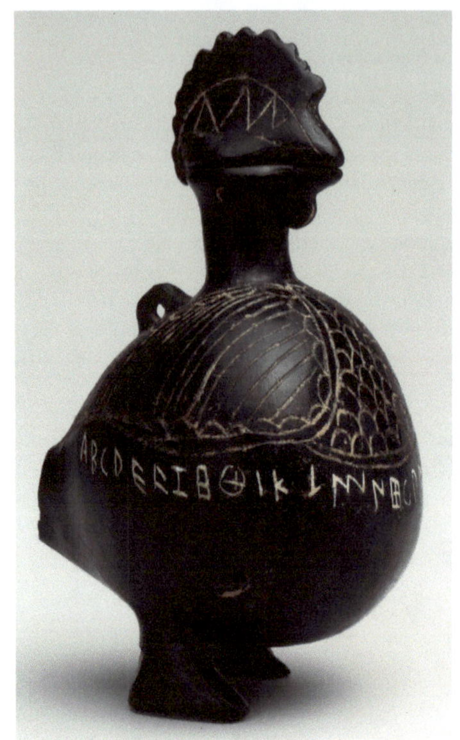

LEFT: *Rooster-Shaped Bucchero Jug,* ca. 650–600 BCE, Etruscan, terracotta, 4.16 inches tall, Metropolitan Museum of Art, New York. Possible abecedarium, found in a tomb, Viterbo, Italy, north of Rome.

LETTER G BECOMES C, D IS DECIDED, AND THE SOUND "EFF" GETS ITS OWN LETTER

Approximately fifty years after the creation of the *Marsiliana Tablet*, the *Rooster-Shaped Bucchero Jug* offers another example of an abecedary, this time reading from left to right. The jug may have served duel purposes: as an ink well, and as a reference tool while practicing the twenty-six letters of the Etruscan alphabet. The rooster's head functioned as a stopper for the ink well. This artifact is one of the few non-funerary items featuring the Etruscan alphabet and may have also served a third purpose—as decoration. When the Etruscans were first introduced to the Euboean Greek alphabet around 750 BCE, it was a new form of technology. As with any innovation, it carried with it a sense of mystery and potential unease. For this reason, some scholars believe the jug may have been regarded as a status symbol, a token of power, or even an object of magic. Euboea, the second-largest island off eastern Greece (after Crete), is where scholar Barry P. Powell suggests the Greek alphabet was first put to use. Like the Phoenicians and Greeks, early

Etruscan writing was typically inscribed from right to left, with occasional examples in boustrophedon style (see page 59). Just as ancient Egyptians modified hieroglyphs to create hieratic and later demotic scripts, the Etruscans adapted and abstracted the Greek alphabet to meet their linguistic needs. Interestingly, some letters borrowed from the Greeks were never actually used in Etruscan writing. Letters 𐌁, 𐌂, 𐌃, and O do not appear in Etruscan texts. The third letter of the Greek alphabet, *gamma* (𐌂), which traces back to Egyptian writing and was known as *gimel* (𐤂) in Phoenician—represented a hard "gah" sound. However, the Etruscan language lacked this sound, so they repurposed the form of the letter to represent a sound that did exist in their speech, resulting in a modified C or Ɔ depending on the script style.

In addition to shaping letters, the Etruscans are attributed with changing how we say the letters. We no longer use word-names, but sound-names: AH, BAY, CAY (KAY), DAY. etc. Change happened quickly (in about one hundred years) before the alphabet moved on for its last major development by the Romans ca. 650 BCE.

𐌀 𐌁 𐌂 𐌃 𐌄 𐌅 𐌆 𐌇 𐌈 𐌉 𐌊 𐌋 𐌌 𐌍 𐌎 𐌏 𐌐 𐌑 𐌒 𐌓 𐌔 𐌕 𐌖 𐌗 𐌘 𐌙

Etruscan alphabet, twenty-six letters, ca. 700 BCE.

ΑΑ Β Γ Δ ΕΕ ΥV Ι Η ⊕⊙ Ι ΚΚ Λ Μ ΝΝ Ξ Ο ΓΠ Ρ Σ Τ ΦΦ Χ ΨΨ Ω

Ionian Greek alphabet, twenty-four letters, including alternative ways to write the letters, ca. 800–500 BCE.

LETTERS AS STATUS

CARS	CLOTHING	UNIVERSITIES	DEGREES
1. T	4. D&G	7. MIT	10. JD
2. BMW	5. LV	8. UCLA	11. PhD
3. L	6. CC	9. Cal	12. MD

1. T, Tesla; 2. BMW, Bavarian Motor Works; 3. L, Lexus; 4. D & G, Dolce & Gabanna; 5. LV, Louis Vuitton; 6. CC, Coco Chanel; 7. MIT, Massachusetts Institute of Technology; 8. UCLA, University of California Los Angeles; 9. Cal, University of California Berkeley; 10. JD, Doctor of Law (Jurisprudence) ; 11. PhD, Doctor of Philosophy; 12. MD, Doctor of Medicine.

MEANWHILE, A KING CREATES A LIBRARY IN ASSYRIA

The last great king of Assyria, Ashurbanipal (668–630 BCE), established the region's largest library: *The Royal Library of Ashurbanipal*. The collection included over 30,000 clay tablets, among them a copy of the *Epic of Gilgamesh*. To request a book, a reader would write the author's name and the title on a piece of clay and hand it to a librarian—an early precursor to the Dewey Decimal System. The library was located in Nineveh, the capital of Assyria, in what is now Mosul, a city in northern Iraq.

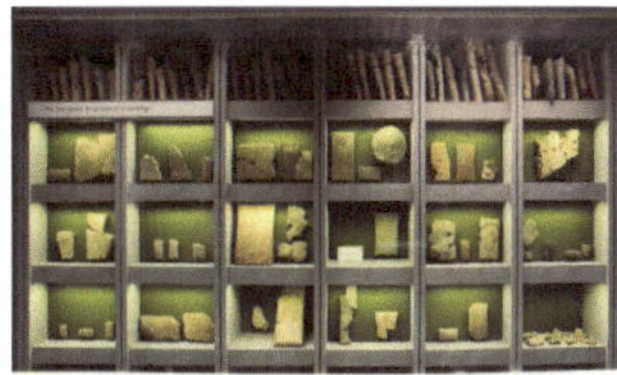

The Library of Ashurbanipal, British Museum, London.

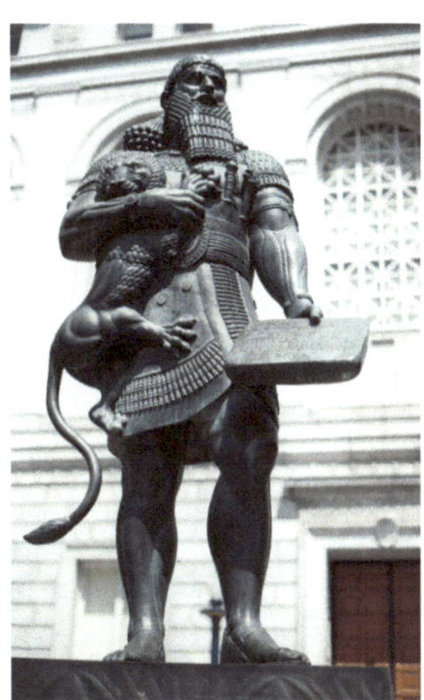

Ashurbanipal, 1988, bronze, Fred Parhad, Civic Center, San Francisco.

16

570 BCE

ARCHAIC LATIN

ROME

Italy

These [Latin inscriptions] are the arts of expression or composition, writing in the strictly physical sense (cutting, painting, or the like, on more or less durable material), and design or arrangement (including integration with the whole object to which the inscription pertains). The history is Roman history in the largest sense, involving men and women in many of their affairs, such as life and death, government, law, religious worship.
— Arthur E. Gordon, *Illustrated Introduction to Latin Epigraphy* (1983)

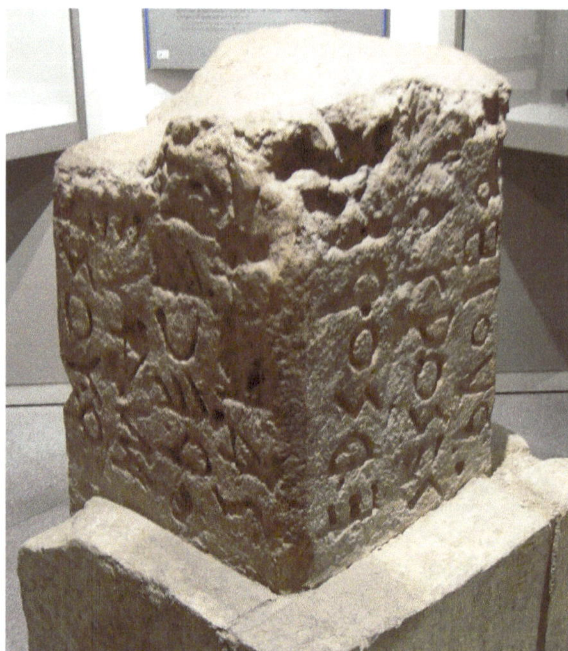

Reproduction, *Lapis Niger (or Black Stone),* black marble, ca. 570-550 BCE.

A SHRINE: FROM MONARCHY TO REPUBLIC

Though the exact origin of the word *Rome* is unknown, the Etruscans referred to the area as *Ruma*, and to the Tiber River that flows through it, as *Rumon*. Some suggest the name derives from *Romulus*, the mythological founder and first king of Rome, but no one knows for certain. In Latin, it is *Roma*; the Greeks called it as *Ρώμη*, meaning "power" or "strength." The *Lapis Niger* is believed to mark a shrine in the Roman Forum and contains one of the earliest known Latin inscriptions. The text, carved on all four sides of a *cippus* (a small stone pillar), is written in boustrophedon style. Cippi were used in ancient Rome and Greece to mark shrines or tombs.

The inscription on the *Lapis Niger* suggests it is dedicated to a king and threatens punishment to anyone who disturbs it—similar to the warning on the *Sarcophagus of Ahiram* (ca. 1000 BCE, see page 42). According to legend, this may be the tomb of Romulus. Like the Egyptians, and Phoenicians before them, the Romans used funerary texts to deter tampering. Throughout the development of the Latin alphabet—from Egyptian hieroglyphs to Phoenician, Greek, Etruscan, and finally ar-

EARLIEST EXAMPLES OF LETTERS C, K, AND Q

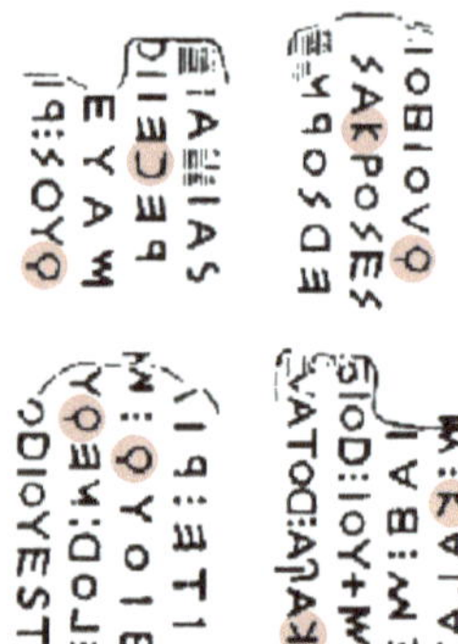

Lapis Niger inscription, letters C, K, and Q highlighted in red.

TRANSLATION

Whosoever (will violate) this (grove), let him be cursed.
(Let no one dump) refuse (nor throw a body...). Let it be lawful for the king (to sacrifice a cow in atonement).

(Let him fine) one (fine) for each (offence). Whom the king (will fine, let him give cows).

(Let the king have a —) herald. (Let him yoke) a team, two heads, sterile...

Along the route... (Him) who (will) not (sacrifice) with a young animal...in ...lawful assembly in grove...

Arthur E. Gordon (1983)

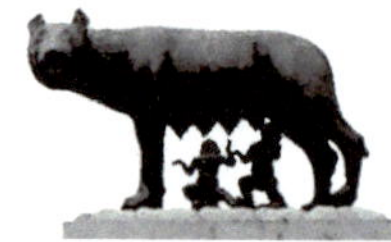

Capitoline She-wolf with Suckling Romulus and Remus. According to legend, Rome was founded by Romulus, twin of Remus (753 BCE).

chaic Latin—boustrophedon writing appears. Derived from the Greek βουστροφηδόν, meaning "to turn like oxen in plowing," boustrophedon refers to writing that alternates direction: left to right, then right to left, and so on. This transitional writing style is also found in early inscriptions from southern Arabian inscriptions, Brahmi texts of South Asia, and the Rongorongo script of Easter Island. Even today, on the Polynesian island of Pentecost in the nation of Vanuatu, the Avoiuli script uses boustrophedon writing as the norm. It's often seen as a transitional form used as ancient writers experimented with how best to structure written language.

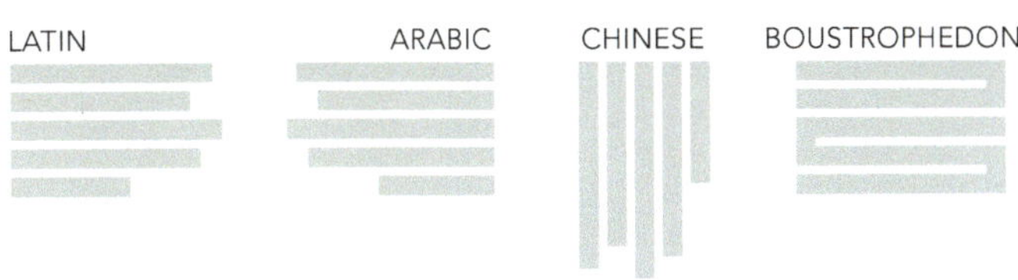

GRAPHIC CONCEPT: Gavin Ambrose and Paul Harris, *The Fundamentals of Typography* (2011).

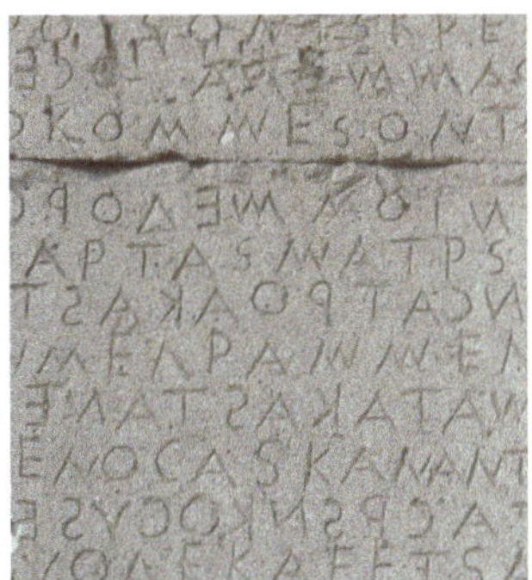

The Gortyn Code (or *The Great Code*), in boustrophedon-style ancient Greek. It discusses the codification of law in the ancient city-state of Gortyn, southern Crete, ca. 450 BCE.

LEONARDO DA VINCI ON WRITING

Leonardo da Vinci (1452–1519), a left-hander, often wrote from right to left in reverse script. He may have done this to prevent smudging the ink and to keep his hand clean. Some believe it was a way to protect his ideas from being copied easily; others suggest it was to avoid scrutiny from the Roman Catholic Church, whose doctrines were often in opposition with his scientific investigations. Whatever the reason, it was a habit he maintained throughout his life—except when writing for others, when he used standard script.

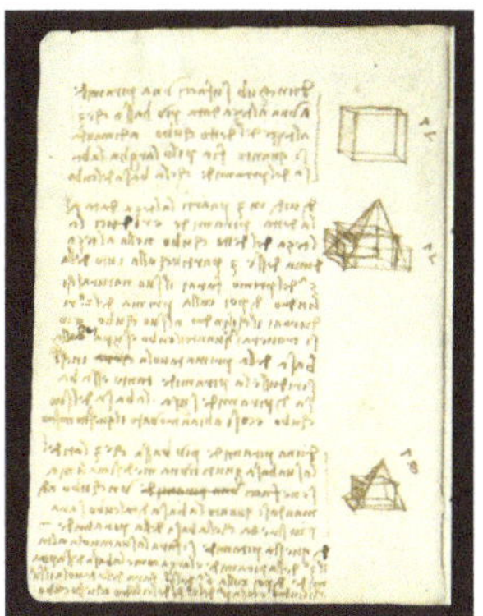

Leonardo da Vinci's Notebook, Codex Forster 1, 1487–1490, National Art Library, Victoria and Albert Museum. DETAIL BELOW.

THROUGHOUT THE HISTORY OF WRITING, BOUSTROPHEDON-STYLE WRITING IS FOUND

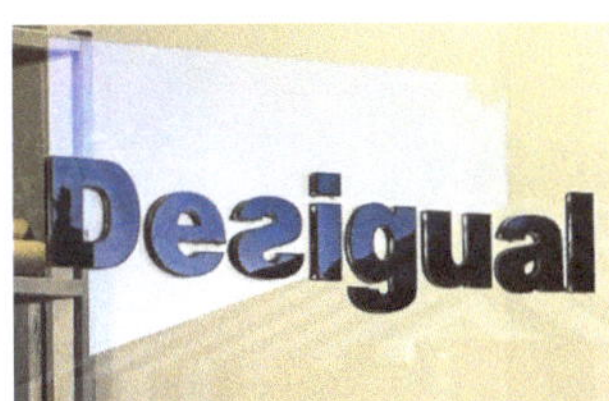

Athens, Greece.

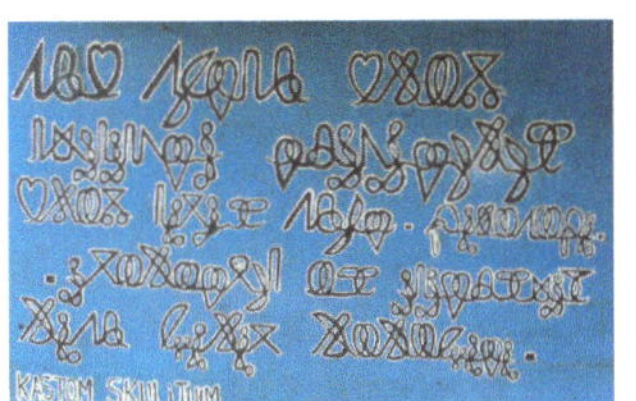

Pentecost Island, Vanuatu.

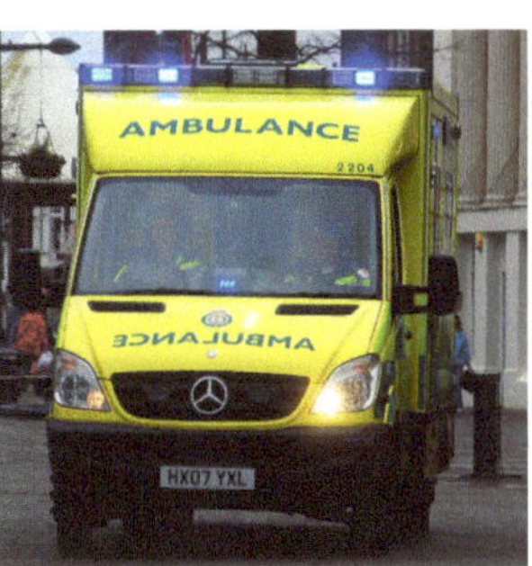

Hampshire, United Kingdom.

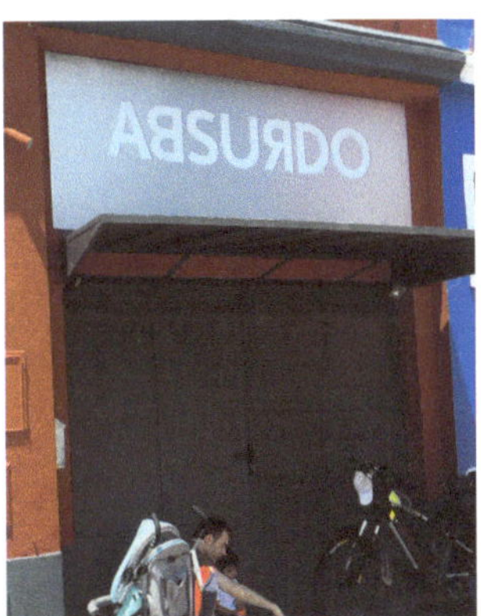

Setúbal, Portugal.

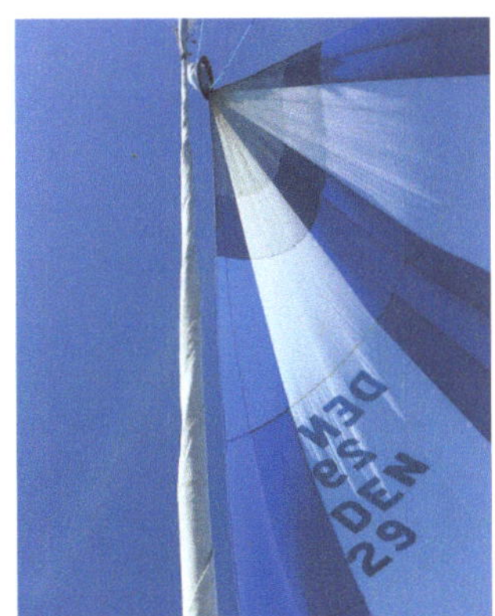

Danish sailing sheet.

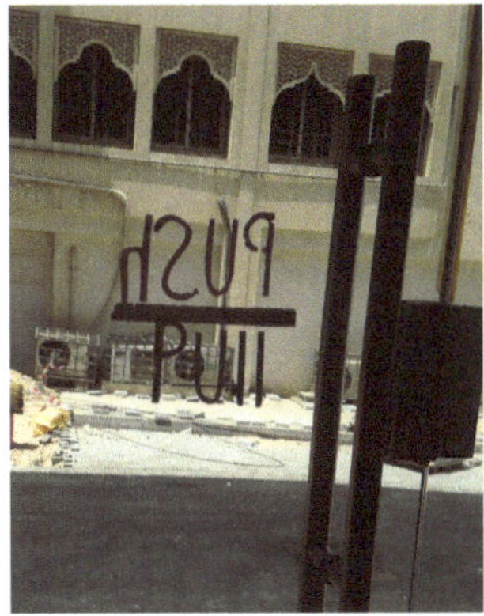

Restaurant door signage, Doha, Qatar.

17

550 BCE

ARCHAIC LATIN

ROME
Italy

The inscription is written from right to left in three lines without word spaces. The text has turned out to be rather difficult to translate, due to both epigraphic and linguistic problems.
—Jón Axel Harðarson, *The 2nd Line of the Duenos Inscription* (2011)

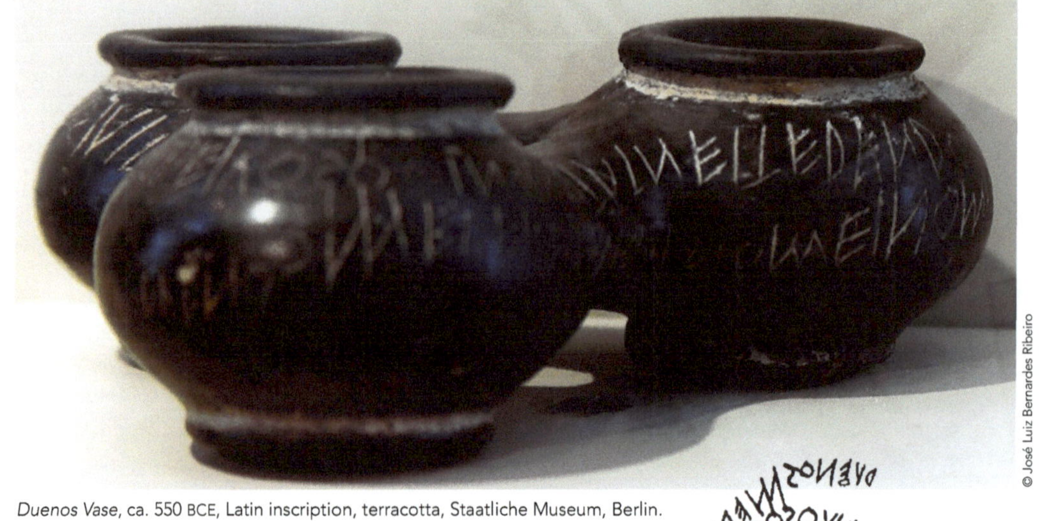

Duenos Vase, ca. 550 BCE, Latin inscription, terracotta, Staatliche Museum, Berlin.

FIFTY WAYS TO INTERPRET AN ARTIFACT

The *Duenos Vase* is made up of three small, connected clay vessels discovered on Rome's Quirinal Hill in 1880. Etched along its sides is an inscription that—along with those on the *Praeneste Fibula* (ca. 650 BCE) and the *Lapis Niger* (ca. 570–550 BCE)—represents one of the earliest known examples of the archaic Latin alphabet. All three inscriptions are written from right to left; however, the text on the *Duenos Vase* must be read with the vessel turned upside down and as one continuous line. Some scholars believe the potter etched the inscription while standing over the soft clay, resulting in the upside-down orientation.

Because the inscription lacks both letter and word spacing and is partially damaged, scholars have struggled to decipher it fully. In fact, there are at least fifty different interpretations, with no consensus on either the meaning of the text or the purpose of the vase. Theories range that it is a love gift, a peace offering, or a funerary object, to a curse, or a container for cosmetics or perfume. Lines 1 and 3 contain recognizable Latin, but Line 2 remains highly debated due to the absence of word breaks. As Arthur E. Gordon writes in *An Illustrated Introduction to Latin Epigraphy*: "Scholars are not agreed as to the purpose of the vase or the meaning of the inscription. The only intelligible phrase seems to be *Duenos med feced*, 'Duenos (or, 'A good man') (has) made me,' the vase (or 'had me made')." What scholars do agree on is that this inscription belongs to the earliest stage of the Latin alphabet, where the letter C represented both the C and G sounds, and that *duenos* means "bonus" or "good" in archaic Latin.

LINE 1: IOVESATDEIVOSQOIMEDMITATNEITEDENDOCOSMISVIRCOSIED

LINE 2: ASTEDNOISIOpETOITESIAIpACARIVOIS

LINE 3: DVENOSMEDFECEDENMANOMEINOMDVENOIMEMEDMALOSTATOD

LINE 1: The person who gives me swears by the gods: If the girl should not be kind / friendly towards you …

LINE 2: and if she does not want to be intimate with you (or enjoy your love), then soothe (her) with the streams (of fragrance)!'

LINE 3: A good man made me as a fine gift for a good man. Let an evil person not steal me!

LETTERS LOOKING UP, LETTERS LOOKING DOWN*

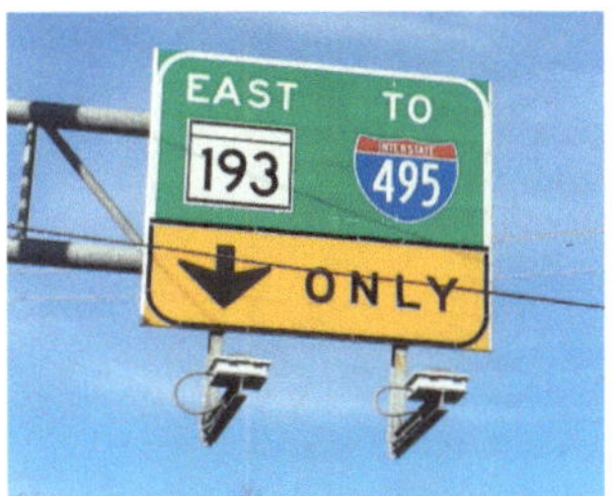

Highway signage, United States.

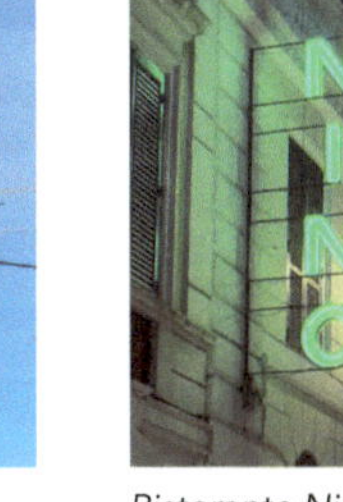

Ristorante Nino dal 1934, Rome, Italy.

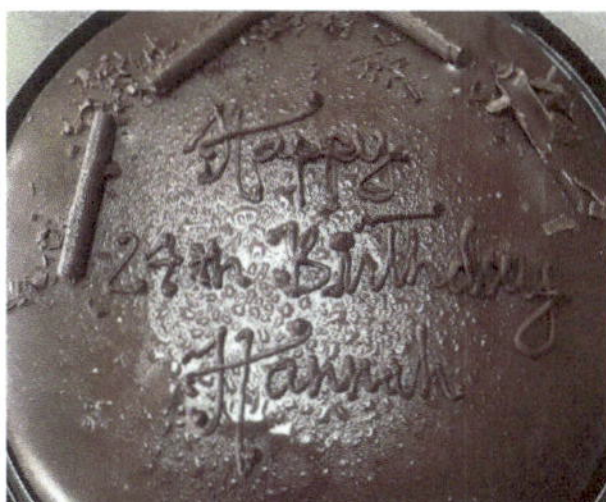

Happy Birthday cake, United States.

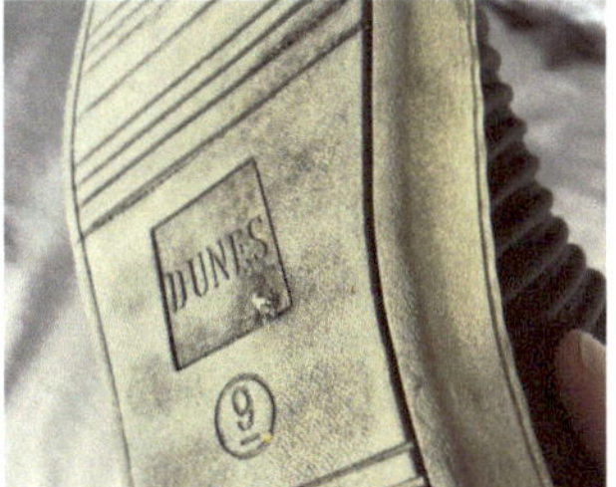

Dunes size 9, United States.

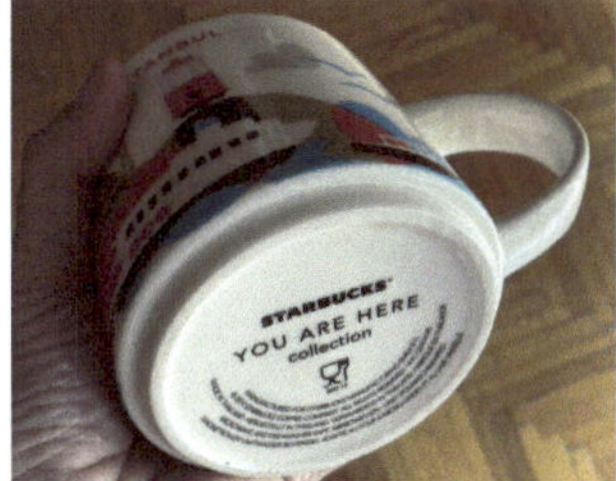

Starbucks mug, Everywhere.

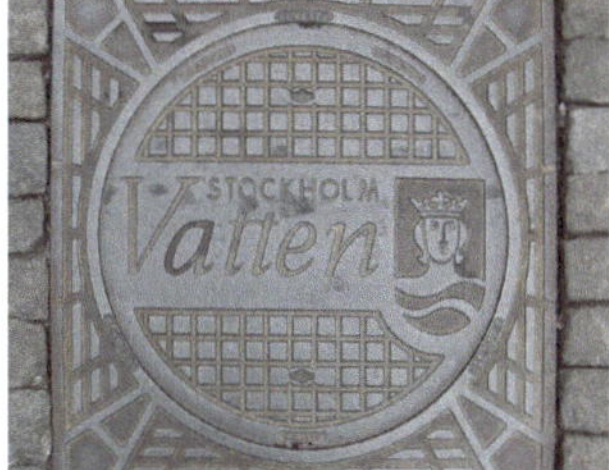

Vatten,"water," Stockholm, Sweden.

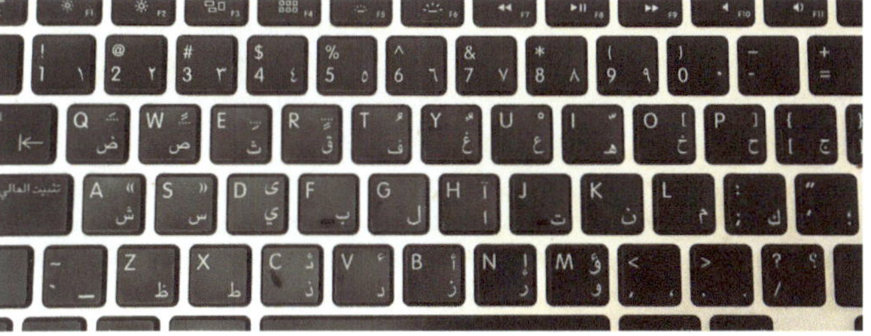

Bilingual keyboard with Arabic and Latin, and Western and Eastern Arabic numerals.

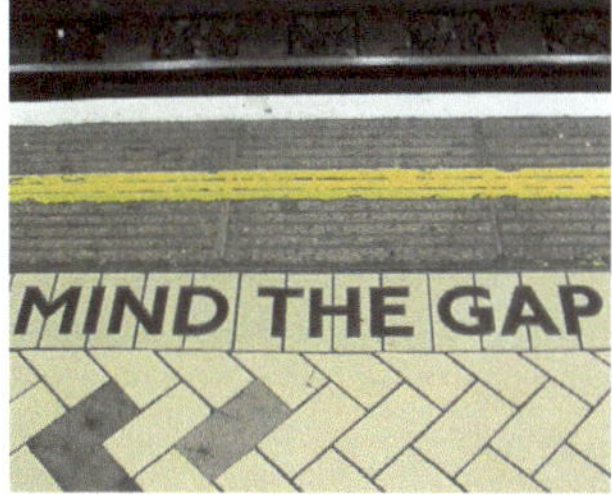

MIND THE GAP, London, England.

*See the *Trajan Column Inscription* (page 66) for designing text when looking up, and read the words of Hermann Zapf (page 76) for inspiration by looking down.

A WORD ABOUT LETTERSPACING

The *Deunos Vase* inscription highlights the importance of letter and word spacing for legibility. Without proper spacing, text can be misread at best—or illegible at worst.

Kerning and tracking are both aspects of letterspacing, but they function differently. *Kerning* adjusts the space between individual pairs of letters, while *tracking* adjusts the spacing uniformly across a line or block of text. Tracking is often referred to more generally as letterspacing. Both increase legibility, but they are applied for different reasons. When setting type in all-caps, some letters naturally sit well together, while others may require a slight nudge in one direction or the other. A quick search online will reveal numerous examples of poor kerning, where unintended spacing changes the meaning of the word or phrase dramatically. Most digital type today include built-in letterspacing. Even so, it never hurts to take a closer look.

As Swiss typeface designer Adrian Frutiger once said: "From all these experiences the most important thing I have learned is that legibility and beauty stand close together and that type design, in its restraint, should be only felt but not perceived by the reader."

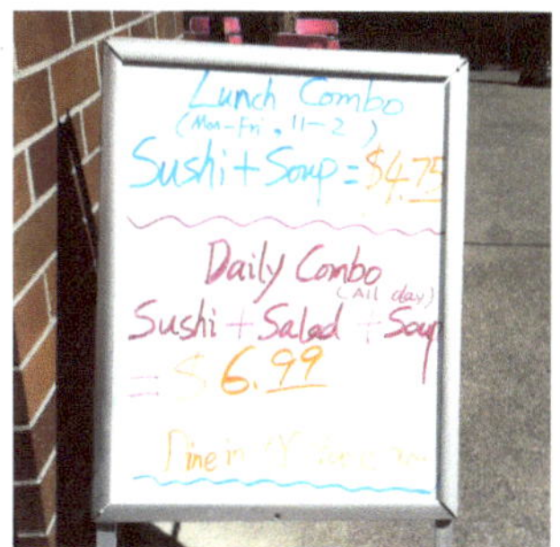

Sushi+Soup, Portland, Oregon.

18

500 BCE

PHOENICIAN and ETRUSCAN

PYRGI
Italy

Etruscan [language] was certainly urban and cosmopolitan, and no doubt farmers used it in the country; but it was not linked with a constant military force, nor indeed a government strong enough to unite the various independent Etruscan-speaking cities behind a single policy.
—Nicholas Ostler,
Ad Infinitum: A Biography of Latin (2007)

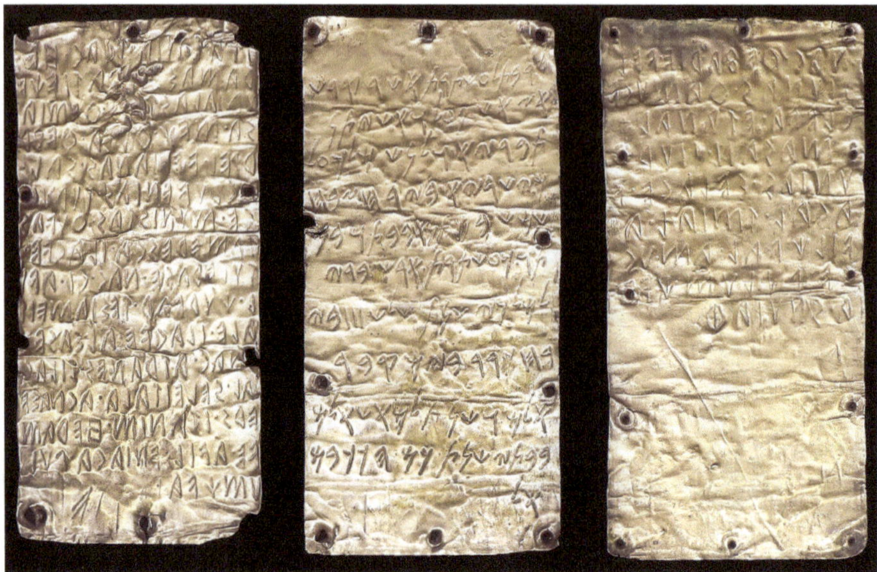

Pyrgi Tablets, ca. 500 BCE, gold, 19.3 cm. x 9 cm., Etruscan, Phoenician (left) and Etruscan (center and right). National Etruscan Museum, Villa Giulia, Rome.

Phoenician text (detail) | Etruscan text (detail) | Etruscan text (detail)

SAME EVENT, DIFFERENT LANGUAGES, ONE ALPHABET

The *Pyrgi Tablets* were discovered in 1964 by Italian archaeologist Massimo Pallottino at an Etruscan sanctuary on the Tyrrhenian Sea coast, in the ancient town of Pyrgi. The find consists of three inscribed gold panels that record a temple dedication to the Phoenician goddess Astarte. Notably, it is the only Etruscan artifact that names a ruler. One panel is written in Phoenician—the language of the Mediterranean, including Carthage and its colonies—while the other two panels are written in Etruscan (sixteen lines and thirty-seven words). Archaeologists initially hoped the Phoenician panel would serve as a direct translation of the Etruscan, but that was not the case. The texts provide separate accounts of the same event, making them parallel rather than bilingual inscriptions. Given the limited understanding of the Etruscan language, the translations are paraphrased. According to the *Museo Nazionale Etrusco*, where the tablets are housed, bronze nails with gold heads were found alongside the tablets, suggesting they were originally affixed to a door. Despite more than thirty scholarly studies attempting to interpret the inscriptions, widespread disagreement persists due to the fragmentary knowledge of Etruscan. However, most scholars agree that the tablets contain a dedication likely tied to a funerary context. Although the Etruscans modeled their twenty-six-letter alphabet on the Greek, as seen in artifacts like the *Marsiliana Tablet* (page 52) and the *Rooster-Shaped Bucchero Jug* (page

56), they did not use the letters B, D, G, or O— sounds absent from their language. By the sixth century BCE, they introduced a new sign for the "eff" sound, resembling an 8, which they placed at the end of the alphabet. Around this time, Rome was growing restless. After a long period of Etruscan dominance, Romans no longer wanted to be ruled by Etruscan kings or a monarchy. They sought a new political system—one governed by elected senators and by the rule of law.

ETRUSCAN WOMEN

Whether married or single, Etruscan women had freedoms and social advantages uncommon in the ancient world. They participated in councils, public events, nude athletics, and dined and drank alongside men at banquets. While the Romans were heavily influenced by Etruscan culture, they differed sharply in their treatment of women—with one exception: Roman women retained the right to inherit wealth from their parents. The "archaic smile," developed by Greek sculptors during the Archaic period (650–480 BCE), was used to make figures appear more lifelike and expressive. This stylistic feature was also adopted by the Etruscans.

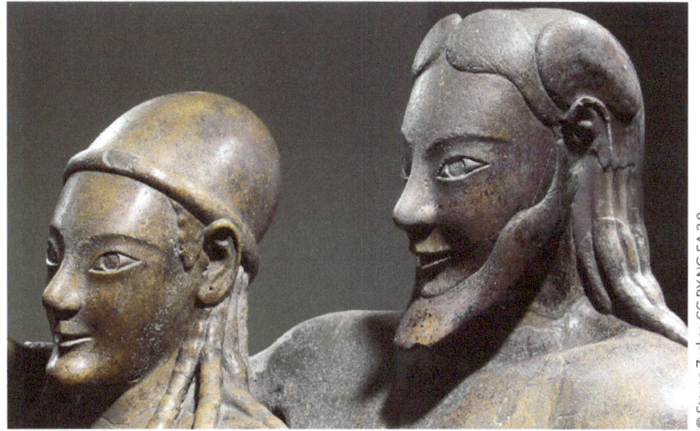

DETAIL: *Sarcophagus of the Spouses*, ca. 520 BCE, Etruscan, painted terracotta, 3 feet 9 inches x 6 feet 7 inches, found in the Banditaccia necropolis (in 400 pieces), Cerveteri. Museo Nazionale di Villa Giulia, Rome.

Etruscan alphabet, twenty-three letters, 5th century, written in boustrophedon style.

SAME FEELING, DIFFERENT LANGUAGE, SAME LETTERS

k 'gezalmel 😍, Abenak
Ya tabe kahayu 🧡, Belarusian
Volim te 💖, Croatian
Ik hou van jou 💘, Dutch
Ma armastan sind 😻, Estonian
Je t'aime 😍, French
Ich liebe dich 😘, German
Aloha Au la 'Oe 💓, Hawaiian
Ti amo 🧡, Italian
Mi luv yuh 💘, Jamaican
Ar lek you 😘, Krio (Sierra Leone)
Es tevi mīlu 💖, Latvia
Mo kontan twa 😍, Mauritian Creole

Ndebele (Zimbabwe) 😻, *Ngiyakuthanda*
Oshiwambo (Namibia) 😘, *Ondikuhole*
Portuguese (Brazilian) 😍, *Eu te amo*
Romanian 💓, *Te iubesc*
Spanish 🧡, *Te amo*
Turkish 😘, *Seni seviyorum*
Uzbek 💖, *Men seni sevaman*
Vietnamese: female/male 😍, *Anh yêu em/Em yêu anh*
Westrobothnian (northern Sweden) 💘, *Ja elschke degg*
Xhosa (South Africa) 🧡, *Ndiyakuthanda*
Yoruba (Nigeria) 😘, *Mo nifee re*
Zulu (South Africa) 😻, *Ngiyakuthanda*

THE LATIN ALPHABET ADAPTS TO DIFFERENT SCRIPTS

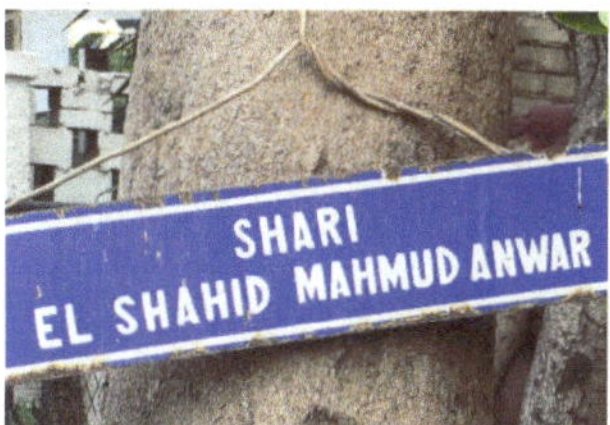

Latin letters spell Arabic words, Cairo, Egypt.

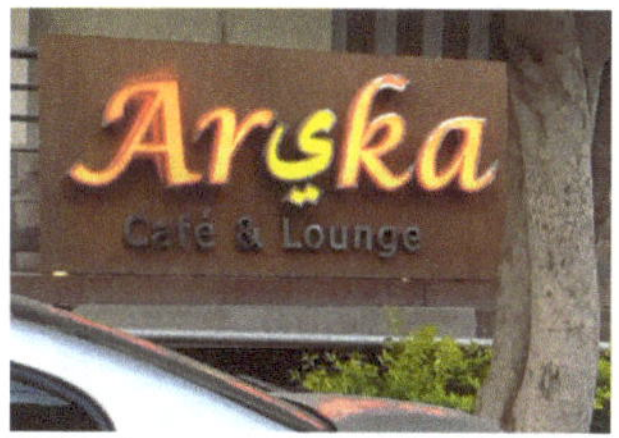

Arabic letter as Latin letter, Cairo, Egypt.

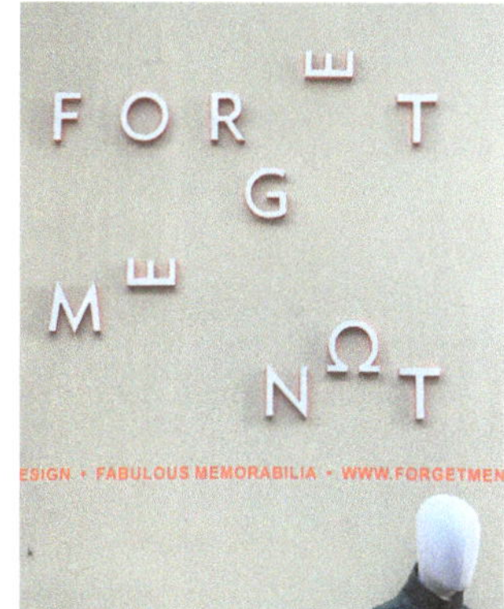

Greek letters as Latin letters, Athens, Greece.

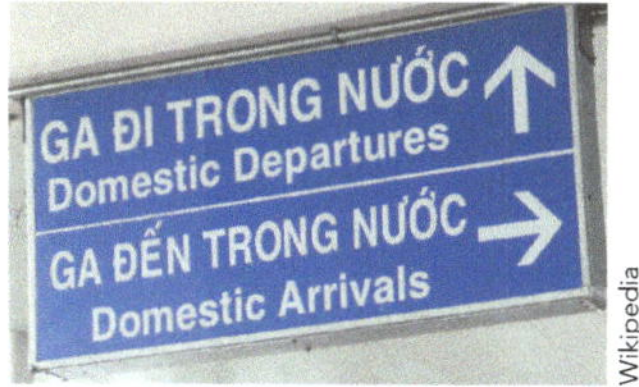

Tan Son Nhat Airport Signage, Ho Chi Minh City (Saigon), Vietnam.

19

400 BCE

CLASSICAL GREEK

PRIENE
Turkey

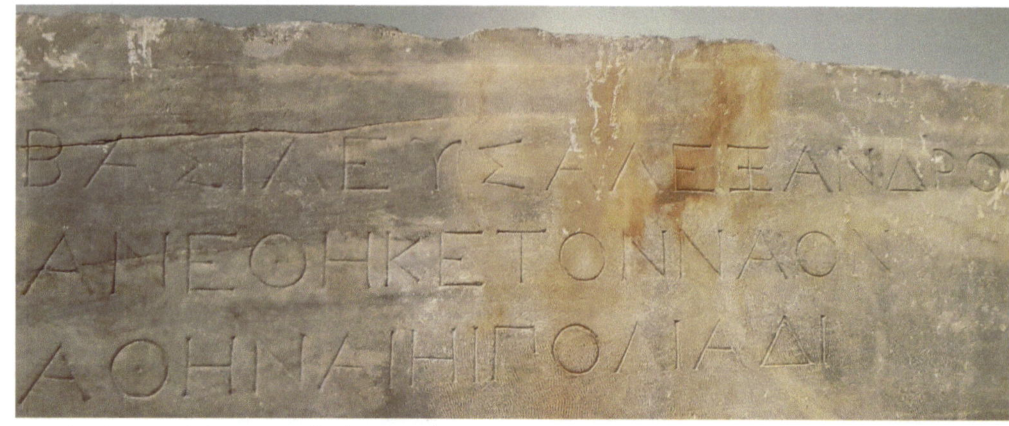

Priene Inscription, ca. 334 BCE, incised lettering, British Museum, London. Dedication of Athena Polias, Priene (southwest coast of Turkey), by Alexander the Great on double-sided marble wall from temple discovered in 1868-9 CE.

TRANSLATION:	**ΒΑΣΙΛΕΥΣ ΑΛΕΞΑΝΔΡΟΣ**	KING ALEXANDER
	ΑΝΕΘΗΚΕ ΤΟΝ ΝΑΟΝ	DEDICATED THE TEMPLE
	ΑΘΗΝΑΙ ΠΟΛΙΑΔΙ	TO ATHENA OF THE CITY

SERIFS EMERGE, LETTERFORMS STRAIGHTEN, BUT IS WRITING A GOOD IDEA

As an embellishment it conferred a ceremonial and ornamental aspect which may be considered particularly appropriate to an imperial inscription. We have not the right to say that the serif was invented for Alexander the Great's inscription, only that this is its first datable appearance.
—Stanley Morison, on the Priene Inscription, *Politics and Script* (1972)

Between 600 and 250 BCE, about a third of Latin letters evolved from their original Greek forms into shapes more recognizable today. Before the fifth century BCE, there were two versions of the Greek alphabet: Ionian and Chalcidian. (*The Iliad* and *Odyssey* were written in Ionian during the cultural renaissance of the eighth century BCE.) In 403 BCE, Athens mandated that all government documents be written in the standardized twenty-four-letter Ionian alphabet, written from left to right with all letters facing right. British typographer and printing historian Stanley Morison identified four primary characteristics of the early Greek alphabet: 1) Squareness of form; 2) Uniformity of stroke; 3) Consistency of structure; 4) Rationality of shapes (i.e., no unnecessary details).

It was around the sixth century BCE, Morison argues, that the "Greco-Roman" alphabet began. The *Priene Inscription* is an exemplifies these four qualities. Its added embellishment—serifs—contributes to a sense of finality in the letterforms. Serifs also act as visual links between letters, making reading smoother and more fluid. For the stone carver, adding a perpendicular finial may have been a logical way to finish the vertical and horizontal strokes— though this remains speculative. Other theories suggest that the embellishments served imperial purposes, lending gravitas to inscriptions. Still others note the influence of nearby Babylonia and Assyria. Merchants from Greek cities like Priene had commercial and political ties with these cultures, where cuneiform, an

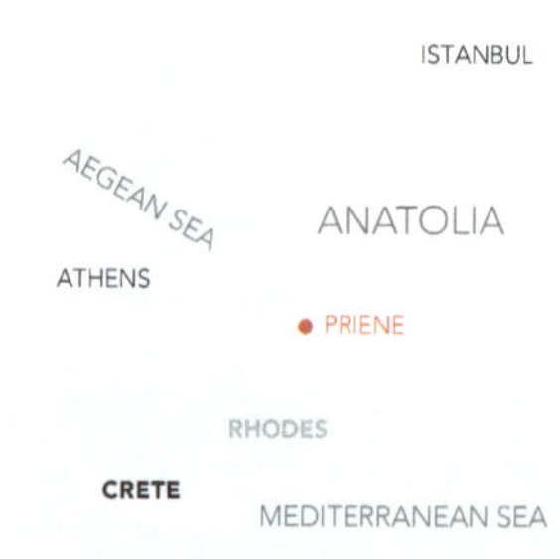

arrow-ended script, may have inspired the development of the serif. The word *serif* is neither Greek nor Latin in origin. Since Holland was a major source of metal type for British printers well into the eighteenth century, type historian Harry Carter theorizes that it may derive from the Dutch "*schreef*, a scratch or flick of the pen." Around this same period, philosopher Socrates (469–399 BCE) questioned whether writing benefited society. His student Plato (c. 429–347 BCE) recorded Socrates' concerns in *Phaedrus*:

> If men learn this, it will implant forgetfulness in their souls; they will cease to exercise memory because they rely on that which is written, calling things to remembrance no longer from within themselves, but by means of external marks. What you have discovered is a recipe not for memory, but for reminder. And it is no true wisdom that you offer your disciples, but only its semblance, for by telling them of many things without teaching them you will make them seem to know much, while for the most part they know nothing, and as men filled, not with wisdom but with the conceit of wisdom, they will be a burden to their fellows.

The Greek alphabet was not only the forerunner of the Etruscan and Latin alphabets but also the parent of the Cyrillic alphabet.

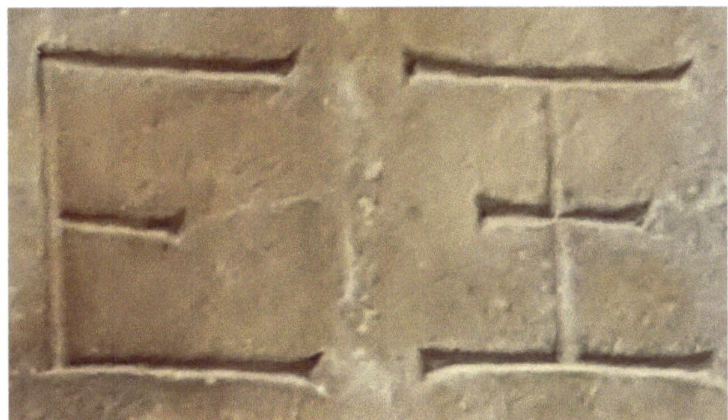

DETAIL, FROM LEFT

STANLEY MORISON'S EARLY GREEK ALPHABET'S FOUR PRIMARY CHARACTERISTICS:

1. SQUARENESS of shapes
2. UNIFORMITY of stroke
3. CONSISTENCY of structure
4. RATIONALITY of shapes, no unnecessary details

ΔA B Γ Δ ϵE YV I H ⊕ʘ I KK Λ M NN Ξ O ΓΠ P ξ T ΦΦ X ΨV Ω

Ionian Greek alphabet, ca. 800–500 BCE, twenty-four letters.

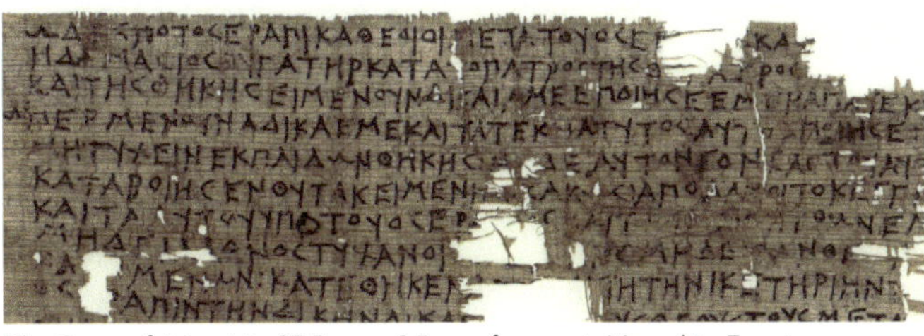

The Curse of Artemisia, 35.5 cm. x 8.5 cm., fragment, Memphis, Egypt, ca. 350–300 BCE, Papyrus Collection, Austrian National Library. From the Ionian Greeks whose culture dominated Memphis, Egypt, particularly after 332 BCE, when Alexander the Great was crowned Pharaoh.

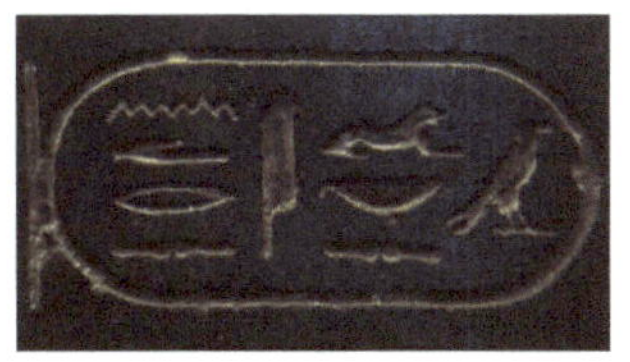

N D R S   I   L K S   A

Alexander the Great, written in Egyptian hieroglyphs inside a cartouche, ca. 332 BCE, reads right to left. Louvre Museum.

SUBSTRATES

Though much of typography today grows out of the fertile ground of computer code, writing substrates, and their physicality, remain.

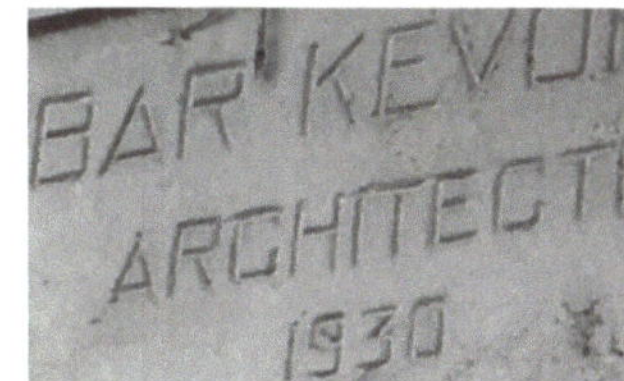

Chiseled marble.

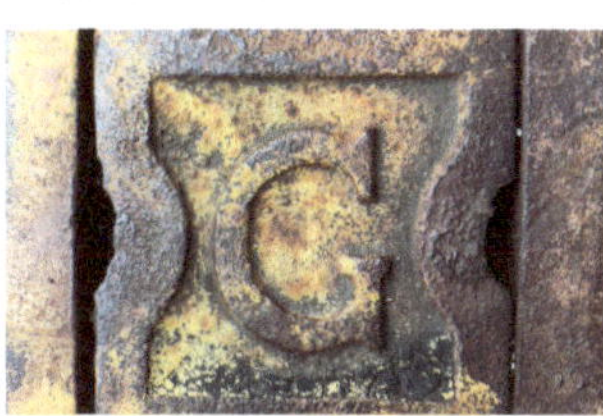

Cast iron.

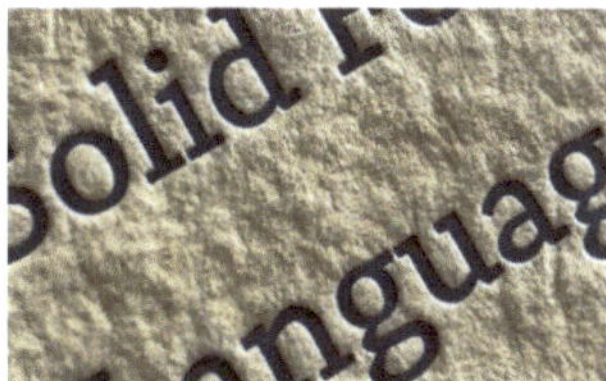

Metal (letterpress) on paper.

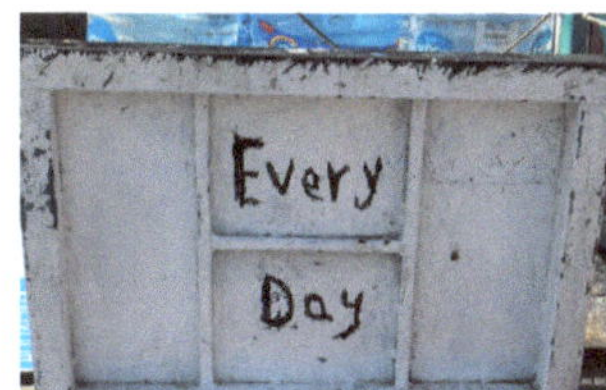

Painted steel.

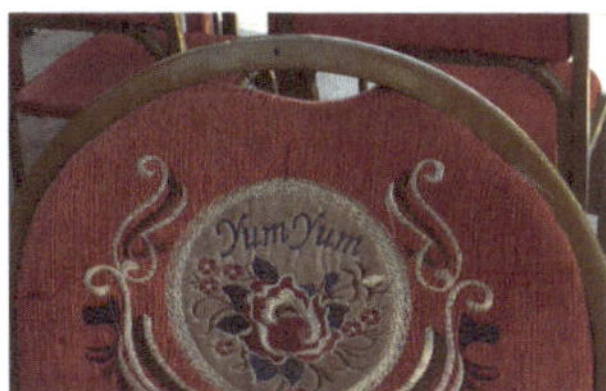

Threaded fabric.

20

200 BCE

HIEROGLYPHS, DEMOTIC and HELLENISTIC GREEK

RASHID
Egypt

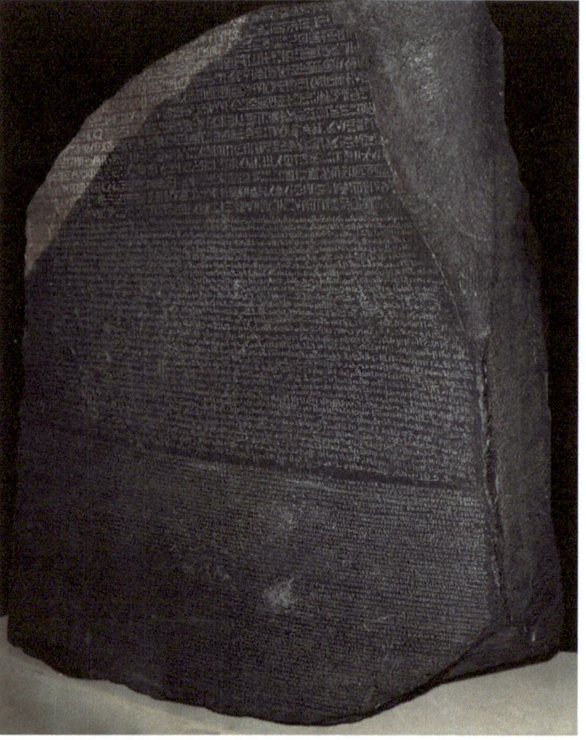

Rosetta Stone, 196 BCE, granodiorite, 45 x 28.5 x 11 inches, discovered in 1799 in Rashid, Egypt. British Museum, London.

By 200 BCE there were twenty-three Latin letters — three had yet to be created: J, V, and W.

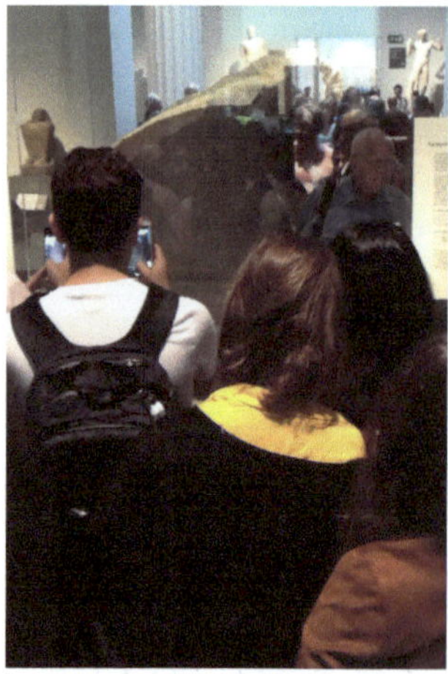

As seen in the British Museum, London.

Hieroglyphic writing is a complex system, a script all at once figurative, symbolic, and phonetic, in one and the same text, in one and the same sentence, and, I might even venture, in one and the same word.
—Jean-François Champollion, *Précis du système hiéroglyphique des anciens Égyptiens* (April 1824)

THE KEY TO UNDERSTANDING EGYPTIAN HIEROGLYPHS

As previously mentioned, hundreds of bilingual and trilingual artifacts were discovered throughout the development of the Latin alphabet. Though not part of that lineage, the *Rosetta Stone* is a critical artifact that unlocked the key to deciphering Egyptian hieroglyphs. For designers and typographers, it also stands as an early example of multilingual, multi-script design. The *Rosetta Stone* is a legal decree (essentially a tax exemption edict) issued from Memphis, a city just south of modern Cairo, to commemorate the first anniversary of the coronation of 13-year-old Ptolemy V Epiphanes on March 27, 196 BCE. It is written in two languages—Egyptian and Greek—and in three scripts: hieroglyphs (used by priests), Demotic (a cursive form of hieroglyphs), and Greek (the administrative language of the Ptolemaic rulers). The stone was discovered by accident in 1799 by French soldiers digging a foundation for a fort during the Napoleonic Wars. Recognizing its importance, their officer, Pierre-François Bouchard, set it aside for shipment to France. However, under the Treaty of Alexandria in 1801, all French-discovered antiquities, including the Rosetta Stone, became British property. It was transported from Rashid (Rosetta) to Portsmouth, then moved to the British Museum in London, where it remains today.

Deciphering the stone was the work of two individuals: Dr. Thomas Young of England and Jean-François Champollion of France. Each brought crucial expertise. Young, a renowned polymath and physicist (praised by Einstein and compared to Newton for discovering light interference in 1801), was also a skilled linguist. Champollion, a master of Latin, Greek, and six other ancient languages including Coptic—a late Egyptian language written in Greek characters—played an equally vital role.

From discovery, scholars recognized the stone had three scripts. The final sentence in the Greek section confirmed the text repeated in all three: This decree shall be inscribed on a stele of hard stone in sacred [hieroglyphic], native [Demotic], and Greek characters and set up in each of the first, second, and third [rank] temples beside the image of the ever-living king.

This confirmation that the stone was bilingual gave scholars clues to begin deciphering hieroglyphs. In 1814, Young analyzed grammar and vocabulary from about 400 languages, including Greek, Latin, and Sanskrit. He was first to compare Demotic with Greek, Demotic with hieroglyphs, and hieroglyphs with Greek. Using this, he decoded a hieroglyphic cartouche spelling "PTOLEMY" (Greek: Ptolemaios), identifying phonetic values for signs P, T, M, Y, and S. He also found hieroglyphs could be read in multiple directions, depending on bird, plant, or animal symbols' orientation (see page 35). Scholars believed hieroglyphs were mostly symbolic, with phonetic elements only for foreign names. In fact, Egyptian hieroglyphs are primarily phonetic.

Between 1814 and 1815, Young determined Demotic evolved from earlier hieroglyphic and hieratic forms, mixing phonetic and symbolic characters. As he wrote: "...it seemed natural to suppose that alphabetical characters might be interspersed with hieroglyphics, in the same way astronomers and chemists have often used arbitrary marks, as compendious expressions of objects frequently mentioned in their sciences." He referred to modern non-phonetic symbols like +, =, $, and %. Young later compiled a dictionary of Demotic.

While scholars translated the fifty-four lines of Greek and the thirty-two lines of Demotic fairly quickly, deciphering hieroglyphs took two more decades. Champollion finally succeeded in 1822. Unlike Young, who believed phonetic elements were limited to foreign names, Champollion correctly theorized hieroglyphs—like Demotic—were a blend of phonetic and symbolic characters. His work laid the foundation for Egyptology. Without Young and Champollion, our understanding of the ancient Egyptian language and culture would be vastly diminished.

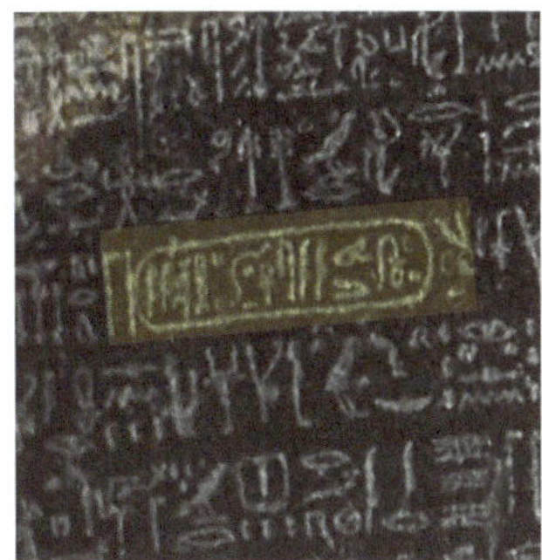

DETAIL: Egyptian hieroglyphs, highlighted in yellow, *King Ptolemy live (in) eternity beloved one of Ptah god,* within a cartouche. This was the key to deciphering hieroglyphics.

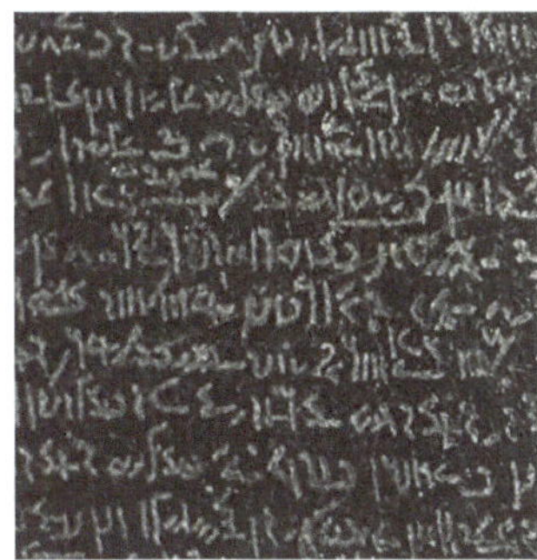

DETAIL: Demotic script.

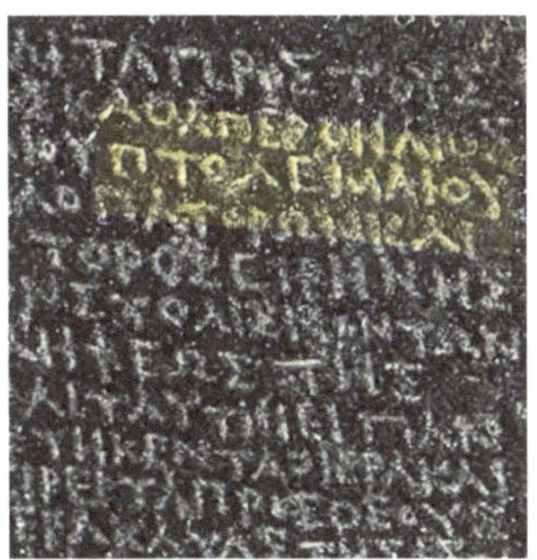

DETAIL: Greek, highlighted in yellow, ΠΤΟΜΑΙΟΥ, meaning *Ptolemy.*

MEANWHILE, IN ALEXANDRIA, THE LONGEST ETRUSCAN TEXT IS FOUND

In 1848, Mahajlo Barić, a retired Croatian living in Vienna, decided to tour Egypt. While shopping in Alexandria, he came across a sarcophagus containing a mummy and purchased it as a souvenir (the sale of Egyptian mummies was popular in the mid-nineteenth century). His purchase turned out to include the oldest surviving linen codex (ancient manuscript) and the longest recorded Etruscan text. Named Liber Linteus Zagrabiensis (Latin for "Linen Book of Zagreb"), dated to around 250 BCE, the manuscript contains 230 lines of Etruscan text and about 1,500 words—1,200 of which are legible. The few words that can be understood suggest it is a religious calendar. The linen had been repurposed as mummy wrapping during the embalming of an Egyptian woman. A papyrus found with the mummy identifies her name as Nesi-hensu, and her husband as Paher-hensu, a tailor from Thebes. Given her husband's profession, it's possible the linen was originally packaging for Etruscan fabric. After Barić's death, his brother Llija donated the linen manuscript to what is now the Archaeological Museum in Zagreb, Croatia.

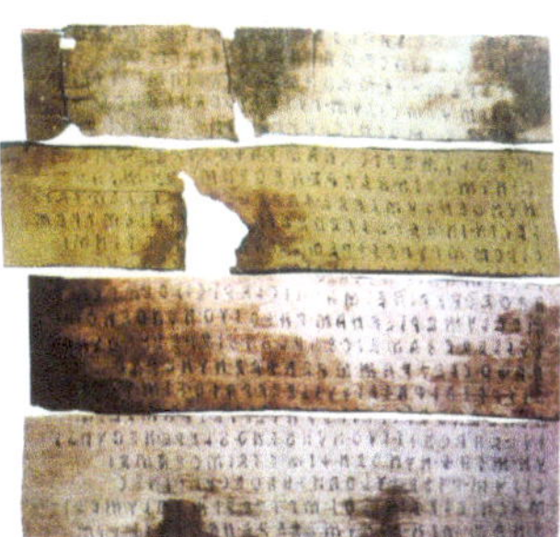

Liber Linteus Zagrabiensis, ca. 250 BCE, linen. Archaeological Museum, Zagreb.

21

100 BCE

EVERYDAY (VULGAR) LATIN and GREEK

POMPEII
Italy

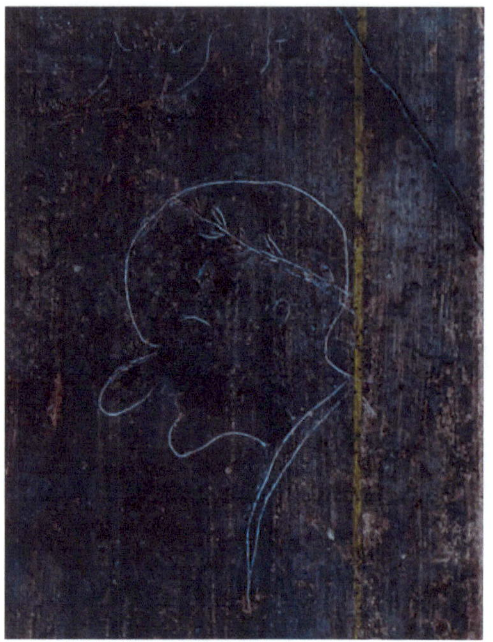

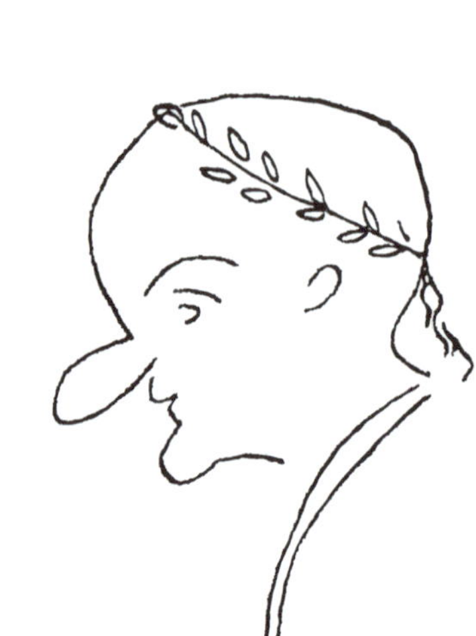

Pompeii Graffiti, RVFVS EST (It's Rufus), ca. 78 BCE, in the atrium on the north wall, Pompeii, Italy.

It recreates the life of the town. It's the voices of the people who were standing there, and thinking this, and writing it. That's why the graffiti are just so special and so enthralling.
— Rebecca R. Benefiel, *Pompeii's Graffiti and the Ancient Origins of Social Media* (2016)

THE VOICES OF EVERYONE

Before Mount Vesuvius erupted in the fall of 79 BCE, approximately fifteen thousand people in Pompeii and five thousand people in Herculaneum were going about their daily lives. On or around October 24th, they were managing shops, caring for children, or sharing a drink with a friend in a café. When the eruption occurred, a pyroclastic surge—where the ratio of gas to ash is higher—swept through the region. Temperatures soared instantly to 572°F (300°C) in Pompeii and 752°F (400°C) in Herculaneum, killing everyone instantly. By the time the eruption ended, Pompeii lay buried under 13 to 16 feet of volcanic ash, and Herculaneum under 50 to 60 feet, leaving thousands of lives entombed. Yet on the walls of shops, cafés, brothels, and homes, their voices live on in the thousands of graffiti inscriptions they left behind. From financial records and insults to declarations of love and well-wishes, the writings of the people of Pompeii and Herculaneum capture vivid, frozen moments of life from two thousand years ago. Scrawled across the walls are tally marks, loan agreements, transactions, and inventory lists—all small in scale but rich in meaning. They left behind everyday expressions, such as "we are cold" or "I was here," as well as insults like *fastuus* ("idiot"), *Fuibus egrotes* ("May you suffer Phoebus") and *Lasius cinedus* ("Lasius is a pervert"). They were expressed in Vulgar Latin—the everyday Latin—and in Greek. As Jacqueline DiBiasie Sammons, Field Director of the Ancient Graffiti Project, notes: "Most Classical literature that we have today was written by elite men... Ancient graffiti gives us the perspective of the other 99% of society. We get an insight into what they were thinking, buying, loving, and desiring." It's also in this graffiti that we see the letter U begin to take on a more rounded shape, evolving from the chiseled V. Today, only one-third of Pompeii and two-thirds of Herculaneum have been excavated.

QUI · SE TUTARI · NESCIT · NESCIT · VIVERE
MINIMUM · MALU (:MALUM) · FIT CONTEMNENDO · MAXIMUM

He who does not know to guard himself does not know how to live
The tiniest trouble, if ignored, becomes tremendous
(the smallest evil becomes the greatest).

Latin, ca. 78 BCE, Graffiti/incised, Herculaneum.

"Mula performs fellatio(?) Antoni(us?).
Fortunata (2 (bronze) asses (coins)),"

Latin, ca. 78 BCE, Graffiti/incised, Pompeii.

Greek abecedarium, ca. 78 BCE, Graffiti/incised, Pompeii.

SALUTE VENIENTIS ("To the health of the one entering"), Latin, ca. 78 BCE, Graffiti/incised, Pompeii.

ROMMIUS RUFUS ("Remnius Rufus"), Latin, ca. 78 BCE, Graffiti/incised, Herculaneum.

ALGEMEMUS ("We are cold"), Latin, ca. 78 BCE, Graffiti/incised, Herculaneum.

ABCDEFGHIKLMNOPQRSTVXYZ

Latin alphabet, ca. 100 BCE, twenty-three letters.

THREE TYPES OF ROMAN CAPITAL LETTERS

ROMAN SQUARE CAPITALS also known as *Capitalis quadrata, capitalis monumentalis* or monumental capitals, and, if carved into stone, as *lapidary* capitals. It is what our capital letters are based on: the circle, square and triangle, contrast between thin and thick strokes, and the formalization of the serif.

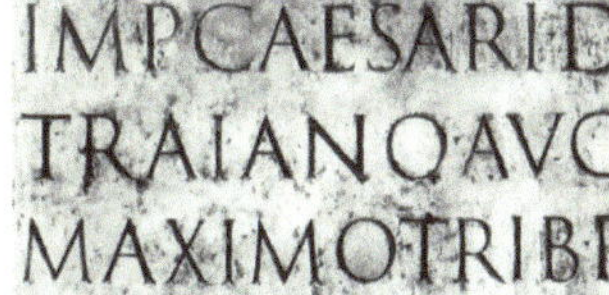

Trajan Column Inscription, 113 CE (see next page) (detail).

RUSTIC CAPITALS also known as *Capitalis rustica, scriptio continua*, or continuous script (no spacing between the words). Rustic capitals are more formal, used for writing or copying literary works with a broad-nib pen on parchment or papyrus.

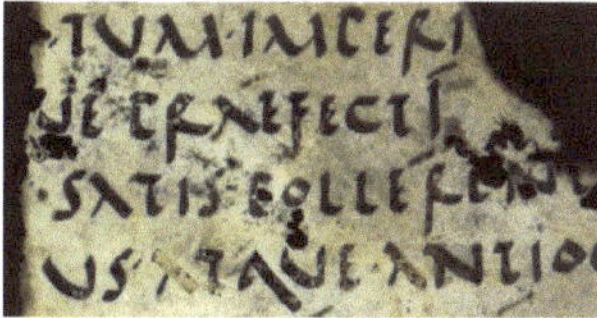

British Library Papyrus 745, ca. 100 CE, oldest example of Latin written on papyrus rather than parchment (detail).

OLD ROMAN CURSIVE also known as *Majuscule cursive* and *Roman Literary Cursive.* Used for daily writing written with a broad-nib pen or brush.

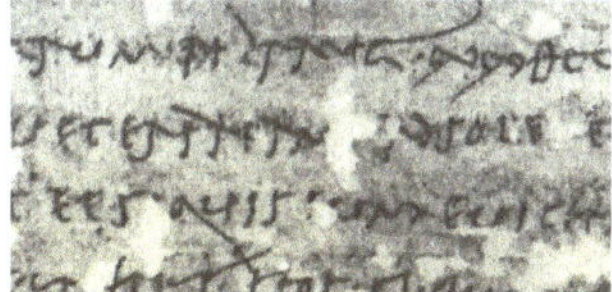

PSI VI 729, Horse sales contract, 77 CE, Old Roman Cursive (detail).

GRAFFITI: ALWAYS AND EVERYWHERE

For additional examples, see page 35 for Semitic graffiti in Egypt (ca. 1850 BCE), page 52 for Greek graffiti in southern Egypt (ca. 590 BCE) and page 71 for Nordic graffiti in Istanbul (ca. 1000 CE).

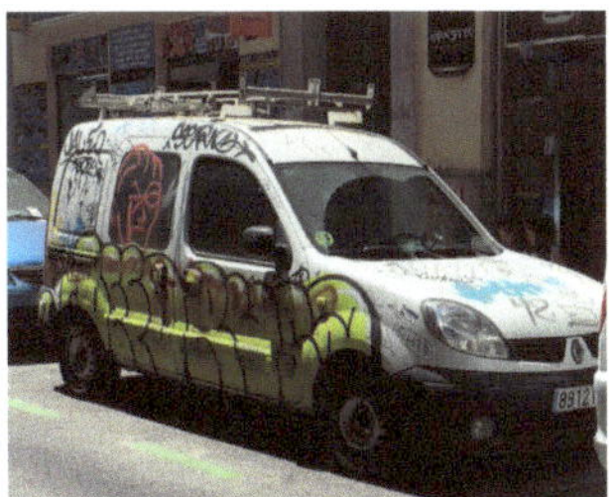

Madrid, Spain

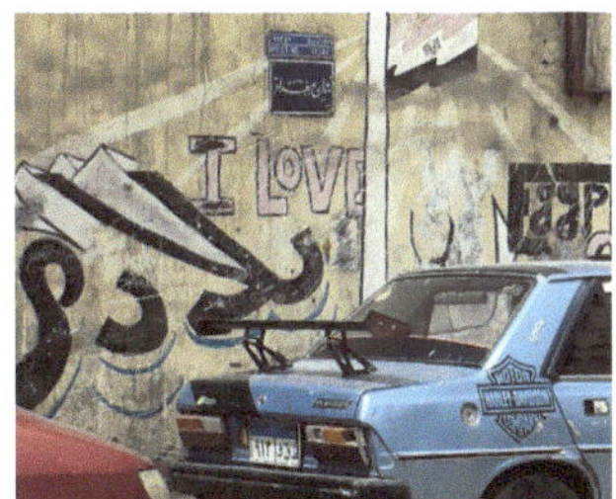

Cairo, Egypt (bilingual)

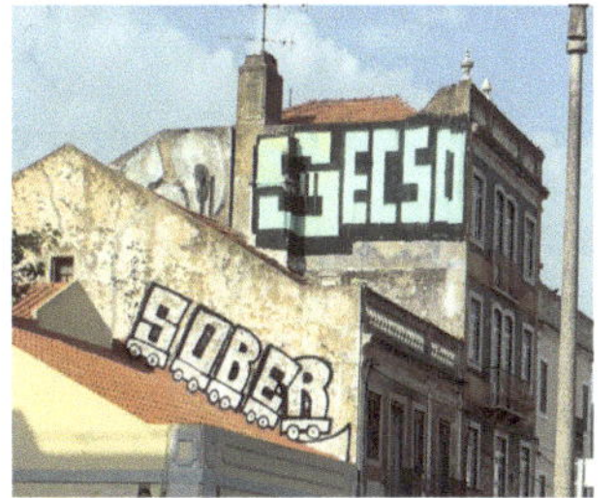

Setúbal, Portugal

22

100 CE

CLASSICAL LATIN

ROMAN EMPIRE

Our letters began their lives as images, while over time becoming abstracted. Many of our capital letters retain aspects of their ancient forms, sometimes with exactly the same consonant sound as in 1000 and 2000 B.C.
—David Sacks, *Letter Perfect: The Marvelous History of Our Alphabet from A to Z* (2003)

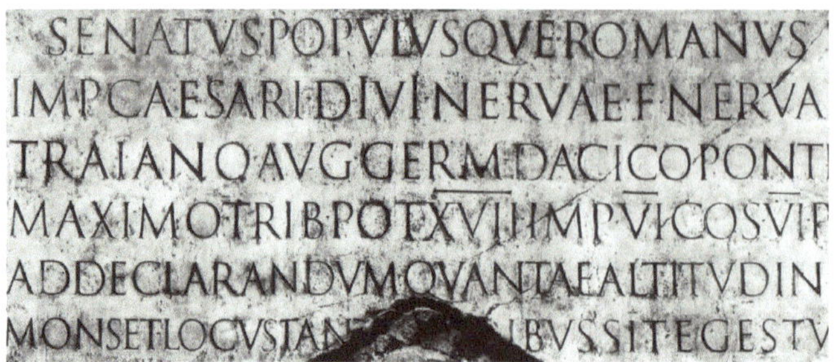

Trajan Column Inscription, 113 CE dedicated, Trajan's Forum, Rome, chiseled text in marble, located over the doorway. As the six lines of text descend the type becomes smaller, making it appear as one size when viewed from the ground.

TRANSLATION

> The Senate and the People of Rome to the
> Emperor, Caesar Nerva, son of the deified Nerva,
> Traianus Augustus, Germanicus, Dacicus, Pontifex
> Maximus, invested with the power of the tribune seventeen times, hailed
> imperator six times, elected consul six times,
> father of the fatherland, to demonstrate how lofty a hill and
> (what area of) ground was carried away for these mighty works.

Translation based on D. R. Dudley, Urbs Roma. 1967: Aberdeen.

A B C D E F G H I K L M N O P Q R S T V X Y Z

Latin alphabet, ca. 100 BCE, twenty-three letters.

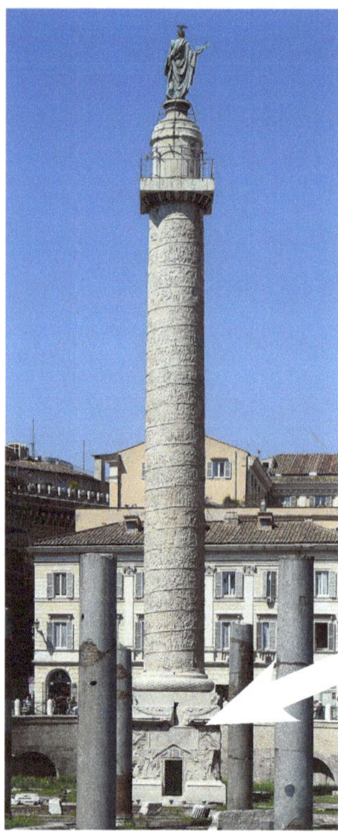

Trajan's Column, 107–113 CE, Trajan's Forum, Rome. Inscription is located above doorway (see white arrow). It is also where the ashes of Emperor Trajan are buried.

THE MOST BEAUTIFUL LETTERS IN THE WORLD

The height of the Roman Empire coincides with what is considered the finest example of Roman square capitals: the *Trajan Column Inscription*, a dedication containing thirty-seven words chiseled into marble. From the first century onward, Latin inscriptions across the Roman Empire (27 BCE–476 CE) became too numerous to count. With the Empire's expansion, the Latin language and its alphabet spread widely. According to Christopher Lightfoot from the Department of Greek and Roman Art at The Metropolitan Museum of Art, the success and proliferation of the Latin alphabet stemmed from the fact that it "was so clear, concise, and easy to read that it came to be adopted by many countries around the world." As it spread, the alphabet had to be adapted to represent new sounds.

In ancient Rome, *Trajan* was pronounced "Trah-yahn-us" and spelled TRAIANUS. The names of Roman gods—Jupiter, Juno, and Janus—were pronounced "Yu-pi-ter," "Yu-no," and "Yahn-nis," and spelled IUPPITER, IUNO, and IANUS. This is because the letters J, V, and W did not exist yet. In classical Latin, the "wah" sound was represented by the letter V, which served as both a vowel and a consonant. For example, *Venus* was spelled VENVS (or informally UENUS) and pronounced "wee-nus." Letters V and U were considered the same letter until modern printing practices began to differentiated them. To represent the "wah" sound,

Romans used **UA**, **UE**, or **UU**, as in *aqua* and *equus*—a sound still heard today in words like *queen* and *squeeze*. The letter **G** was probably a Roman invention, as the Etruscan alphabet they inherited lacked the "gee" sound. The Etruscans likely used **C** in place of **G**; the Romans added a small spur to **C** to create **G**, distinguishing the two letters.

BRITANNIA
ROME
CONSTANOPLE
ATHENS
CARTHAGE
MEDITERRANEAN SEA
BABYLON
ALEXANDRIA
ASWAN

Roman Empire, ca. 117 CE

A SHORT INTRODUCTION TO RUNES

As the Latin alphabet spread north, it gradually replaced the Runic alphabet (ca. 100–800 CE), also known as FUÞARK, named after its first six letters. This script was used by the Vikings to write early Germanic languages. Elder Futhark is considered the oldest version of the runic writing system.

ᚠᚢᚦᚨᚱᚲᚷᚹᚺᚾᛁᛃᛇᛈᛉᛊᛏᛒᛖᛗᛚᛜᛞᛟ

f u þ a r k g w h n i j ï p R s t b e m l ng d o

FUÞARK (or Runic) alphabet, ca. 100–800 CE, twenty-four characters.

AND A SHORTER INTRODUCTION TO UNCIAL: THE SMALL LETTERS

Uncial script was used as early as the third century BCE by the Greeks and later adopted by the Romans, who developed it into a more rounded and freely written style. Some scholars believe its name comes from the Latin *literae uniciales*, meaning "inch-high letters." It was a rounded form of uppercase (*majuscule*), though not entirely—certain letters such as a, d, h, i, and q began to take on lowercase (*minuscule*) characteristics, including the appearance of ascenders and descenders. Uncial became the Latin "book hand," as opposed to a "business hand," and survived the fall of Rome by becoming the writing style of the Roman Catholic Church.

a b c d e f g h i k l m n o p q r s t u x y z

Uncial script with twenty-three-letters, used from the 4th to 8th century CE.

TRAJAN'S COLUMN'S LETTERFORMS TODAY

RETAIL

BARNEYS NEW YORK

VICTORIA'S SECRET

HIGHER EDUCATION

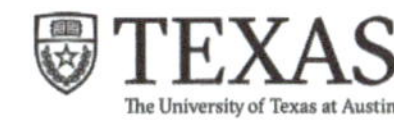

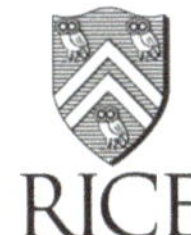

ENTERTAINMENT

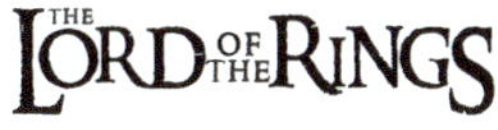

TITANIC

ABCDEFGHIJKLMNOPQRSTUVWXYZ

Trajan Typeface, Adobe Co., 1989, designed by Carol Twombly, inspired by the *Trajan Column Inscription*. Only uppercase.

MEANWHILE, EGYPT SUPPLIES ROME WITH GRANITE

Between the first and third centuries CE, the Romans operated a quarry at Mons Claudianus in Egypt's Eastern Desert, about 650 kilometers southeast of Cairo. They extracted granodiorite—granito del foro—which was transported to Rome across the desert, down the Nile, and across the Mediterranean. The stone was widely used in the city, notably in Nero's Domus Transitoria, Trajan's Forum, the Basilica Ulpia (112 CE), and the Pantheon (113–125 CE), whose sixteen portico columns each stand 12 meters tall and weigh 60 tons.

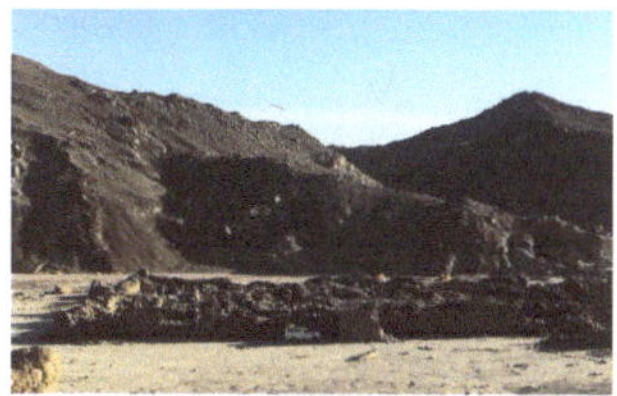

Remnants of the miners' village, Mons Claudianus, Eastern Desert, Egypt.

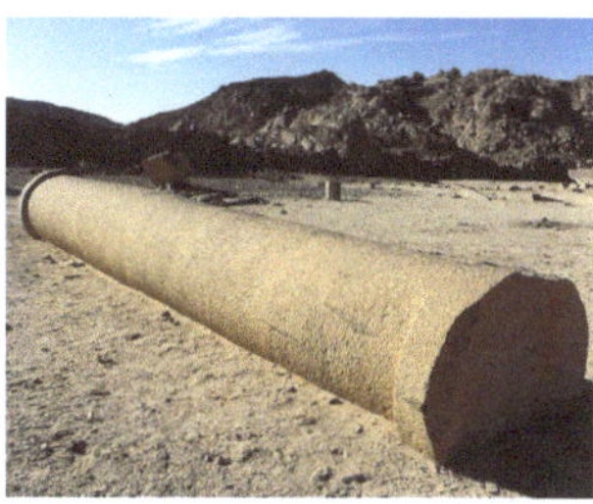

Mons Claudianus, Eastern Desert, Egypt.

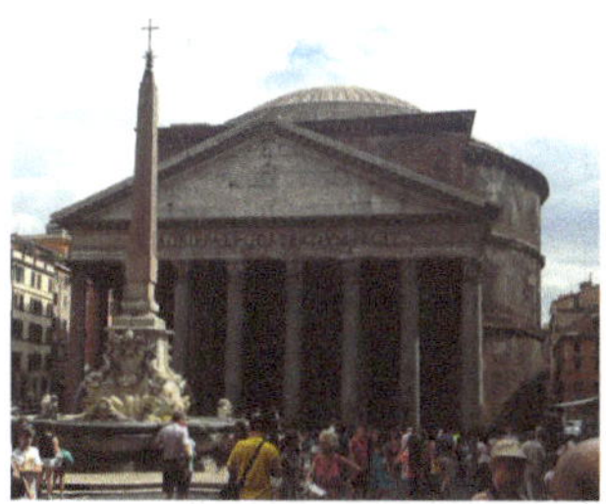

Pantheon, 113–125 CE, Rome.

23

800 CE

MEDIEVAL LATIN

CAROLINGIAN EMPIRE

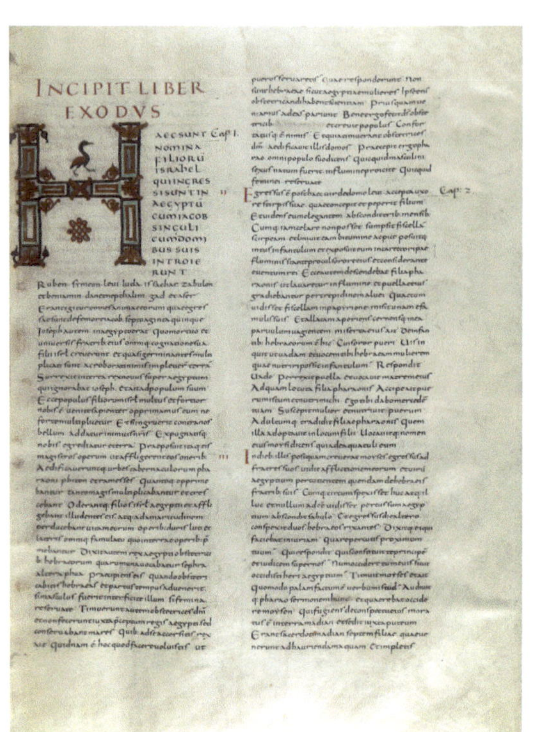

Moutier-Grandval Bible, f.26r, Benedictine Abbey of St. Martin, Tours, France, ca. 830-840 CE, 510 x 375 mm, Latin, parchment, British Library.

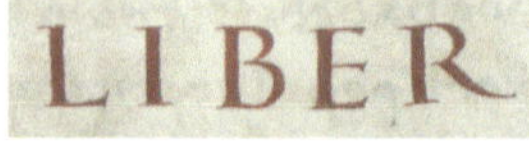

Roman square capitals

Uncial script

Carolingian minuscule

The *Moutier-Grandval Bible* (left) lays the foundation for modern page design, illustrating three levels of typographic hierarchy based on color, scale, and handwriting style. At the top, in red, is the three-word headline: INCIPIT LIBER EXODUS ("Here begins the book of Exodus") , written in large Roman square capitals. Below that, the introductory line begins with an ornate capital H, followed by uncial: [H]AEC SUNT NOMINA FILIORUM ISRAHEL QUI INGRESSI SUNT IN AEGYPTUM ("These are the names of the sons of Israel who entered Egypt"). The main body of the text appears in a smaller size and is written in Carolingian minuscule (see the example of the name *joseph* above). In medieval Latin manuscripts, words ending in M were sometimes indicated by placing a bar over the preceding vowel—such as in the word AEGYPTUM ("Egypt") in the example below.

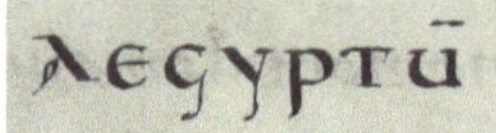

In these hide-outs of culture and learning, which were not all part of the early church system, the Roman manuscript styles continued to have a place.
—Alexander Nesbitt,
The History and Technique of Lettering (1957)

HIERARCHY, HARMONY, AND THE HEAVENLY

With the fall of the Roman Empire, and the rise of the Roman Catholic Church—which became the state religion in 380 CE— Europe underwent dramatic change as power shifted across the continent. From 500 to 800 CE, waves of migration spread across the region in what became known as the "wandering of the peoples," or *Völkerwanderung* in Germans. During this period of declining Roman influence, both its culture and handwriting began to fade. However, the twenty-three-letter Latin alphabet and language were preserved and propagated by the Roman Catholic Church through its monasteries and cloisters. As Roman authority waned, new writing styles emerged—hybrids of monumental and cursive forms. By 800 CE, the Carolingian Empire was at its height, encompassing what is now France, Germany, and northern Italy. It was led by a charismatic and influential leader named Charlemagne, whose name derives from the French *Charles-le-Magne*, meaning "Charles the Great." Reigning from 768 to 814 CE, Charlemagne held many titles: King of the Franks and the Lombards, Holy Roman Emperor, and "Father of Europe." In 789 CE, Charlemagne launched an initiative that would bring order and consistency to the diverse and chaotic handwriting styles of the time. The result was *Carolingian minuscule*—named after the Carolingian dynasty and described as *minuscule* due to its small size. Compared to uncial and square capitals, it was more compact and significantly more legible.

While uncial had modified seven letters and semi-uncial seven more, Carolingian minuscule refined the entire alphabet, laying the foundation for the lowercase letters we use today. By the late ninth century, Christian missionaries working in Slavic-speaking regions—wanting their congregants to understand their services—developed the Cyrillic alphabet, based on Greek capital letters. Meanwhile, the Arabic script, second only to the Latin alphabet in global use today, spread rapidly during the Arab conquests of the seventh and eighth centuries, fueled by the expansion of Islam and the influence of the Qur'an. Like early Cyrillic, Hebrew, and Arabic, the Latin alphabet spread largely through religion. As the Roman Empire ended around 476 CE, Romance languages blossomed. From Latin, five major languages emerged, each with new sounds that required new written forms: Spanish (470 million speakers), Portuguese (250 million), French (150 million), Italian (90 million), and Romanian (25 million).

EARLY EUROPEAN SCRIPTS

UNCIAL

Harley Gospels, ca. 575 CE, Latin, probably Aachen, Germany (detail).

INSULAR MAJESCULE

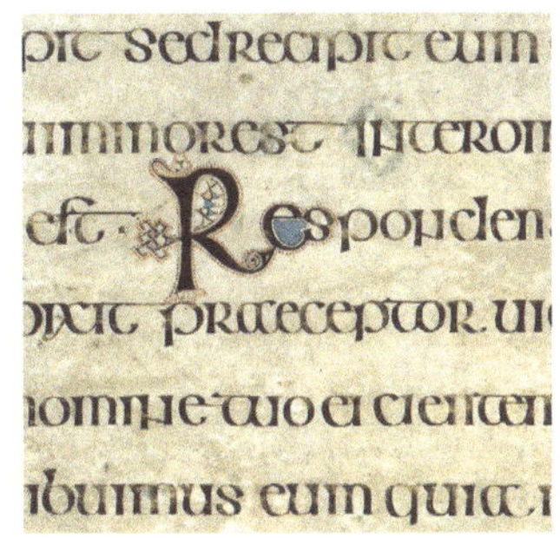

Book of Kells, ca. 800 CE, Latin (detail).

CAROLINGIAN

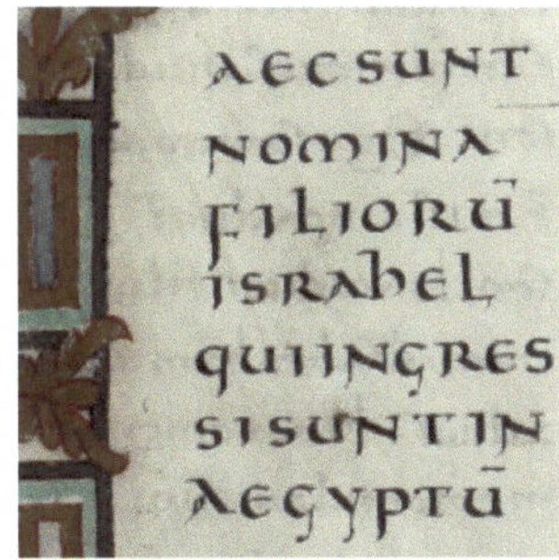

Moutier-Grandval Bible (from facing page). Note the unicial H in ISRAHEL—a step in representing today's lowercase h (detail, from facing page).

MODERN HIERARCHICAL DESIGN ON SCREENS AND OUTSIDE

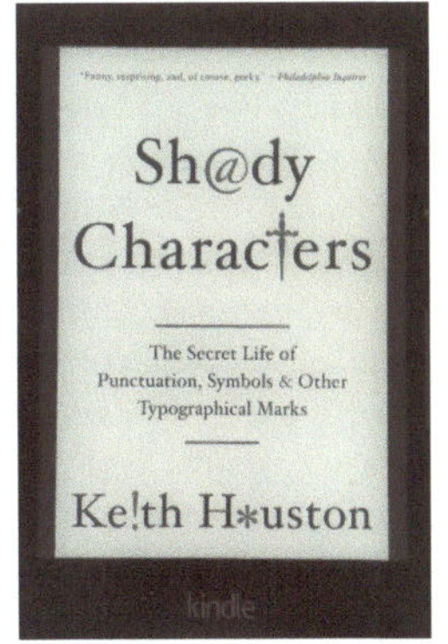

Shady Characters, Kindle book cover.

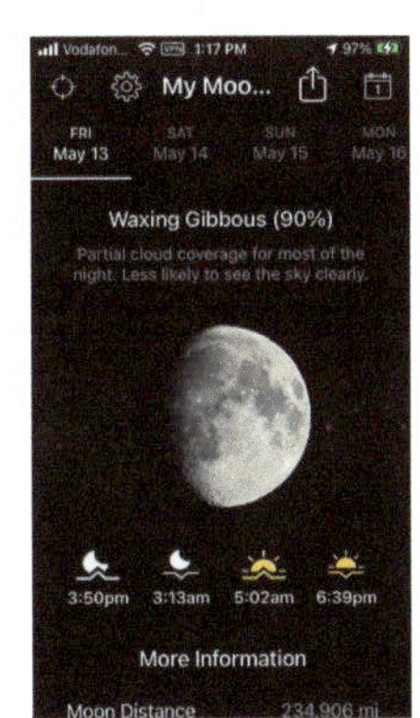

MoonPro, app screenshot (accessed May 2022).

Moderna Museet, Outdoor signage, Museum of Modern Art, Stockholm.

IMPORTING A NEW TECHNOLOGY

Papermaking began in China around 100 CE.. By the 600s, the knowledge had spread to Korea and Japan, and by the 700s, to the Arab world. Many Arabic manuscripts made from linen and flax have survived. Despite this long tradition, papermaking remained unknown in Europe until after 1000 CE.

PARCHMENT: Made from untanned sheep, goat, or calf skin; used since ancient Egypt.
VELLUM: A finer parchment made from calfskin.
PAPER: Made by soaking wood, cloth, or plant fibers.

The earliest surviving European document on paper (below) is a mandate written in Greek and Arabic. It was issued by Countess Adelaide, first wife of Roger, Norman king of Sicily. The red spot at the bottom is her wax seal. The original document is heavily damaged—only two-thirds survives.

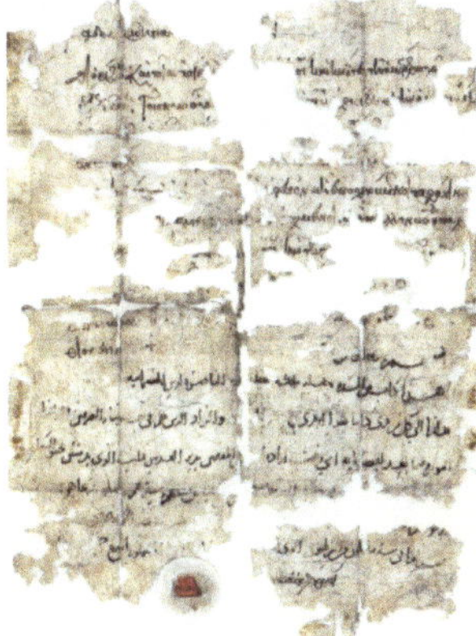

Adelaide's Bilingual Mandate of 1109 CE, in Greek and Arabic, after restoration in 1995. In its present state it measures 37.5 cm. high by 27 cm. wide. Palermo, Archivio di Stato, Tabulario dell'Ospedale Grande di Palermo, Tabulario dei monasteri di San Filippo di Fragalà e di Santa Maria di Maniaci, number 9.

24

1000–1500 CE

OLD ENGLISH

ENGLAND

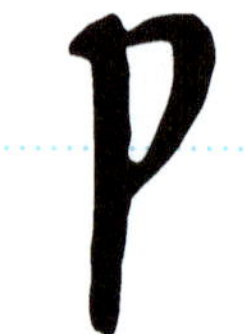

Anglo-Saxon letter, *wyn*, or *wen*. It would disappear from English writing about 1300, and be replaced by the Norman double U.

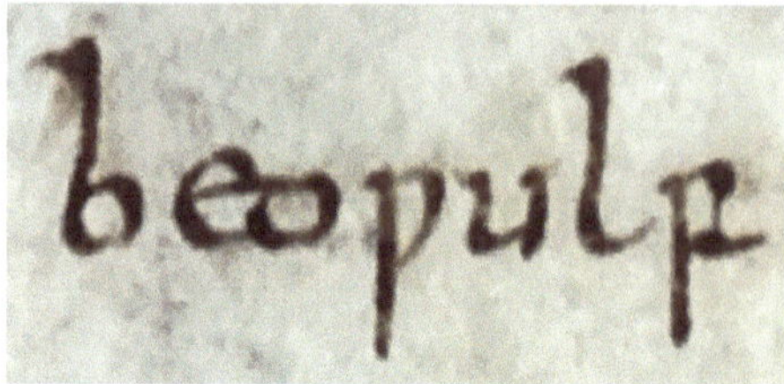

The word *Beowulf* from page 3 of the text, where the Anglo-Saxon letter *wyn*, ƿ, is used for the "wah" sound. British Library, London (detail).

LEFT: Opening page, *Beowulf*, ca.1000, parchment, British Library, London. It is a three-thousand-plus line epic poem, the longest in Old English.

The greatest literary masterpiece is no more than an alphabet in disorder.

—Jean Cocteau (1889-1963)

A NEW LETTER—W—AND A REVOLUTIONARY INVENTION

From 500–1500 CE, the twenty-three-letter Latin alphabet saw the end of antiquity and the rise of modern Europe. By 1500 CE, it was being used by thirty Western and Central European languages. The Norman Invasion of 1066 had a profound effect on Old English, particularly through the influence Old French. In Old English, the "wah" sound was originally represented by the Anglo-Saxon letter *wyn* or *wen* (ƿ), which traces its roots back to the Phoenician *waw* character (Y). This sound was common in the Germanic languages of Northern Europe. Remember, in ancient Latin, the letters **U** and **V** were interchangeable—both reflected the same "wah" sound. By the 14th century, scribes began representing the "wah" with either two **u**'s or two **v**'s. With the invention of metal type, printers created a new character formed by nearly touching or overlapping two V's: **VV**, **VV**, which evolved into the letter **W**. The name reflects its origin: *double U* in English, for its handwritten form, and *double vé* in French, for its printed form. By the late 1500s, the letter **W** was officially recognized as part of the English alphabet, and remains the only letter with more than one syllable. It was not until the late 19th century that the letter **W** was added to the French alphabet. Even today, the letter W does not appear in the Italian or Spanish alphabets; it is only used for foreign words.

Around 1440, Johannes Gensfleisch zur Laden zum Gutenberg, a goldsmith from Mainz, Germany, revolutionized the world by combining three key technologies: metal movable type, oil-based ink with the right viscosity, and a printing press. This combination dramatically increased the speed and scale at which information could be reproduced and shared. Gutenberg's invention helped fuel the Italian Renaissance, with Venice emerging as the center of book production. It also played a crucial role in the Protestant Reformation. In 1517, German theologian Martin Luther—critical of the Catholic Church—wrote, printed, and distributed his Ninety-Five Theses in Wittenberg. Just seventeen days later, as the story goes, printed copies reached London. For the first time, ideas could spread quickly across vast regions, empowering the masses and democratizing access to information. It is important to note, however, that book printing existed long before Gutenberg. In Korea, movable metal type had been used nearly a century earlier. In China, during the 1040s—while the Normans were conquering England—Bī Shēng was developing movable porcelain type. And in Europe, long before Gutenberg, books were printed from woodblocks, engraved metal plates, and drawings. However, these earlier methods allowed for little to no editing. Gutenberg's key innovation was individual metal letters—known as sorts—that could be rearranged, edited, or corrected. As S.H. Steinberg writes in *Five Hundred Years of Printing*: "What was epoch-making in Gutenberg's process was the possibility of editing, sub-editing, and correcting a text which was (at least in theory) identical in every copy: in other words, the uniform edition preceded by critical proofreading." The common expression "out of sorts" comes from this era, referring to the shortage of a particular letter in a printer's type case. With the printing press came the standardization of the alphabet, paving the way for modern typography.

Drawing of one of Koberger's presses, Albrecht Dürer, 1511.

A TIMELINE OF TYPOGRAPHY

TYPOGRAPHIC FORM	ORIGIN	TIME PERIOD
Uppercase	Roman Empire, Rome	ca. 100 CE
Lowercase	Christian scribes, Holy Roman Empire	ca. 800 CE
Italics	Italian Renaissance	ca. 1500 CE

uu

Hand-written miniscule double u

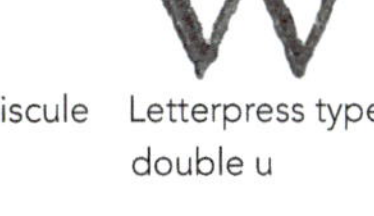

Letterpress type double u

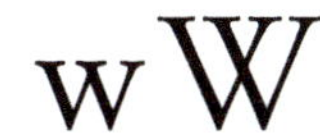

Digital type: Adobe Garamond **W** in lowercase and uppercase, designed by Robert Slimbach in 1989. Based on Claude Garamond's (ca. 1510–1561 CE) old-style typeface, Garamond (see page 77).

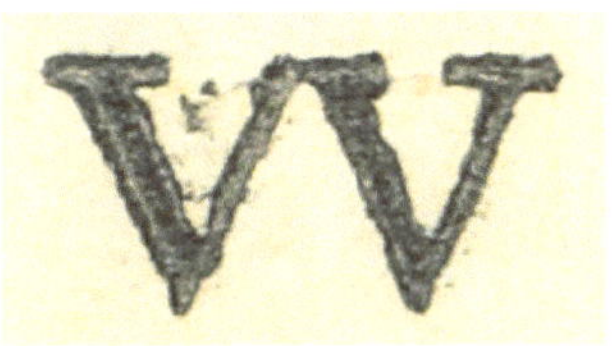

DETAIL: Two uppercase **V**'s create the **W** in *William* (see right).

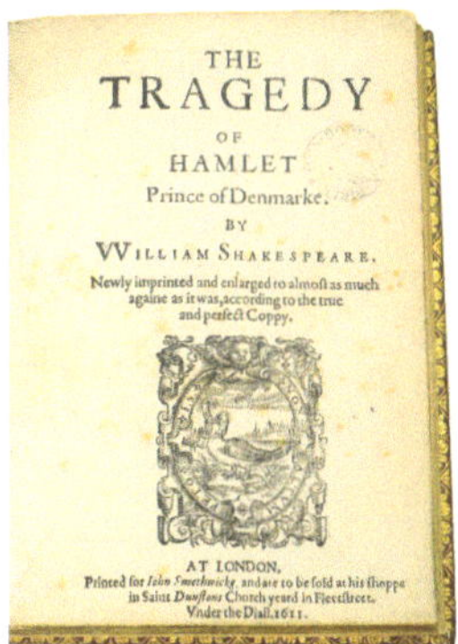

THE
TRAGEDY
OF
HAMLET
Prince of Denmarke.
BY
VVILLIAM SHAKESPEARE.
Newly imprinted and enlarged to almost as much againe as it was, according to the true and perfect Coppy.

AT LONDON,
Printed for *Iohn Smethwicke*, and are to be sold at his shoppe in Saint *Dunstons* Church yeard in Fleetstreet.
Vnder the Diall. 1611.

RIGHT: Title page of *The Tragedy of Hamlet*, 1611 CE, Bodleian Library, Oxford University. Note the ligatures and the interchangeably use of the letters **I** and **V** for **J** and **U**, respectively (see Iohn and Vnder in the bottom three lines).

MEANWHILE, IN SPAIN AND SARDINIA

In 1492, Jewish communities across Spain—and in Alghero, Sardinia, where the Phoenicians had settled 2,300 years earlier—were expelled. Ferdinand II of Aragon (1452–1516), known as Ferdinand the Catholic and ruler of Sardinia, forced Jews from their homes and communities. The ketubah (Jewish marriage contract) below was discovered in Sardinia, hidden in a book binding.

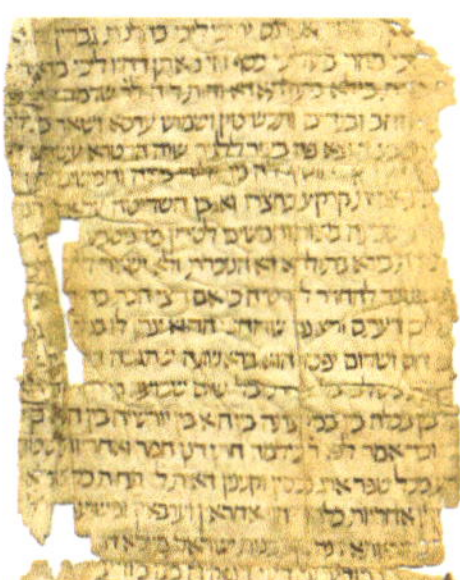

Ketubah (Jewish marriage contract), parchment, 1300–1499 CE, 44.4 cm. x 26.6 cm. University Library of Sassari, Sardinia, Italy. Written in Hebrew, the contract records the marriage between Shelomò, son of Zare of Carcassona, and Bella di Merwanha.

AND, IN THE HAGIA SOFIA, CONSTANTINOPLE (ISTANBUL)

Sometime during the Viking Age (793–1066 CE), an elite unit of Varangian Guards—originating from northern Russia and Scandinavia—were stationed at the Hagia Sofia, hired to protect the Byzantine emperor. Perhaps out of boredom, some of them etched their names in runes (see page 71) into the marble balustrades. Two inscriptions survive. Scholar Elisabeth Svärdström suggests one, *ftan*, may be the name "Halfdan," the Nordic name of the carver. The second inscription, according to scholar Mats G. Larsson, could be interpreted as: "Ari m(ade these runes)."

25

1500 – 1650 CE

SPANISH

MEXICO and PERU

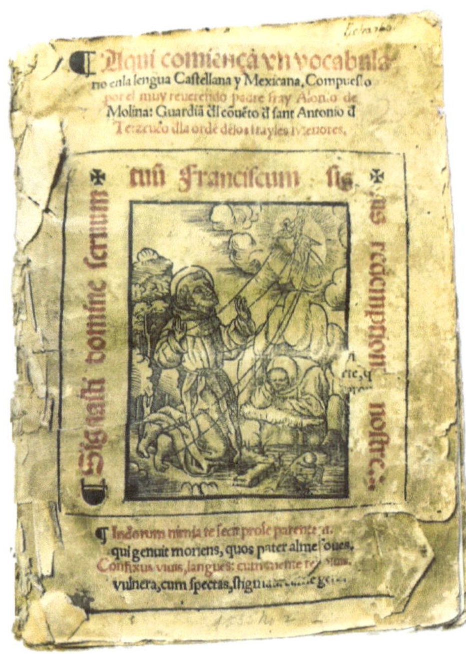

LEFT: Title page, *Vocabulario en lengua castellana y mexicana,* 1555 CE, written and printed by Alonso de Molina (1514–1579), a Franciscan friar and grammarian, Rare Books and Special Collection, Library of Congress. This was the first dictionary printed in the New World (Mexico City) and the first to use the vocabulary of the indigenous American language, Nahuatl.

Note the continued interchange of the letters **V** and **U** (e.g., *VOCABVLARIO, Lengva, nueua*) and the absence of an uppercase **J**.

AN OLD LETTER, U, BECOMES A NEW LETTER, V, WHILE PRINTING FLOURISHES

The dictionary itself is a masterwork of lexicography and is critical for scholars, linguists, and archaeologists studying both the history of the language and how its was spoken and understood in the sixteenth century.
—John Hessler, *Nahuatl as it was: an exploration of the great dictionary of Alonso de Molina* (2001)

As spoken Latin declined and medieval Romance languages like French and Spanish emerged, the Latin alphabet adapted to new sounds. The letters **V** and **J**—once considered variants of **U** and **I**—became distinct. Norman scribes (speaking Norman-French), working with English scribes after the Norman Conquest, played a key role in modifying and standardizing English spelling. By 1300 CE, English had absorbed thousands of Norman French words. In medieval writing, **U** and **V** were used interchangeably—remember, in ancient Rome, they were the same letter. Around this time, **J** also began to be consistently used as a consonant in Spanish. With colonization and proselytization moving westward, the first printing press in the Western Hemisphere was established in 1539 by the Jesuits at the Casa de la Primera Imprenta de América in Mexico City. This marked the growing use of both majuscule (uppercase) and minuscule (lowercase). In 1584, Italian printer Antonio Ricardo (ca. 1540–1606), after working with the Jesuits in Mexico City, established a printing press in Lima, Peru. By this point (ca. 1557), punctuation, including periods, hyphens, commas, colons, plus accents and ligatures, had come into common use. It would take nearly another century (ca. 1640) for the press to reach what would become the United States. Meanwhile in Italy, birthplace of Christianity, banking, and accounting, Venice became a center of printing innovation. It was the first city outside Germany with a press and became a hub. Two foundational type styles, roman and italic, were developed here, along with the first Greek and Hebrew typefaces. Innovations in book design also emerged, including title pages, pagination, and printed music. Still, many books printed before 1480 retained manuscript design. They lacked title pages, pagination, and illustrated material, such as initial caps, which were still drawn by hand. As typographer Stanley Morison observed in *First Principles of Typography*: "The history of printing is in large measure the history of the title-page." Within twenty years of

Gutenberg's invention, presses had spread across Europe, especially in cities thriving in trade, banking, shipping, and legal or ecclesiastical authority. By 1500, Venice had become the book-publishing capital of Europe, with approximately 150 presses in operation. Among the most influential printers of the era was Aldus Manutius, who revolutionized bookmaking in Venice. He made books more accessible and refined, reshaping how people read and thought. Between Gutenberg's press (ca. 1440) and 1500, an estimated 10 to 20 million books were printed. By 1600, that number had risen to 150–200 million volumes, comprising roughly 1.25 million unique titles—about two books per European. The economic effects were profound. According to one analysis, cities with printing presses in the late 1400s grew at least sixty percent faster than those without. From 1500 to 1800, cities with access to printing saw twenty-five percent faster growth, fueled by increased access to information, innovation, and trade. This surge in literacy and demand for books also spurred advancements in type design. Humanist scripts, in contrast to earlier Gothic or Blackletter scripts (such as in Gutenberg's Bible), offered greater legibility, clarity, and beauty. One of the most enduring legacies of the era is the typeface designed by Claude Garamond (ca. 1480–1561), whose elegant letterforms remain in wide use today as Garamond.

Claude Garamond's Second Great Primer Roman Type, sixteenth century, cast from original matrices (the original copper molds used to form the letters) by the Plantin-Moretus Museum, Antwerp.

A B C D E F G H I K L M N O P Q R S T V X Y
a b c d e f g h i k l m n o p q r s ſ t u v x z
Æ æ œ & ff ffi ffl fi fl œ Qu ſh ſi ſl ſſ ſſi ſt
1 2 3 4 5 6 7 8 9 0

EVOLUTION OF THE LETTER V

1 2 3 4 5 6 7 8 9 10 11 12

1. Phoenician, 11th cent. BCE. 2. Phoenician, 9th cent. BCE. 3. Greek, 8–7th cent. 4. Etruscan, 7th cent. 5. Roman, 3rd cent. 6. Roman, 113 CE. 7. Rustic, Roman, 1st cent. 8. Cursive, Roman, 1st cent. 9. Uncial, English, 8th cent. 10. Minuscule, Carolingian, 9th cent. 11. Minuscule, Humanist, 15th cent. 12. Printing Type, Italian, late 15th cent.

Chart: Lyn Davies (2006).

THE TITLE PAGE: THEN AND NOW

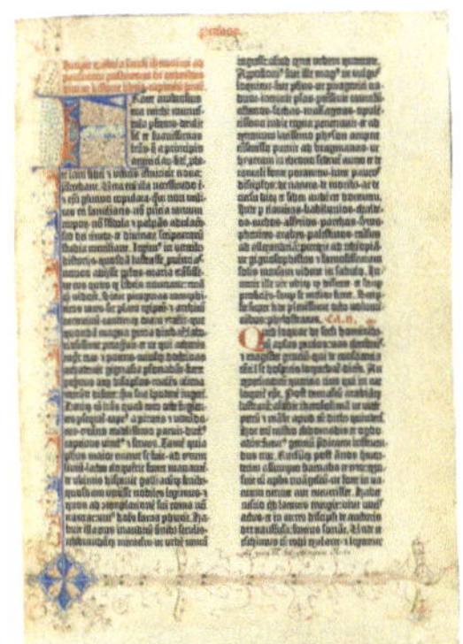

Gutenberg's Bible, 1454 CE, Latin.

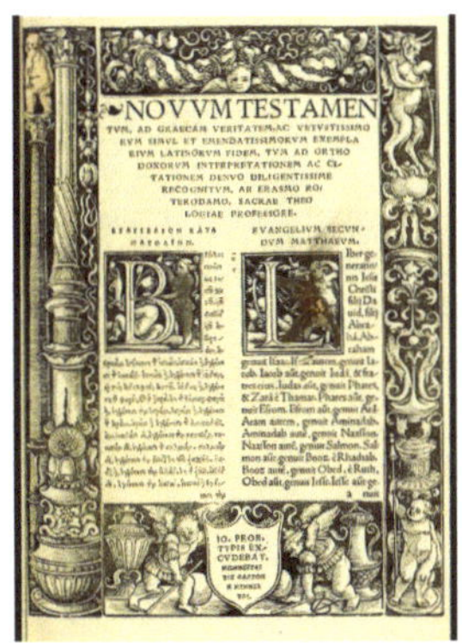

Erasmus's Novum Testamentum, 1519 CE, bilingual: Greek and Latin.

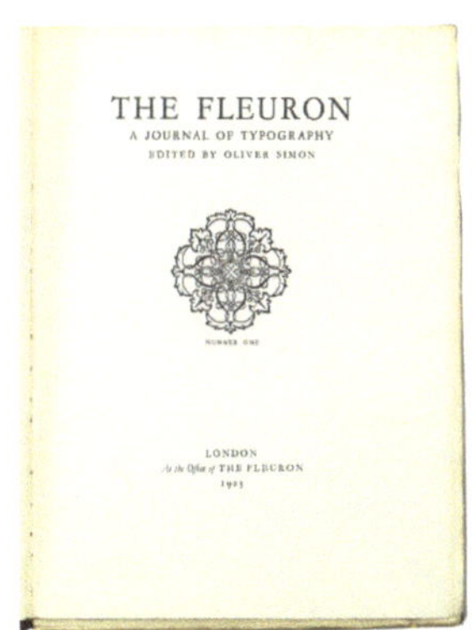

The Fleuron, 1923, British English.

EARLY PRINTING TYPES: UP CLOSE

BLACKLETTER, GERMANY

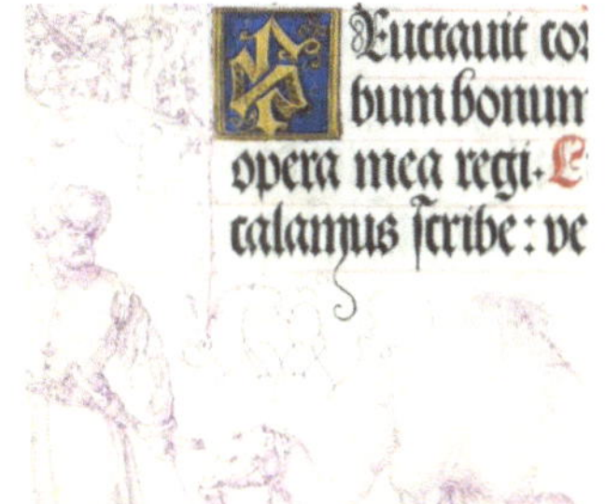

Prayer Book of Maximilian, 1514–1515, Munich, Germany. Albrecht Dürer created the marginal drawings (detail).

HUMANIST, ITALY

Eusebuis' De Evangelica Praeparatione, Nicholas Jenson, Venice, 1470 (detail).

ROMAN and **ITALIC**, ITALY

Book of the Holy Gospel of Our Lord and God Jesus Christ, bilingual edition in Latin and Syriac. Vienna, Austria, 1555 (detail). Syriac, along with Latin and Greek, was one of the most important languages of early Christianity (1st century CE).

26

1650–1800 CE

AMERICAN ENGLISH

UNITED STATES

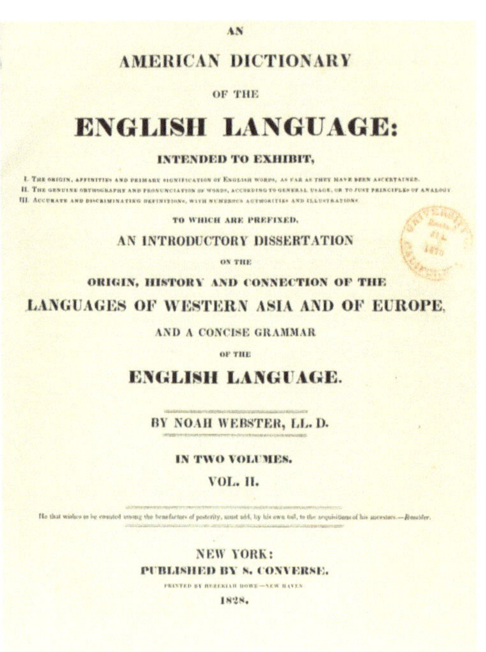

AN
AMERICAN DICTIONARY
OF THE
ENGLISH LANGUAGE:
INTENDED TO EXHIBIT,
I. The origin, affinities and primary signification of English words, as far as they have been ascertained.
II. The genuine orthography and pronunciation of words, according to general usage, or to just principles of analogy.
III. Accurate and discriminating definitions, with numerous authorities and illustrations.
TO WHICH ARE PREFIXED,
AN INTRODUCTORY DISSERTATION
ON THE
ORIGIN, HISTORY AND CONNECTION OF THE
LANGUAGES OF WESTERN ASIA AND OF EUROPE,
AND A CONCISE GRAMMAR
OF THE
ENGLISH LANGUAGE.
BY NOAH WEBSTER, LL. D.
IN TWO VOLUMES.
VOL. II.
He that wishes to be counted among the benefactors of posterity, must add, by his own toil, to the acquisitions of his ancestors.—Rambler.
NEW YORK:
PUBLISHED BY S. CONVERSE.
PRINTED BY HEZEKIAH HOWE—NEW HAVEN.
1828.

American Dictionary of the English Language, Noah Webster, 1828 CE.

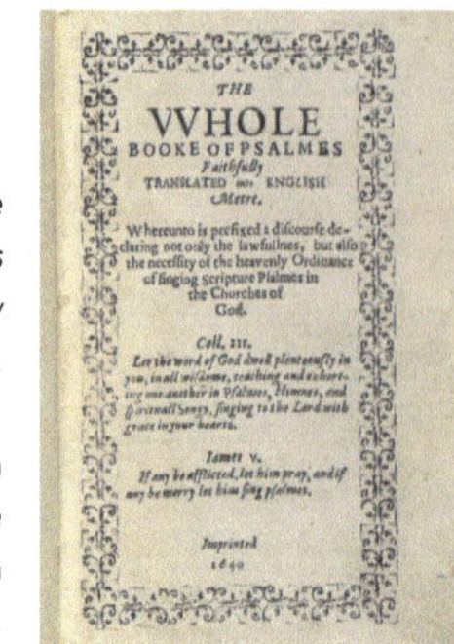

THE
VVHOLE
BOOKE OF PSALMES
Faithfully
TRANSLATED into ENGLISH
Metre.
Whereunto is prefixed a discourse declaring not only the lawfullness, but also the necessity of the heavenly Ordinances of singing scripture Psalmes in the Churches of God.
Coll. III.
Let the word of God dwell plenteously in you, in all wisdome, teaching and exhorting one another in Psalmes, Himnes, and spirituall Songs, singing to the Lord with grace in your hearts.
James v.
If any be afflicted, let him pray, and if any be merry let him sing psalmes.
Imprinted
1640

RIGHT: Title Page, *The Whole Booke of Psalmes* (also known as *The Bay Psalm Book*), 1640 CE, Cambridge, Massachusetts: Matthew Day for Stephen Day, (sig. *1r). It is the first book printed in British North America.

J. This letter has been added to the English Alphabet in modern days; the letter I being written formerly in words where J is now used. It seems to have had the sound of *y*, in many words, as it still has in the German. The English sound of this letter may be expressed by *dzh*, or *edzh*, a compound sound coinciding exactly with that of *g*, in *genius*; the French *j*, with the articulation *d* preceding it. It is the tenth letter of the English Alphabet.

The letter J. heading in the *American Dictionary of the English Language*, it is now official! (detail).

THE LAST LETTER, J— HALLELUJAH

The letter **J** is the tenth letter in the modern English alphabet—and yet the last letter to be fully accepted. Although it first arrived in England with the French following the Norman Conquest of 1066, it took centuries for **J** to become integrated into English. Old English had no "jay" sound, but French loanwords like *jolly* and *juice* gradually introduced the consonant. In Old French, the word for "justice" was iustice, pronounced something like "joos-tee-seh." In Spanish, it was *iusticia*, pronounced "hoo-tee-see-a," both deriving from the Latin *iustitia*. Over time, the Latin "yeh" sound softened to a "hah" sound in medieval Spanish, eventually becoming *justicia*. Here, J was used as a consonant, while I remained a vowel. Modern Spanish continues this tradition: **J** carries the "hah" sound, and **H** is silent. Following the invention of printing in the 1470s, Spain became the first country to consistently use **J** as a consonant. Though consonantal **I** (which evolved into **J**) originated in Italy, the modern Italian alphabet consists of only 21 letters—omitting **J**, **K**, **W**, **X**, and **Y**, which are used only in foreign words. Still, it took several hundred years for **J** to be recognized as a distinct letter with its own shape and sound, especially in uppercase form. It wasn't until 1640 that **J** appeared in the English alphabet, at a time when grammarians debating whether to expand the traditional 24-letter set. Even as late as 1755, Samuel Johnson's *Dictionary of the English Language* lists only 24 letters, treating **J** and **V** as variants of **I** and **U**, respectively. It wasn't until Noah Webster's American dictionary in 1828, and others like it, that **J** and **V** were fully accepted into the modern English alphabet. It is important to remember that widespread literacy is a recent development. In 1820, only about twelve percent of the world's population could read and write. Today, the reverse is true. In American English, **J** is the fourth least-used letter, ranking just above **Z**, **Q** and **X**.

Ottmar, you've done it again!
A line o' type!
—Whitelaw Reid, publisher,
New York Tribune, July 3, 1886

EVOLUTION OF THE LETTER J

1 2 3 4 5 6 7 8 9 10 11 12

1.Phoenician, 11th cent. BCE. 2. Phoenician, 10th cent. BCE. 3. Greek, 8th cent. 4. Etruscan, 7th cent. 5. Roman, 2nd cent. 6. Roman, 1st CE. 7. Uncial, Italian 6th–7th cent. 8. Insular, 8th cent. 9. Minuscule, Carolingian 9th cent. 10. Gothic, Dutch 15th cent. 11. Printing Type, French, 17th cent. 12. Printing Type, English, 18th cent.

Chart: Lyn Davies (2006).

ANOTHER REVOLUTIONARY INVENTION: THE LINOTYPE

In 1886, in Baltimore, Maryland, a German-born watchmaker named Ottmar Mergenthaler (1854–1899), brought precision and mechanization to the printing process. His groundbreaking invention, the Linotype machine, used brass matrices linked to a keyboard. Each matrix contained a specific "code" and was used to cast a single line of type—hence the name "line-o'-type." Theses lines were molded in a lead alloy that could be easily reset. If a typo occurred, only that single line needed to be recast, rather than an entire page. Once used, each matrix was automatically returned to its proper place by its uniquely notched teeth. The Linotype revolutionized printing by replacing Gutenberg's painstaking hand-setting of individual letters with a fast, efficient system of and machine-set type.

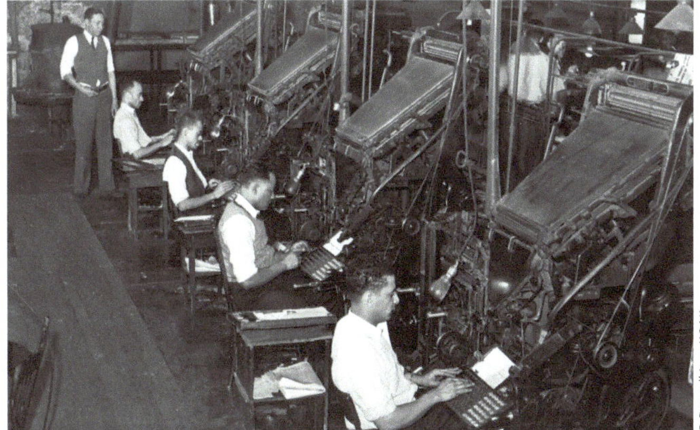

Linotype operators of the *Chicago Defender*, an African-American newspaper, April, 1941. Thomas Edison referred to the Linotype as "the eighth wonder of the world."

THE LINOTYPE MATRIX

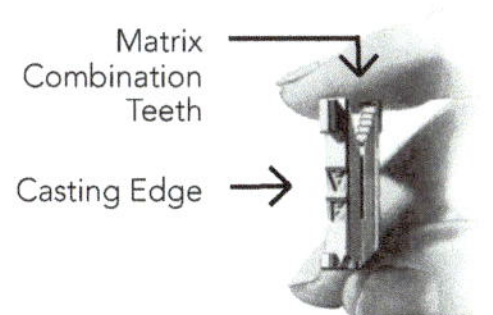

HAWAI'IAN ALPHABET, 1822

THE ALPHABET.

VOWELS. Names.	SOUND. Ex. in Eng.	Ex. in Hawaii.
A a ... ä	as in father,	la—sun.
E e ... a	— tele,	hemo—cast off.
I i ... e	— marine,	marie—quiet.
O o ... o	— over,	ono—sweet.
U u ... oo	— rule,	nui—large.

CONSONANTS.	Names.	CONSONANTS.	Names.
B b	be	N n	nu
D d	de	P p	pi
H h	he	R r	ro
K k	ke	T t	ti
L l	la	V v	vi
M m	mu	W w	we

The following are used in spelling foreign words:

F f	fe	S s	se
G g	ge	Y y	yi

1

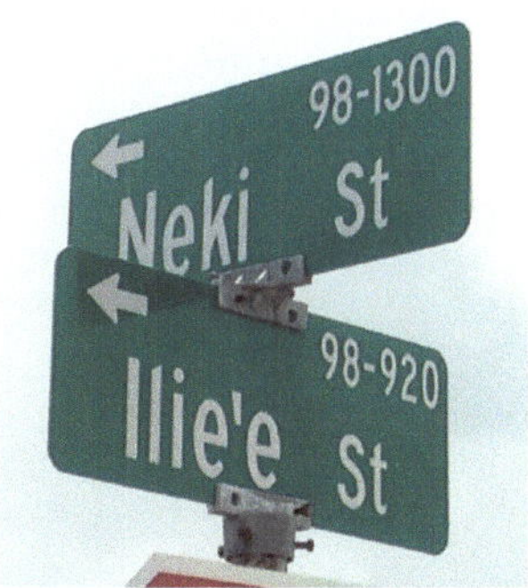

Street signage, Hawai'i.

MEANWHILE, IN HAWAI'I, USA

The first European to reach the Hawaiian Islands was British explorer James Cook in 1778, though some argue it was Spaniard Ruy López de Villalobos in 1542. Under the American Board of Commissioners for Foreign Missions, Congregational and Presbyterian missionaries followed. They were instructed "to obtain adequate knowledge of language; to make them acquainted with letters," and "to give them the Bible with skill to read it..." By 1820, missionaries began using the Latin alphabet to render oral Hawaiian into written form, producing a printed Bible. By 1825, they adopted a twelve-letter alphabet: A, E, I, O, U, H, K, L, M, N, P, and W. Letters B, D, G, R, S, T, V, and Z were placed on a supplementary list but rarely used. Within twenty years, they were printing not only hymnals and sermons, but textbooks on astronomy, anatomy, mathematics, and natural history. Printing helped preserve Hawaiian history and genealogy. Today, the official Hawaiian alphabet includes eighteen letters: A, E, I, O, U, Ā, Ē, Ī, Ō, Ū, H, K, L, M, N, P, W, and the 'okina (')—a glottal stop. This is why we pronounce Hawai'i as "ha-WHY-ee." Simultaneously, American businesses were establishing sugar plantations requiring labor forces. Workers arrived from Japan, China, and the Philippines. By 1896, 25% of Hawai'i's population was Japanese, while the Native Hawaiian population was being devastated—especially by smallpox brought by European settlers. Between 1770 and 1920, the Native Hawaiian population declined from 300,000 to 24,000. By 1894, Sanford Ballard Dole, son of Protestant missionaries, led a committee that overthrew Queen Lili'uokalani. The Kingdom of Hawai'i, which had remained independent, was annexed by the United States in 1898, and the Hawaiian language was subsequently banned. In 1959, Hawai'i became the 50th U.S. state.

AFTERWORD

During a visit to Italy, I made studies of old inscriptions in Rome and Florence. My attention was caught especially by marble inscriptions on the floor of the Santa Croce Church in Florence. Every day, most people walked over these inscriptions so unmindfully. I got the inspiration one day to use these simple forms without serifs for a typeface.
—Hermann Zapf,
Alphabet Stories, 2007

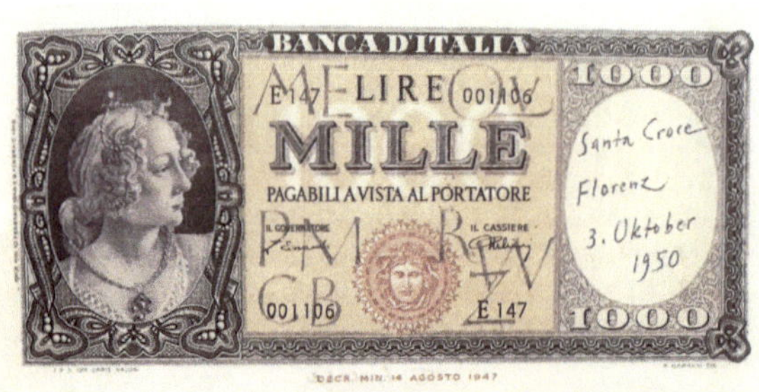

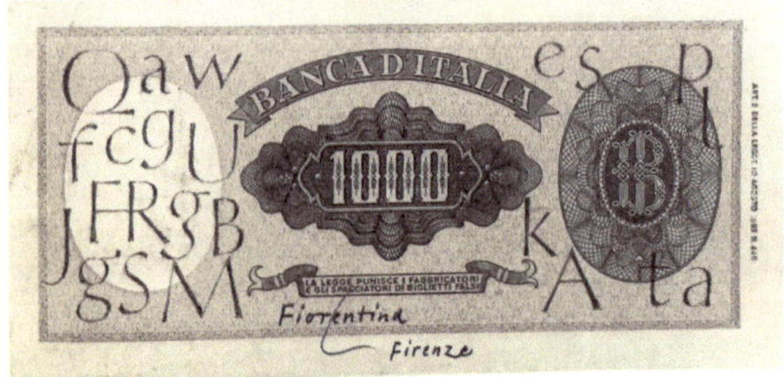

Sketches © Hermann Zapf (1950)

Front (top) and back (above) of an Italian 1000 lire banknote, on which Zapf made early sketches for a new serif-less Roman typeface. Hermann Zapf, 1950.

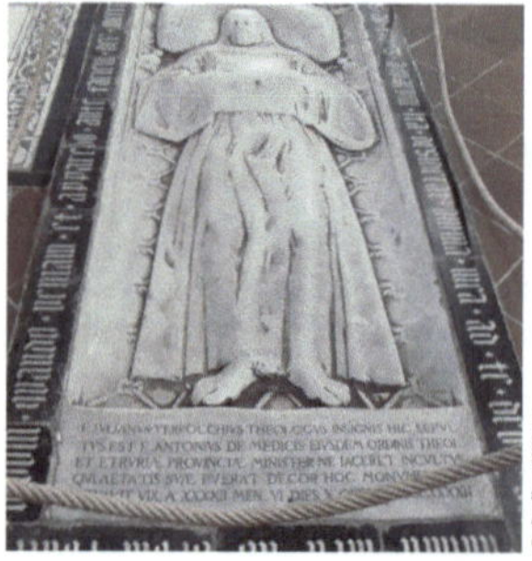

© Saiko (2011)

The inspiration for Zapf's font, Optima, came from the marble inscriptions on the floor of the Santa Croce Church in Florence, Italy (above).

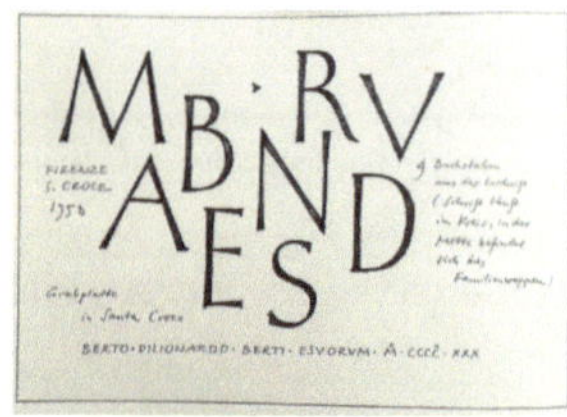

These sketches, above and left, eventually became the typeface Optima Roman.

GOING TO THE PAST TO REIMAGINE THE FUTURE

Artists and designers have always drawn connection, knowledge, and inspiration from the past. Whether graphic designers, fashion designers, or architects, the past can inform the future—if we are aware of it. The pictograms, ideograms, logograms, and phonograms—the communication tools of the ancients—still endure. They continue to evolve alongside society and cultural. As we've seen in modern pictograms, from a breastfeeding woman to a WiFi symbol (see page 31), the ideas of the ancient Egyptians still resonate.

Looking to the past offers more than just visual inspiration. It provides timeless stories that lend depth and meaning to how we understand the world today. The identity for Bluetooth, a wireless technology that allows users to share data between devices, is one such example. It encapsulates both ancient symbolism and modern function. In 1996, industry leaders from Intel, Ericsson, and Nokia met to develop a standard for short-range radio communication. Their goal was to improve connectivity and collaboration across devices and industries. At this meeting, Intel's Jim Kardach proposed the name *Bluetooth* as a temporary code name. He later explained: "King Harald Bluetooth… was famous for uniting Scandinavia, just as we intended to unite the

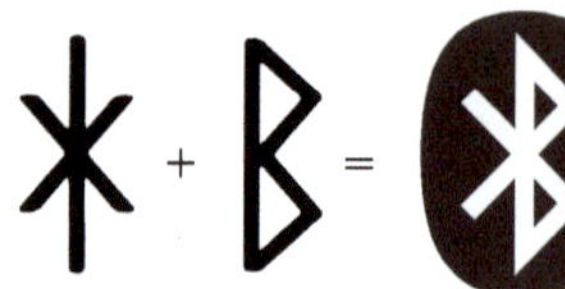

Combining two runes, the initials of King Harald *"Bluetooth,"* from the Younger futhark runic alphabet (ca. 800s CE): (ᚼ) *hagall* and (ᛒ) *bjarkan* (though his real last name was Gormsson) were used to create the twenty-first century identity, *Bluetooth*, a wireless technology company.

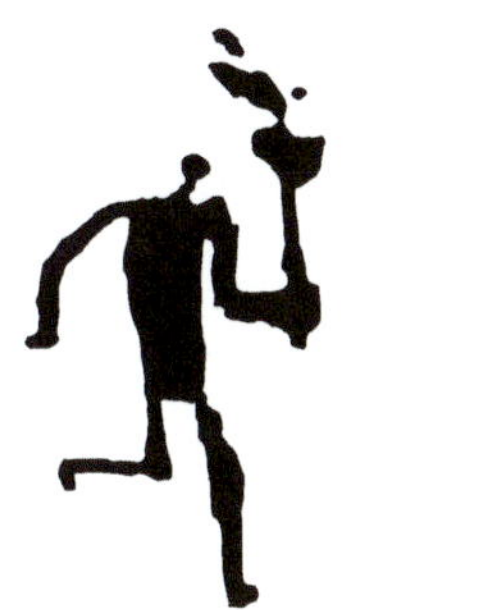

1994 Winter Olympics Sports Pictogram, Lillehammer, Norway.

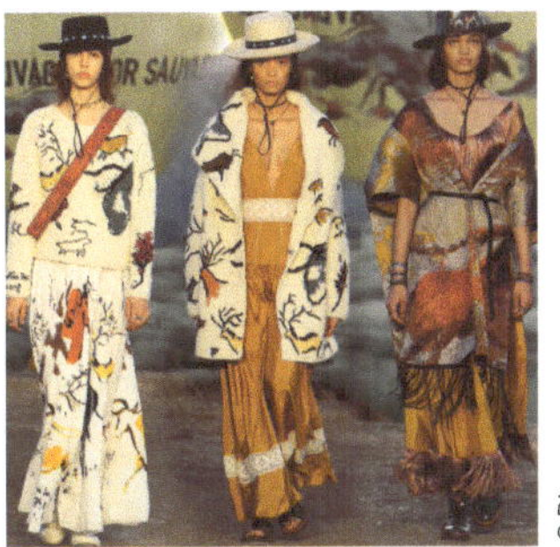

The Dior Cruise 2018 Collection, by Maria Grazia Chiuri.

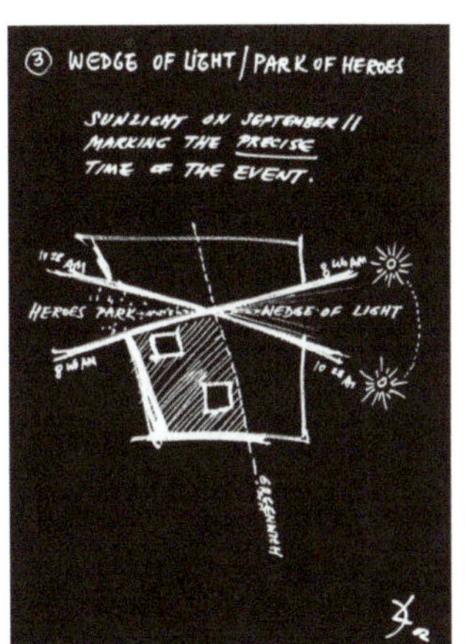

Wedge of Light, Original Plan for Ground Zero, 2002, Daniel Libeskind.

PC and cellular industries with a short-range wireless link." King Harald, who united Denmark with Norway in 958 CE, also had a dead tooth with a bluish-gray tint—hence the nickname "Bluetooth." The name was only meant to be provisional until the marketing team found "something really cool." But nothing better emerged. Alternatives like PAN (Personal Area Networking) had too many search hits online, and RadioWire posed trademark challenges. And so, the name Bluetooth stuck.

The visual identity followed. Drawing from the king's nickname, designers merged two ninth-century Scandinavian runes (see page 67): Hagall (ᚼ) and Bjarkan (ᛒ)—the initials of Harald Bluetooth. The result is a concept that seems improbable, yet works beautifully: a thousand-year-old story reimagined as a twenty-fist-century brand.

Graphic designer Sarah Rosenbaum also found inspiration in the distant past. She created the sports pictograms for the 1994 Winter Olympics in Lillehammer, Norway, based on 4,000-year-old rock carvings from Rødøy Island—home to the oldest known image of a skier.

Similarly, fashion designer and Dior creative director Maria Grazia Chiuri looked to prehistory for her debut 2018 collection. Inspired by the cave art of Lascaux, France (see page 24), she wrote: "At Dior, I spend my time simultaneously looking backwards and forwards. It's important to know everything — to recognize the history and rich heritage of the house and use this to determine a new future."

Architect Daniel Libeskind, a lead designer of the new World Trade Center complex in Lower Manhattan, also turned to ancient traditions for inspiration. In his original master plan, he incorporated the concept of a "Wedge of Light," echoing how ancient builders aligned monuments like Stonehenge with celestial events. On the solstices, the sun aligns with the center of Stonehenge, marking the shortest or longest day of the year. Similarly, Libeskind arranged five smaller buildings around the 1,776-foot Freedom Tower (a nod to the year of American independence) so that, each year on September 11, a shaft of light would shine between the buildings from 8:46 a.m.—when the first plane struck the North Tower—until 10:28 a.m., when it collapsed.

Today, the Latin alphabet includes roughly six hundred characters—and when counting mathematical, scientific, or borrowed characters, the number exceeds one thousand. One thing is certain: the alphabet will continue to change. Whether an accountant or a king, a priest or a poet, a typographer or a designer, people will always seek new ways to communicate. And as long as communication evolves, so too will the alphabet.

TODAY'S HIEROGLYPHS

We continue to use four fundamental systems of communication that originated with ancient hieroglyphs: pictograms, ideograms, logograms, and phonograms. These categories often overlap—but each represents a unique way we visually convey meaning.

PICTOGRAM

A simple image that represents a word or idea. These are direct, visual representations, such as emojis or public signage, understood regardless of language.

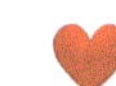 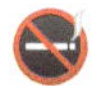 

IDEOGRAM

A character or symbol that represents an idea or thing without expressing a specific sound. This includes no-smoking signs, typographic symbols (&, $, @), or emoticons made from keyboard characters.

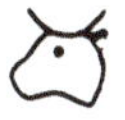

Egyptian, *aleph,* "ox," 1900 BCE

LOGOGRAM

A written symbol or character that represents a word or phrase. It conveys meaning through a symbol, regardless of pronunciation—like "4" for "four" in English or "quattro" in Italian (see pages 29 and 31).

b4 r u hungry?

PHONOGRAM

A symbol that represents a sound, syllable, or phoneme. Most of the modern alphabet is phonographic, with letters corresponding to sounds in spoken language.

¯_(~›.~)_/¯

Though we can't predict how the alphabet will evolve—especially as it adapts to screen-based and interactive media—we do know this: it will evolve, shaped by the changing needs of its users.

GLOSSARY

And we designed it all into the Mac. It was the first computer with beautiful typography.
—Steve Jobs, Stanford Commencement Address, 2005

ABECEDARY *A primer for learning the alphabet and the language of letters, symbols, and type.*

Æ æ **AESC** A ligature of A and E (or a and e), pronounced "ash." Originating in Old English to represent a diphthong vowel (two vowel sounds combined), it is still used in Danish and Icelandic alphabets (see page 37).

& & & **AMPERSAND** A character and ligature meaning "and." It derives from the Latin *et* and evolved from the handwritten combination of the letters e and t (see page 37).

Type **BLACKLETTER** Also known as Gothic script, Blackletter evolved from Carolingian minuscule and was the first metal type used in Gutenberg's Bibles. It was prevalent throughout Europe from the 11th to 17th centuries. As Robert Bringhurst noted, "They are the typographic counterpart of the Gothic style in architecture" (see page 77).

BOUSTROPHEDON A method of writing in which alternate lines are written in opposite directions—left to right, then right to left—mimicking the motion of oxen plowing a field. From Greek ***βουστροφηδόν*** (see page 59).

CHARACTER A graphic symbol, such as a letter, numeral, or hieroglyph, used in writing or printing to convey meaning.

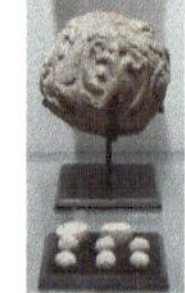

CLAY ENVELOPE Used in ancient Mesopotamia around 3300 BCE to securely store clay tokens representing a business transaction. The envelope could not be tampered with (see page 26).

CODEX An early form of the book; handwritten and typically on parchment, it contained multiple pages two-sided pages and replaced the scroll.

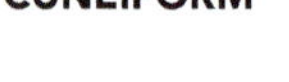

CUNEIFORM One of the world's oldest writing systems, developed by the Sumerians, ca. 3500–3200 BCE. The term comes from Latin for "wedge-shaped" (see page 35).

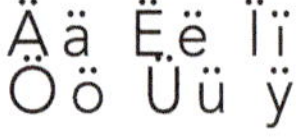

DEMOTIC A simplified version of Egyptian script, ca. 650 BCE-ca. 400 CE, appearing in the center text of the Rosetta Stone (see page 66–68).

Ä ä Ë ë Ï ï Ö ö Ü ü ÿ **DIAERESIS UMLAUT/** Two dots above a letter. As a diaeresis, it separates adjacent vowels (e.g., naïve); as an umlaut, it indicates a vowel sound shift (e.g., German über) (see page 37).

DIGRAPH A pair of letters that together form a single sound (phoneme), such as th, ch, and sh.

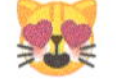 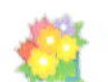  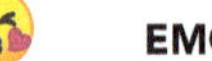

EMOJI From the Japanese e (picture) + moji (character). Modern pictographs used in digital communication. First developed by Shigetaka Kurita in 1999 for Japanese cell phones (see page 81).

; –) **EMOTICON** A visual facial expression created using standard keyboard characters. Popularized with early internet use (see page 81).

Avenir Light 8/10 **FONT** A specific style, weight, and size of type within a typeface. *Avenir Light 8-point on 10-point leading* refers to font name, weight, and spacing. It is what you are reading.

GLOTTAL STOP A sound produced when the vocal cords stop airflow, such as in "uh-oh." In Hawaiian, the *'okina* (') represents this sound (see page 79).

➔ ? ! # $ % & **GYLPH** A visual symbol or mark conveying meaning—often as part of a writing or typesetting system.

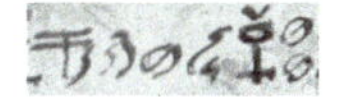 **HIERATIC** From Greek, *hieratikós*, meaning "sacred, priestly." A cursive form of Egyptian hieroglyphs used from 3200 BCE to 200 BCE, primarily written with ink and a reed pen. Used in both secular and sacred contexts (see pages 36–37, 38).

HUMANIST A Renaissance-inspired typeface style with open, hand-drawn, forms. Also known as Venetian (see pages 76–77).

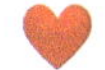 £ © = **IDEOGRAM** A picture, or symbol, that represents a thing or an idea, not necessarily linked to sound. In Egyptian hieroglyphs, certain images represented abstract ideas like power or governance (see pages 27, 29, 33, 81).

Text set in italics **ITALIC** A type style with slanted letterforms, originally based on Renaissance handwriting. First used by Aldus Manutius in Venice, 1500 CE. Used for emphasis.

KERNING The spacing between individual characters in a word. Good kerning improves readability (see page 61).

LEADING (LINE SPACING) The vertical space between lines of text. Affects text clarity and aesthetics.

ABCDEFG **MAJUSCULE** An uppercase or capital letter. From Latin *majuscula littera,* meaning "somewhat larger letter" (see pages 69, 72–73).

abcdefg **MINUSCULE** A lowercase letter. From Latin *minusculus,* meaning "rather small" (see pages 72–73, 75).

 **PICTOGRAM** A visual symbol that represents a physical object (something you can see, touch, hear, etc). Used in early writing systems like hieroglyphs and cuneiform (see pages 28–35).

PUNCTUATION Standardized marks (periods, commas, dashes, etc.) used in writing to clarify structure and meaning.

LETTER A symbol that represents a spoken sound within an alphabet system.

ff fi fl ffi ffl **LIGATURE** A single glyph combining two or more letters. Some typefaces, like Adobe Garamond, include ligatures; others, like Avenir, do not (see page 37).

平 & $ **LOGOGRAM** A letter, symbol, or sign that represents a word or morpheme. For example, the Chinese character for "peace" is a logogram (see page 31).

ᚠᚢᚦᚨᚱ **RUNES** Letters used by early Germanic and Norse peoples (ca. 150 CE–1200 CE), prior to the Latin alphabet (see pages 71, 75–81).

ABC **SANS SERIF** A typeface without serifs —those small strokes or feet at the ends of letterforms. *Sans* is French for "without."

ABC **SERIF** A small stroke or decorative flourish at the end of a larger stroke in a letterform. From Dutch *schreef*, meaning "line or stroke of the pen."

ñ **TILDE** A diacritical mark used in languages such as Spanish. In *mañana* ("tomorrow"), the tilde changes the sound of "n" to "nyah."

s t a r t r e k **TRACKING** The overall spacing between characters in a word or sentence. Affects visual rhythm and legibility (see page 61).

TYPEFACE The design of a set of characters, encompassing serif or sans serif, roman or italic, and light to bold styles.

TYPE FAMILY A group of related typefaces that vary in weight and style. For example:
Avenir Light, *Avenir Light Oblique*
Avenir Medium, *Avenir Medium Oblique*
Avenir Black, ***Avenir Black Oblique***
Each version, in a specific size, is a font.

TYPE CLASSIFICATION A system for grouping typefaces into major categories: Serif, Sans Serif, Script, and Decorative.

UPPERCASE and **LOWERCASE** See *Majuscule* and *Minuscule*.

VISUAL IDENTITY The design elements—such as color, typography, or logo—that establishes the look and feel (visual tone) of a brand, organization, or product (see pages 18, 27, 29, 35, 37, 41, 45, 47, 49, 51, 55, 57, 59, 63, 71, 73, 81).

ƿ **WYNN** or **WYN** A runic letter used in Old English for the "w" sound, eventually replaced by the Norman *double u* (uu) around 1300 CE (see page 76).

LIST OF ILLUSTRATIONS

* public domain

FM Photo grid by author
FM Animal, Graffiti, ca. 78 BCE, House of the Stags, Herculaneum, Italy (IV.21) 83, Abb. 228, © The Graffiti Project.
18 Logo, National Institute of Design, India, designer Adrian Frutiger; Photo, National Institute of Design, the author
20-21 Illustrated map by the author
22-23 Family Tree illustration by the author
24-25 El Castillo Cave Paintings, ca. 39,000 BCE, Spain, Photos © Cuevas Culturade Cantabria; Photos by the author; Thirty-two Prehistory Geometric Signs, © Genevieve von Petzinger
26 Early Sumerian tokens, ca. 4000 BCE, © Denis Schmandt-Besserat
27 Photos by the author
28 Kish Tablet, Uruk period (3500 BCE), © British Museum, London
29 I [heart] New York logo*, Milton Glaser, 1976; America Runs on Dunkin, advertising campaign, © Hill Holiday, 2006; [eye] [heart] T[ea] packaging, Copenhagen, designer unknown, 2012; Ramses and Horus, ca.1297–1213 BCE, Egyptian Museum, photo by the author; To be or not to be: symbols and pictures representing words, illustration by the author; IBM Rebus, poster, Paul Rand designed it in 1981, produced in 1982; © IKEA Advertisement, designer unknown,1985
30 Bone and Ivory Tags, ca. 3400-3200 BCE, photo © Günter Dreyer
31 Monumental Hieroglyphs, 3250 BCE, El-Khawy, Elkab, Egypt, © Egypt Ministry of Antiquities; photos by the author
32 Blau Monuments, 3300–3000 BCE, British Museum, © Trustees of the British Museum; illustrated map by the author
33 Illustrations, © David Diringer, The Alphabet: A Key to the History of Mankind; Student Exercise Tablet,* cuneiform, clay, Sumerian, ca. 2000-1500 BCE, Metropolitan Museum of Art; photos by the author; IKEA Directions, © IKEA
34 Narmer Palette,* ca. 3100 BCE, slate, Hierakonpolis, Egypt, Egyptian Museum, Cairo, illustrations by the author
35 French Cartouche,* 1645; Italian Cartouche,* ca. 1700s; British Coat of Arms,* 1837; Egyptian Coat of Arms, 1984; Atlanta Falcons Logo, © National Football League, USA; Chicago Bulls Logo, © National Basketball Association, USA; Lacoste Logo, © Sporloisirs SA; Twitter Logo © X Corp, USA; PUMA Logo, © PUMA, Inc.; Penguin Books Logo, © Penguin Random House
36 The Tale of Sinuhe, ca.1991–1786 BCE, Egyptian Museum, photo by the author
37 Disk, Enheduanna, ca. 2300 BCE, © Penn Museum; photos by the author
38 Wadi el-Hôl Alphabetic Inscription 2 (Vertical Inscription), ca. 1850–1700 BCE © Egypt Ministry of Antiquities; illustrated map by the author
39 Evolutionary illustrations based on the research of John Colman Darnell et al. 2005; Egyptian hieroglyphs by Sir Alan Gardiner
40 Sandstone Sphinx, ca.1800–1700 BCE, © British Museum; illustrated map by the author
41 Sandstone Sphinx, ca.1800–1700 BCE, © British Museum; Double-sided limestone ostracon, 1400 BCE, photo © Nigel Strudwick; Phaistos Disk, Side B,* ca. 1800-1600 BCE, Archaeological Museum of Heraklion
42 Sarcophagus of Ahiram, King of Byblos, ca. 1000 BCE, limestone, Phoenician, National Museum of Beirut, and detail, photos by the author; illustrated map by author
43 Phoenician illustrated alphabet by the author; Byblos photos by the author; oldest papyri: © Pierre Tallet
44 Mesha' Stele (Moabite Stone),* 841 or 842 BCE, The Louve Museum
45 All photos by the author
46 Nora Stone,* ca. 825 BCE, Sardinia, Phoenician, Museo Archeologico Nazionale, Cagliari; Nuraghe Tower, Is Paras, Isili, Sardinia, Italy, ca. 1500 BCE, photo © Norbert Nagel
47 Photos and illustrated map by the author
48 Dipylon Inscription,* Greece, ca. 740 BCE, National Archaeological Museum of Athens; Photos by the author; Transcription of Dipylon,* (Powell), 1988
49 Photos by the author; Ionic Greek alphabet illustration by the author; Principles of Design illustrations by the author
50 Nestor's Cup,* ca. 725 BCE, clay, ancient Greek, Late Geometric Period, The Archaeological Museum of Pithecusa, Ischia
51 Drawn translation,* Photos by the author
52 Marsiliana Tablet,* Greek/Etruscan, ca. 700 BCE, National Archaeological Museum, Florence; drawn alphabet;* proportional illustration by the author
53 Photos of keyboards by the author; Greek to Latin chart by the author; photo, Ponte Di Badia Vulci,* Viterbo, Italy; photo, A cuniculus by Garofoli*
54 Praeneste Fibula,* ca. 650 BCE, Museo Preistorico Etnografico Luigi Pigorini
55 Illustrations, Archaic Latin alphabet,* ca. 600 BCE, Archaic Latin alphabet,* ca. 300 BCE; Name as Maker logos: © Ben + Jerry's; © McDonalds; © Ford; © Walt Disney; © Harley-Davidson; © Fisher-Price; © L.L.Bean; © John Deere; © Levi-Strauss; bottom photo of Abu Simbal by the author; top photo of Abi Simbal, detail *
56 Rooster-Shaped Bucchero Jug,* ca. 650–600 BCE, Etruscan, terracotta, Metropolitan Museum of Art;
57 Etruscan alphabet,* ca. 700 BC; Ionian Greek alphabet,* ca. 800–500 BCE; Letters as Status logos: © Tesla, © Bavarian Motor Works, © Lexus, © Dolce & Gabanna Holding, © Louis Vuitton Malletier S.A. (LVM), © Chanel Company, © Massachusetts Institute of Technology, © University of California Los Angeles, © University of California Berkeley; The Library of Ashurbanipal;* photo, Ashurbanipal, 1988, bronze, © Fred Parhad
58 Reproduction, Lapis Niger* (or Black Stone), black marble, ca. 570-550 BCE; Lapis Niger inscription*; Capitoline She-wolf with Suckling Romulus and Remus*
59 Graphic Concept: © Gavin Ambrose and Paul Harris, The Fundamentals of Typography; The Gortyn Code* (or The Great Code), ca. 450 BCE; boustrophedon photos by the author; photo

of Pentecost Island*; photo, Hamp shire, United Kingdom*; Leonardo da Vinci's Notebook, Codex Forster 1, 1487–1490, National Art Library, Victoria and Albert Museum (no. MSL/1876/Forster/141/1/026v)

60 Duenos Vase, ca. 550 BCE, terracotta, Staatliche Museum, Berlin, © José Luiz Bernardes Ribeiro; Duenos inscription*

61 Photos by the author

62 Pyrgi Tablets,* ca. 500 BCE, gold, National Etruscan Museum, Villa Giulia, Rome; Pyrgi Tablets inscriptions*

63 Faces (detail), *Sarcophagus of the Spouses*,* c. 520 BCE, Etruscan, painted terracotta, Museo Nazionale Etrusco di Villa Giulia, Rome; photo © Steven Zucker, CC BY-NC-SA 2.0; Etruscan, twenty-three-letter alphabet;* sidebar photos, top three by author, bottom photo is in the public domain

64 Priene Inscription,* ca. 334 BCE, British Museum, London; illustrated map by the author

65 The Curse of Artemisia,* Memphis, Egypt, ca. 350–300 BCE, Papyrus Collection, Austrian National Library; Alexander the Great,* ca. 332 BCE, Egyptian hieroglyphs within a cartouche, Louvre Museum; sidebar photos of substrates by the author: carved type in marble, type molded into iron, metal type impressed on paper, drawn type on steel, type embroidered into fabric.

66 Rosetta Stone,* 196 BCE, British Museum, London; Photo, Rosetta Stone as seen in the British Museum by the author.

67 Details of Rosetta Stone (by the author); Liber Linteus Zagrabiensis,* ca. 250 BCE, linen, Archaeological Museum, Zagreb

68 Pompeii Graffiti,* RVFVS EST (It's Rufus), ca. 78 BCE, in the atrium on the north wall, Pompeii, Italy (photo and line drawing)

69 QUI · SE TUTARI · NESCIT · NESCIT · VIVERE MINIMUM · MALU (:MALUM) · FIT CONTEMNENDO · MAXIMUM,* Latin, Graffiti/incised, Herculaneum; "Mula performs fellatio(?) Antoni(us?); Fortunata (2 (bronze) asses (coins)),"* Latin, ca. 78 BCE, Graffiti/incised, Pompeii; Greek abecedarium,* ca. 78 BCE, Graffiti/incised, Pompeii; SALUTE VENIENTIS* ("To the health of the one entering"), Latin, ca. 78 BCE, Graffiti/incised, Pompeii; Photos of graffiti in Madrid, Spain, Cairo, Egypt (bilingual), and Setúbal, Portugal by the author; Trajan Column Inscription,* 113 CE (detail); British Library Papyrus 745,* ca. 100 CE, oldest example of Latin written on papyrus rather than parchment* (detail); PSI VI 729, Horse sales contract,* 77 CE, Old Roman Cursive

70 Trajan Column Inscription,* 113 CE dedicated, Trajan's Forum, Rome, chiseled text in marble; Trajan's Column, 107–113 CE, Trajan's Forum, Rome

71 Map, Roman Empire ca. 117 CE, by the author; FUÞARK (or Runic) alphabet,* ca. 100–800 CE; Uncial script,* 4th to 8th century CE; Logos that use Trajan: © The University of Texas, © Rice University, © The Lord of the Rings, © Titanic; Trajan Typeface, © Adobe Co., 1989, designed by Carol Twombly; photos of remnants of miners' village, Mons Claudianus, Eastern Desert, Egypt, and the Pantheon, Rome by the author

72 Moutier-Grandval Bible,* f.26r, Benedictine Abbey of St. Martin, Tours, France, ca. 830-840 CE, Latin, parchment, British Library

73 Harley Gospels,* ca. 575 CE, Latin, probably Aachen, Germany (detail); Book of Kells,* ca. 800 CE, Latin (detail); Moutier-Grandval Bible (detail); photos of Shady Characters, Kindle bookcover, United States National Park Service, Website homepage, screenshot, Moon-Pro, app screenshot, Moderna Museet, Outdoor signage, Museum of Modern Art, Stockholm, by the author; Adelaide's Bilingual Mandate of 1109,* after restoration in 1995. Palermo, Archivio di Stato, Tabulario dell' Ospedale Grande di Palermo, Tabulario dei monasteri di San Filippo di Fragalà e di Santa Maria di Maniaci, number 9

74 Opening page, Beowulf,* ca.1000, parchment, British Library, London; The word Beowulf from page 3 of the text, British Library, London (detail)

75 Drawing of one of Koberger's presses,* Albrecht Dürer, 1511; Hand-written miniscule double u; Letterpress type W*; Digital type, © Adobe Garamond W in lower- and uppercase, designed by Robert Slimbach, 1989, after Claude Garamond's (ca. 1510–1561 CE) old-style typeface, Garamond; Two upper-case V's* create the W in William (detail, from right); Title Page, The Tragedy of Hamlet,* 1611 CE, Bodelian Library, Oxford University; Ketubah,* a Jewish marriage contract, parchment, between 1300–1499 CE, University Library of Sassari, Sardinia, Italy

76 Evolution of the letter V © Lyn Davies; *Vocabulario en lengua castellana y mexicana,** 1555 CE, written and printed by Alonso de Molina (1514–1579), Rare Books and Special Collection, Library of Congress.

77 Claude Garamond's second Great Primer Roman type,* sixteenth century, cast from original matrices (the original copper molds of the letters) by the Plantin-Moretus Museum, Antwerp; Gutenberg's Bible,* Vol. 1, f.1, 1454 CE, title page; Novum Testamentum,* 1519 CE, title page; The Fleuron,* 1923, title page; Prayer Book of Maximilian,* 1514–1515, Munich, Germany; Albrecht Dürer created the marginal drawings (detail);* Eusebuis' De Evangelica Praeparatione, Nicholas Jenson, Venice,* 1470 (detail); Book of Holy Gospel of Our Lord and God Jesus Christ,* Bilingual: Latin/Syriac, Vienna, Austria, 1555 (detail)

78 American Dictionary of the English Language,* Noah Webster, 1828 CE; Evolution of the letter J © Lyn Davies; Title Page, The Whole Booke of Psalmes* (also known as The Bay Psalm Book), 1640 CE, Cambridge, Massachusetts

79 Linotype operators of the Chicago Defender, an African-American newspaper, April, 1941 © Russell Lee; The Linotype matrix illustration*; Chart, Hawaiian Alphabet,* 1822; Street signage, Hawai'i.*

80 Sketches, © Hermann Zapf, 1950; Front

and back of 1000 Lire banknote, © Hermann Zapf, 1950; Photo, Santa Croce, tomba sul pavimento 76 Giuliano Verrocchio; Sailko (2011); Evolution of Bluetooth logo chart by the author

81 1994 Winter Olympics Sports Pictogram, Lillehammer, Norway, © Sarah Rosenbaum, 1994; Cruise 2018 Collection, © Dior, Maria Grazia Chiuri, 2017; Wedge of Light, Original Plan for Ground Zero, 2002, © Studio Daniel Libeskind

BM Photo by the author; Drawing of an Animal and of a Rooster (right),* Herculaneum, Italy, ca. 79 CE, The Graffiti Project.

FM Photo grid by author

BIBLIOGRAPHY

OPENING QUOTES

Bringhurst, Robert, *The Elements of Typographic Style*, 3rd ed. (Vancouver: Hartley & Marks Publishers, 2004).

Sacks, David, *Letter Perfect: The Marvelous History of Our Alphabet From A to Z.* (New York, NY: Broadway Books, 2003).

INTRODUCTION

Diringer, David, *The Alphabet: A Key to the History of Mankind.* (New York, NY: Philosophical Library, 1948).

Bringhurst, *The Elements of Typographic Style.*

Kemp, Barry J., *Ancient Egypt: Anatomy of a Civilization.* (New York, NY: Routledge, 1991).

Sacks, *Letter Perfect.*

Greisner, Walter, *Adrian Frutiger Remembered.* Linotype, Font Designer Gallery. D. Stempel AG. https://www.linotype.com/720-34866/adrian-frutiger-remembered.html.

Type Directors Club. *Adrian Frutiger: A Tribute by Matthew Carter.* Vimeo video, 1:15:52. May 8, 2017. https://vimeo.com/216594178

Alderson, Rob, *Typographer Adrian Frutiger Dies Aged 87.* (Dezeen, December 21, 2016). https://www.dezeen.com/2015/09/14/adrian-frutiger-obituary-life-work-font-designer-typography-univers-london-street-signs/.

PrintMag. *"designed in California": Tracing the history of socially conscious design.* PRINT Magazine. (2018, January 12). https://www.printmag.com/environment/designed-in-california-tracing-the-history-of-socially-conscious-design/

I

40,000–10,000 BCE

VISUAL EXPRESSION

TED. *Why Are These 32 Symbols Found in Caves All over Europe, Genevieve Von Petzinger.* YouTube, December 18, 2015. https://www.youtube.com/watch?time_continue=+724&v=hJnEQCMA5Sg.

12.5 Different Types of Communication. Principles of Management. University of Minnesota Libraries Publishing edition, 2015. This edition adapted from a work originally produced in 2010 by a publisher who has requested that it not receive attribution., October 27, 2015. https://open.lib.umn.edu/principlesmanagement/chapter/12-5-different-types-of-communication/.

Woods, Christopher. *Visible Language: Inventions of Writing in the Ancient Middle East and Beyond.* (Chicago: Oriental Institute Museum Publications. Number 32. The Oriental Institute of the University of Chicago, 2010).

Frutiger, Adrian, *Signs and Symbols: Their Design and Meaning.* (New York, NY: Van Nostrand Reinhold, 1989).

Sacks, *Letter Perfect.*

D'Arcy, Patrick, *What the Mysterious Symbols Made by Early Humans Can Teach Us about How We Evolved.* ideas.ted.com, June 7, 2017. https://ideas.ted.com/what-the-mysterious-symbols-made-by-early-humans-can-teach-us-about-how-we-evolved/

I I

8500–4000 BCE

PHYSICAL OBJECTS

Schmandt-Besserat, Denise, *From Accounting to Writing.* (sites.utexas.edu. Briscoe Center for American History, The University of Texas at Austin, April 25, 2005). https://sites.utexas.edu/dsb/tokens/from-accounting-to-writing/.

Editors, The. *The World's Oldest Writing.* (Archaeology Magazine, 2016). https://www.archaeology.org/issues/213-1605/features/4326-cuneiform-the-world-s-oldest-writing.

Frutiger. *Signs and Symbols.*

Rensberger, Boyce, *History of Writing May Be Written in Sumerian Tokens of Trade.* (The Washington Post, December 6, 1993).

https://www.washingtonpost.com/archive/politics/1993/12/06/history-of-writing-may-be-written-in-sumerian-tokens-of-trade/1b94481f-ecbb-41d5-958d-d6f1d-215bca8/?utm_term=.729a034c3bd1.

IEC 60417 - 5009, Stand-by - International Organization for Standardization. Online Browsing Platform (OBP). ISO. Accessed September 1, 2022. https://www.iso.org/obp/ui#!iec:grs:60417:5009.

https://interbrand.com/work/wi-fi/

1
3500 BCE
PICTOGRAPHIC
Robinson, A., *The Story of Writing: Alphabets, Hieroglyphs and Pictograms.* (New York, NY: Thames & Hudson, 1999).

Woods, *Visible Language: Inventions of Writing in the Ancient Middle East and Beyond.*

Choi, E. Kwan, *Babylonian Culture and Tablets.* (Iowa State University, Department of Economics). http://www2.econ.iastate.edu/classes/econ355/choi/bab.htm.

Diringer, *The Alphabet: A Key to the History of Mankind.*

Editors, The. *The World's Oldest Writing.* Archaeology Magazine.

Spar, Ira, *The Origins of Writing.* (Metmuseum.org. Department of Ancient Near Eastern Art, The Metropolitan Museum of Art, October 2004). http://www.metmuseum.org/toah/hd/wrtg/hd_wrtg.htm.

Rebus Collection. *Reading Rebus.* (The Graduate Center, City University of New York). https://readingrebus.com/rebus-collection/.

Mitchell, Larkin, *Earliest Egyptian Glyphs.* (Archaeology Magazine archive. Archaeological Institute of America, 1999). http://archive.archaeology.org/9903/newsbriefs/egypt.html.

2
3400 BCE
HIEROGLYPHS
Davies, Lyn. *A is for Ox: A Short History of the Alphabet.* (Great Britain: The Folio Society, 2006).

Mitchell, Larkin, *Earliest Egyptian Glyphs.*

Kemp, Barry. *Ancient Egypt: All That Matters.* (London: Camelite House, 2015).

Shaw, Ian, *Ancient Egypt: A Very Short Introduction.* (Oxford University Press, 2004).

Woods, Christopher. *Visible Language: Inventions of Writing in the Anceint Middle East and Beyond.*

Connolly, Bess. *Yale Archaeologists Discover Earliest Monumental Egyptian Hieroglyphs.* (Yale News. Yale University, Office of Public Affairs & Communications, June 20, 2017). https://news.yale.edu/2017/06/20/yale-archaeologists-discover-earliest-monumental-egyptian-hieroglyphs.

American Institute for Graphic Arts, *Symbol Signs.* https://www.aiga.org/resources/symbol-signs.

Bringhurst, *The Elements of Typographic Style.*

3
3300–3000 BCE
PROTO–CUNEIFORM
Stein, Jil J. Foreword. *In Visible Language: Inventions of Writing in the Ancient Middle East and Beyond.* (Chicago: Oriental Institute Museum Publications. Number 32. The Oriental Institute of the University of Chicago, 2010).

Woods, *Visible Language: Inventions of Writing in the Ancient Middle East and Beyond.*

Diringer, *The Alphabet: A Key to the History of Mankind.*

4
3000 BCE
HIEROGLYPHS
Bahia Shehab Interview: Art As a Tool for Change. Lousiana Channel, 2016. https://www.youtube.com/watch?v=I72idm-Davb4&ab_channel=LouisianaChannel.

Diringer, *The Alphabet: A Key to the History of Mankind.*

Davies, Lyn. *A is for Ox: A Short History of the Alphabet.* (Great Britain: The Folio Society, 2006).

Ancient Egypt: Hieroglyphs and Writing Systems | National Museums Liverpool. (YouTube. National Museums Liverpool, 2020). https://www.youtube.com/watch?v=I0C4BYy_EWQ.

Jevons, Frank Byron, *A History of Greek Literature: From the Earliest Period to the Death of Demosthenes.* Internet Archive. (London : C. Griffin, 1886). https://archive.org/details/historyofgreekli00jevoiala/page/52.

Connolly, *Yale Archaeologists Discover Earliest Monumental Egyptian Hieroglyphs.*

Gardiner, Sir Alan H., *List of Egyptian Heiroglyphs,* digitized: http://www.egyptianhieroglyphs.net/gardiners-sign-list/

5
1900 BCE
HIERATIC SCRIPT
Abdel-Hamid Youssef, Ahmad. *From the Pharaoh's Lips: Ancient Egyptian Language in the Arabic of Today.* (Cairo: American University in Cairo Press, 2003). 4.

Parkinson, R.B., Translator. *The Tale of Sinuhe and Other Ancient Egyptian Poems, 1940–1640 BC.* (Oxford: Oxford University Press, 1997).

Sacks, *Letter Perfect.*

Gardiner, Sir Alan H., *Notes on The Story of Sinuhe.* (Paris: Librairie Honeré Champion, 1916). Lines 129-141. http://www.etana.org/sites/default/files/coretexts/15243.pdf

Roberson, Joshua Aaron, *A Very Brief Introduction to Hieratic.* (Egyptology Forum, 2018). http://www.egyptologyforum.org/bbs/Stableford/Roberson,%20A_Very_Brief_Introduction_to_Hieratic.pdf.

Bringhurst, *The Elements of Typographic Style.*

Binkley, Roberta, *Biography of Enheduanna, Priestess of Inanna.* (Enheduanna. Center for Digital Discourse and Culture at Virginia Tech University, 1998). http://www.cddc.vt.edu/feminism/Enheduanna.html.

Hafford, Brad, *Artifact of the Month: Ceremonial Stone Disk (Disk of Enheduanna).* (Penn Museum Blog. Penn Museum, June 2012). https://www.penn.museum/blog/museum/ur-digitization-project-item-of-the-month-june-2012/.

Wells, J.C., *Orthographic Diacritics and Multilingual Computing.* (Article published in *Language Problems and Language Planning,* 24.3, 2001). http://www.phon.ucl.ac.uk/home/wells/dia/diacritics-revised.htm

6
1850–1700 BCE
EARLY ALPHABETIC
Darnell, John Coleman, *Wadi el-Hol.* In Willeke Wendrich (ed.), UCLA Encyclopedia of Egyptology, Los Angeles, 2013). http://digital2.library.ucla.edu/viewItem.do?ark=21198/zz002dx2tj

Sacks, *Letter Perfect.*

Wilford, John Noble, *Discovery of Egyptian Inscriptions Indicates an Earlier Date for Origin of the Alphabet.* (New York Times, November 13, 1999).

Davies, *A is for Ox: A Short History of the Alphabet.*

Oldest Alphabet Found in Egypt. (BBC News. BBC, November 15, 1999). http://news.bbc.co.uk/2/hi/middle_east/521235.stm.

Gardiner, Sir Alan H., *List of Egyptian Heiroglyphs,* digitized: http://www.egyptianhieroglyphs.net/gardiners-sign-list/

Himelfarb, Elizabeth J. *First Alphabet Found in Egypt.* (Archaeology Institute of America, 2000). http://archive.archaeology.org/0001/newsbriefs/egypt.html.

7
1800–1300 BCE
EARLY ALPHABETIC and HIEROGLYPHS

Ikram, Salima, *Ancient Egypt: An Introduction.* (New York, NY: Cambridge University Press, 2009).

Azevedo, Joaquim, *The Origin and Transmission of the Alphabet.* (MA Theses, Andrews University, June 1994).

Diringer, David, *The Alphabet: A Key to the History of Mankind.*

Borschel-Dan, Amanda, *First Written Record of Semitic Alphabet from 15th Century BCE Found in Egypt."* (The Times of Israel, May 22, 2018). https://www.timesofisrael.com/first-written-record-of-semitic-alphabet-from-15th-century-bce-found-in-egypt/.

Howitt, Caitlin, *Archaeologies of the Greek Past: Linear B.* (Joukowsky Institute for Archaeology & the Ancient World, Brown University). https://brown.edu/Departments/Joukowsky_Institute/courses/greekpast/4690.html.

The Editors, Phaistos Disc. (Academic Dictionaries and Encyclopedias, 2010). https://en-academic.com/dic.nsf/enwiki/117741.

The Editors, Phaistos Disc. (Academic Dictionaries and Encyclopedias, 2010). https://en-academic.com/dic.nsf/enwiki/117741.

The Editors of Encyclopaedia. Hyksos. (Encyclopedia Britannica, 8 Nov. 2017). https://www.britannica.com/topic/Hyksos-Egyptian-dynasty

The Editors, Ancient Egyptian City Located in Nile Delta by Radar. (BBC News. BBC, June 21, 2010). https://www.bbc.co.uk/news/10367930.

Tdondich, 10 Ways to Say Thank You in Japanese. (Nihongo Master, August 8, 2021). https://blog.nihongomaster.com/thank-you-in-japanese/.

8
1000 BCE
PHOENICIAN

Diringer, The Alphabet: A Key to the History of Mankind.

Sacks, Letter Perfect.

Davies, A is for Ox: A Short History of the Alphabet.

Lehmann, Reinhard G., Calligraphy and Craftsmanship in the AHIROM Inscription: Considerations on Skilled Linear Flat Writing in Early First Millennium Byblos. (Academia.edu, May 25, 2014). https://www.academia.edu/4306363/Calligraphy_and_Craftsmanship_in_the_Ahirom_inscription_Considerations_on_skilled_linear_flat_writing_in_early_first_millennium_Byblos.

Gaudet, John, *The Pharaoh's Treasure: The Origin of Paper and the Rise of Western Civilization.* (New York: NY, Pegusus Books Ltd., 2016).

Editors, *An Introduction to Papyrus: Ancient and Modern.* (The University of Michigan Papyrus Collection, Papyrus Making 101: Rediscovering the Craft of Making Ancient Paper, May 4, 2004). https://apps.lib.umich.edu/papyrus_making/pm_intro.html.

Marouard, Gregory, and Pierre Tallet, *The Harbor of Khufu on the Red Sea Coast at Wadi Al-Jarf, Egypt (NEA 77/1."* (Near Eastern Archaeology, August 29, 2015). https://www.academia.edu/6248978/THE_HARBOR_OF_KHUFU_on_the_Red_Sea_Coast_at_Wadi_al-Jarf_Egypt_NEA_77_1_.

Stille, Alexander, *The World's Oldest Papyrus and What It Can Tell Us About the Great Pyramids.* (Smithsonian Institution, October 1, 2015). https://www.smithsonianmag.com/history/ancient-egypt-shipping-mining-farming-economy-pyramids-180956619/.

9
850 BCE
PHOENICIAN in ARCHAIC GREEK LETTERS

Walsh, William Pakenham, *The Moabite Stone: The Substance of Two Lectures.* (The British Library. George Herbert, 1872). http://access.bl.uk/item/viewer/ark:/81055/vdc_100041480016.0x000001#?c=0&m=0&s=0&cv=5&xywh=648%2C487%2C534%2C368.

Diringer, David., *The Alphabet: A Key to the History of Mankind.*

The Palestine Exploration Fund. (biblicalstudies.org.uk, January 21, 1870). https://biblicalstudies.org.uk/pdf/pefqs/1869-71_061.pdf.

Lemaire, André, *House of David' Restored in Moabite Inscription.* (Center for Online Judaic Studies, September 21, 2016). http://cojs.org/how_i_discovered_the_-house_of_david-_inscription-_gila_cook-_cojs/.

Britannica, The Editors of Encyclopaedia, *Cyrillic alphabet.* (Encyclopedia Britannica, 20 May 2020). https://www.britannica.com/topic/Cyrillic-alphabet.

10
825 BCE
PHOENICIAN

Diringer, *The Alphabet: A Key to the History of Mankind.*

Cross, Frank Moore. *An Interpretation of the Nora Stone.* (The University of Chicago Press, Bulletin of the American Schools of Oriental Research. No. 208, Dec 1972).

Ring, Trudy, ed. *International Dictionary of Historic Places: Volume 3, Southern Europe.* (London and New York: Rutledge, 1995).

Pilkington, Nathan, and Department of History. *A Note on Nora and the Nora Stone.* (Bulletin of the American Schools of Oriental Research, Vol 365, February 1, 2012). https://www.journals.uchicago.edu/doi/10.5615/bullamerschoorie.365.0045.

McDonald's Egypt Story. (McDonald's Egypt). https://www.mcdonalds.eg/About.

SAR Motors, Kigali, Rwanda. (SAR Motors). https://www.japanesecartrade.com/sarmotor/.

Our History in the KSA. (ExxonMobil, July 28, 2017). https://corporate.exxonmobil.com/en/Locations/Saudi-Arabia/Our-history-in-the-KSA.

11
750 BCE
ARCHAIC GREEK

Binek, Natasha M., *The Dipylon Oinochoe Graffito: Text or Decoration? (Hesperia: The Journal of the American School of Classical Studies at Athens,* Vol. 86, No. 3, July-September 2017).

Powell, Barry B., *The Dipylon Oinochoe and the Spread of Literacy in Eighth-Century Athens.*(Kadmos, vol. 27, no. 1, 1988, pp. 71-94). https://doi.org/10.1515/kadmos-1988-0109

Diringer, *The Alphabet: A Key to the History of Mankind.*

Sacks, *Letter Perfect.*

Britannica, The Editors of Encyclopaedia. *Ionic Alphabet.* (Encyclopedia Britannica, 17 Oct. 2016). https://www.britannica.com/topic/Ionic-alphabet.

Herodotus, *Book V.* (University of Chicago: Loeb Classical Library Edition, Chapters 55-96, 1922). https://penelope.uchicago.edu/Thayer/E/Roman/Texts/Herodotus/5c*.html.

McCauley, Jim. *The Story of the Tour De France Logo.* (Creative Bloq, July 7, 2017). https://www.creativebloq.com/logo-design/tour-de-france-logo-71515677.

12
725 BCE
ARCHAIC GREEK

Jevons, Frank Byron. *A History of Greek Literature from the Earliest Period to the Death of Demosthenes.* (New York: Charles Scribner's Sons, 1892.)

Murray, A.T., translator, *Iliad* by Homer, Book 11, Line 635. (Cambridge, MA:

Harvard University Press; London, William Heinemann, Ltd. 1924). http://www.perseus.tufts.edu/hopper/text?doc=Perseus%3Atext%3A1999.01.0134%3Abook%3D11%3Acard%3D616

Mora, Faustino, *Archaeologies of the Greek Past: Nestor's Cup.* (Joukowsky Institute for Archaeology, Brown University). https://brown.edu/Departments/Joukowsky_Institute/courses/greekpast/4695.html.

Britannica, The Editors of Encyclopaedia, *Aristophanes Of Byzantium.* (Encyclopedia Britannica, 17 May 2017). https://www.britannica.com/biography/Aristophanes-of-Byzantium.

West, M. L., *Aristophanes of Byzantium's Text of Homer.* (Classical Philology, January 2017 112:1, 20-44, University of Chicago Press). https://www.journals.uchicago.edu/doi/epdf/10.1086/689961

Sacks, *Letter Perfect.*

Gaunt, Jasper, *Nestor's Cup and Its Reception.* (Leiden, Koninklijke Brill NV., *Voice and Voices in Antiquity*, 2017).

Faraone, Christopher A., *Taking the "Nestor's Cup Inscription" Seriously: Erotic Magic and Conditional Curses in the Earliest Inscribed Hexameters.* (Classical Antiquity, Volume 15, Issue 1, April 1996).

Dean, Paul, *EXtreme Type Terminology, Part 4: Numeral and Puncuation.* (I Love Typography, November 9, 2020). https://ilovetypography.com/2008/04/25/extreme-type-terminology-part-4/.

Houston, Keith, *The Mysterious Origins of Punctuation.* (BBC Culture, BBC, September 2, 2015). https://www.bbc.com/culture/article/20150902-the-mysterious-origins-of-punctuation.

Lockwood, John Francis, and Nigel Wilson. *Aristophanes (2), of Byzantium, Librarian of Alexandria, c. 257–180 BCE.* (Oxford Classical Dictionary, December 22, 2015). https://oxfordre.com/classics/view/10.1093/acrefore/9780199381135.001.0001/acrefore-9780199381135-e-770.

Lukas, Paul, *All-CAPS TYPOGRAPHY IS DOOMED.* (The New Republic, June 24, 2013). https://newrepublic.com/article/113578/using-all-caps-worst-form-emphasis.

13
700 BCE
ARCHAIC GREEK and ETRUSCAN
Sacks, *Letter Perfect.*

Diringer, *The Alphabet: A Key to the History of Mankind.*

Robinson, Andrew, *The Story of Writing: Alphabets, Hieroglyphs and Pictograms.* (New York, NY: Thames & Hudson, 1999).

Huntsman, Theresa, *Etruscan Language and Inscriptions."* (Metmuseum.org, The Met, June 2013). https://www.metmuseum.org/toah/hd/etla/hd_etla.htm.

14
650 BCE
ARCHAIC LATIN
Jevons, Frank Byron, *A History of Greek Literature: From the Earliest Period to the Death of Demosthenes.* Internet Archive. (London : C. Griffin, 1886). https://archive.org/details/ahistorygreekli02jevogoog/page/42/mode/2up

Anderson, Lisa M., *Replica of the Praeneste Fibula.* (Division of Asian and Mediterranean Art, Harvard University). https://harvardartmuseums.org/art/286341.

Who Made the Praeneste Fibula? (Archaeology Magazine, 2009). https://archive.archaeology.org/online/features/hoaxes/praeneste_fibula.html.

Wood, Wesley, *Interpuncta Verba: Reassessing the Role of Punctuation in the Latin Classroom.* (The Classical Journal Forum, September 15, 2015). http://www.thecjforum.com/blog/category/pedagogy/2.

Diringer, David, *The Alphabet: A Key to the History of Mankind.*

Gordon, Arthur Ernest, *Illustrated Introduction to Latin Epigraphy* . (Internet Archive. Berkeley : University of California Press, January 1, 1983. https://archive.org/details/illustratedintro0000gord/page/75/mode/1up.

On the Etruscan eff sound, and FH
PDF (in folder), p223
Penney Archaic and Old Latin from Clackson 2013 Companion to the Latin Language

Dillon, Matthew P.J., *A Homeric Pun from Abu Simbal.* (Zeitschrift fur Papyrologie und Epigraphik 118, 1997). http://www.uni-koeln.de/phil-fak/ifa/zpe/downloads/1997/118pdf/118128.pdf

Fischer-Bovet, Christelle, *Army and Society in Ptolemaic Egypt.* (Cambridge University Press, 2014).

15
600 BCE
ETRUSCAN
Bonfante, Larissa, *Reading the Past: Ancient Writing from Cuneiform to the Alphabet.* (Berkeley, University of California Press, 1990).
https://archive.org/details/readingpastancie0000unse/page/n5/mode/2up

Davies, *A is for Ox: A Short History of the Alphabet.*

Daniels, Peter T. (Editor), William Bright (Editor). *The World's Writing Systems Illustrated Edition.* Oxford University Press; Illustrated edition (February 8, 1996).

Bonfante, Larissa, *Etruscan History Gets a Rewrite.* (Times Higher Education, May 19, 2000).
https://www.timeshighereducation.com/books/etruscan-history-gets-a-rewrite/156223.article

Carroll, Andrew, *Etruscan Numbers.* (Ancient History Encyclopedia, January 23, 2017). https://www.ancient.eu/video/1074/

Civic Center: Ashurbanipal. (Public Art and Architecture from Around the World, January 24, 2012). https://www.artandarchitecture-sf.com/tag/fred-parhad.

16
570 BCE
ARCHAIC LATIN
Gordon, Arthur E., *Illustrated Introduction to Latin Epigraphy.* (Berkeley: University of California Press, 1983).

The Ohio State University, Knowledge Bank. *CIL 6.36840–Lapis Niger–boustrophedon* (August 2016). https://kb.osu.edu/handle/1811/99479

Rectors and Visitors of the University of Virginia, *Lapis Niger* (2008). http://archive1.village.virginia.edu/spw4s/RomanForum/GoogleEarth/AK_GE/AK_HTML/TS-009.html

Explore Leonardo Da Vinci's Notebooks: Codex Forster I. (Victoria and Albert Museum). https://www.vam.ac.uk/articles/explore-leonardo-da-vinci-codex-forster-i#?c=&m=&s=&cv=&xywh=-867%2C-111%2C3209%2C2211.

17
550 BCE
ARCHAIC LATIN
Harðarson, Jón Axel, *The 2nd Line of the Duenos Inscription.* (Edizioni dell'Orso s.r.l., 2011).

Conway, R. Seymour, *The Duenos Inscription.* (The American Journal of Philology, Volume 10, No. 4, January 1, 1889). https://archive.org/details/jstor-287059/page/n1/mode/2up

Gordon, Arthur E., *Notes on the Duenos-Vase Inscription in Berlin.* (California Studies in Classical Antiquity 1 January 1975; 8 53–72). doi: https://doi.org/10.2307/25010682

Gordon, Arthur E., *Illustrated Introduction to Latin Epigraphy.* (Internet Archive. Berkeley : University of California Press, January 1, 1983). https://archive.org/details/illustratedintro0000gord/page/78/mode/2up.

18
500 BCE

PHOENICIAN and ETRUSCAN

Ostler, Nichola, *Ad Infinitum : A Biography of Latin.* (Internet Archive. New York : Walker & Co : Distributed by Holtzbrinck, January 1, 1970). https://archive.org/details/adinfinitumbiogr0000ostl/page/56/mode/2up?view=theater.

Schmitz, Philip C., *The Phoenician Text from the Etruscan Sanctuary at Pyrgi.* (Journal of the American Oriental Society, vol. 115, no. 4, 1995). www.jstor.org/stable/604727.

Zamora Lopez, Jose Angel, *Pyrgi Revisited. An Analysis into the Structure and Formulae of Pyrgi's Phoenician Text.* (Studi Epigrafici e Linguistici sul Vicino Oriente Antico, 2016).

Pygri Tablets. (Museo Nazionale Etrusco di Villa Giulia). https://www.museoetru.it/masterpieces/lamine-doro-da-pyrgi.
Becker, Jeffrey, A., *Sarcophagus of the Spouses (Rome) in Smarthistory,* August 8, 2015, accessed November 11, 2022, https://smarthistory.org/sarcophagus-of-the-spouses-rome/.

Knoppers, Gary N., *The God in His Temple: The Phonecian Text From Pygri as a Funerary Inscription.* (The University of Chicago, Journal of Near Eastern Studies, 51 no. 2, 1992).

Diringer, *The Alphabet: A Key to the History of Mankind.*

Ager, Simon, *I Love You in Many Languages.* (Translations of I love you in many languages). https://omniglot.com/language/phrases/iloveyou.htm.

I Love You Translated. (Western Abenaki Dictionary, 2008). http://westernabenaki.com/dictionary/reciprocal.php?variablewa=gezalm&variablewa1=gezalme&variablewa2=gezal&variablewa3=gezalmi&variablewa4=gezalma&variableen=love&variableen3=loved&variableen4=loved.

19
400 BCE
CLASSICAL GREEK

Morison, Stanley, *Politics and Script: Aspects of Authority and Freedom in the Development of Graeco-Latin Script from the Sixth Century B.C. to the Twentieth Century A.D.* (The Lyell Lectures, 1957. Edited and Completed by Nicholas Barker, Oxford University Press, 1972).

Sacks, *Letter Perfect.*

Carter, Harry, *A View of Early Typography Up to About 1600.* (Hyphen Press by arrangement with Oxford University Press, 2002).

Cooper, J. M., editor, *Compete Works. Phaedrus.* pp. 551-552. Indianapolis IN: Hackett. https://newlearningonline.com/literacies/chapter-1/socrates-on-the-forgetfulness-that-comes-with-writing

Hackforth, Reginald, translator, *Plato on Writing* (1952). http://websites.umich.edu/~lsarth/filecabinet/PlatoOnWriting.html.

20
200 BCE
HIEROGLYPHS, DEMOTIC and HELLENISTIC GREEK

Robinson, Andrew, *Cracking the Egyptian Code: The Revolutionary Life of Jean-François Champollion.* (United Kingdom: Thames & Hudson, 2012).

Maitland, Margaret, *Emojis vs. Hieroglyphs: Why Is Ancient Egyptian Writing Still Dismissed as Primitive Almost 200 Years after Its Decipherment?* (The Eloquent Peasant, October 11, 2019). http://www.eloquentpeasant.com/2015/06/02/emojis-vs-hieroglyphs/.

Young, Joanna, *6 Things You Need to Know about Egyptian Hieroglyphs.* (HieroEducation, November 6, 2015). https://www.hieroeducation.co.uk/blog/7/9/2015/6-things-you-need-to-know-about-egyptian-hieroglyphs.

Werning, Daniel A., and Eliese-Sophia Lincke Lincke, eds., *The Rosetta Stone Online: Section 38.* (The Rosetta Stone Online Project. Institut für Archäologie, Humboldt-Universität zu Berlin). http://rosettastone.hieroglyphic-texts.net/sections/section-38/.

Liber Linteus. (Wikipedia. Wikimedia Foundation). https://en.wikipedia.org/wiki/Liber_Linteus.

21
100 BCE
EVERYDAY (VULGAR) LATIN and GREEK

LaFrance, Adrienne, *Pompeii's Graffiti and the Ancient Origins of Social Media.* (The Atlantic, Atlantic Media Company, March 30, 2016). https://www.theatlantic.com/technology/archive/2016/03/adrienne-was-here/475719/.

Benefiel, Rebecca R., Director, *The Ancient Graffiti Project.* (cf. Voegtle, 115-116, 2012). http://ancientgraffiti.org/Graffiti/results.

Eska, Joseph F., *The Language of the Latin Inscriptions of Pompeii and the Question of an Oscan Substratum.* (*Glotta* 65, no. 1/2,: 146–61, 1987). http://www.jstor.org/stable/40266785.

Andrews, Robin, *This Is How a Volcano's Pyroclastic Flow Will Kill You.* (*Forbes Magazine*, June 4, 2018). https://www.forbes.com/sites/robinandrews/2017/01/08/this-is-how-a-volcanos-pyroclastic-flow-will-kill-you/?sh=7ed9f72132cd.

Porter, J.R., *A Sampling of Graffiti and Other Public and Semi-Public Texts from Pompeii and Herculaneum.* (2021). https://www.academia.edu/36829610/A_Sampling_of_Graffiti_and_Other_Public_and_Semi_Public_Texts_from_Pompeii_and_Herculaneum

Voon, Claire. *Help Build a Database of Ancient Graffiti from Pompeii and Herculaneum.* (Hyperallergic, February 21, 2018). https://hyperallergic.com/426566/ancient-graffiti-project-crowdfunding-pompeii-herculaneum/.

Ohlson, Kristin, *Reading the Writing on Pompeii's Walls.* (Smithsonian.com, July 26, 2010). https://www.smithsonianmag.com/history/reading-the-writing-on-pompeiis-walls-1969367/.

The British Museum, *Life and Death in Pompeii and Herculaneum.* (The British Museum, film, 2013). https://www.britishmuseum.org/pompeii-live.

Ancient Scripts: Rustic Capitals, Old and New Roman Cursive. (Dartmouth Ancient Books Lab. Dartmouth College, May 25, 2016). https://sites.dartmouth.edu/ancientbooks/2016/05/25/ancient-fonts-rustic-capitals-old-and-new-roman-cursive/.

Coleman-Norton, Paul Robinson, and Frank Card Bourne, eds., *The Twelve Tables.* Translated by Allan Chester Johnson. (Avalon Project: Documents in Law, History and Diplomacy. Yale Law School, 1961). https://avalon.law.yale.edu/ancient/twelve_tables.asp.

Death and Burial. (Odyssey. Michael C. Carlos Museum, Emory University). https://carlos.emory.edu/htdocs/ODYSSEY/ROME/d&b.html.

Robinson, Olivia. *The Roman Law On Burials and Burial Grounds.* (Irish Jurist (1966-) 10, no. 1 (1975): 175–86). http://www.jstor.org/stable/44026221.

Parents of the Roman Alphabet: Phoenicians and Greeks." (Development of the Roman Letterform. Graphic Design History, 2011). http://www.designhistory.org/Handwriting_pages/Evolution.html.

22
100 CE
CLASSICAL LATIN

Sacks, *Letter Perfect.*

Scenes 126–148 from Trajan Column. (Trajan's Column Scenes CXXVII-CLV, 127-155). http://www.trajans-column.org/?flagallery=trajans-column-scenes-cxxvii-clv-127-155#PhotoSwipe1570362154003.

Lightfoot, Christopher, *Roman Inscriptions.* (In Heilbrunn Timeline of Art History. New York: The Metropolitan Museum of Art, February 2009). http://www.metmuseum.org/toah/hd/insc/hd_insc.htm

Elder Futhark Runic Alphabet. (The Viking

Rune, 2008). https://www.vikingrune.com/2008/11/elder-futhark-runes/.

Ager, Simon, *Runic Alphabet* (Runic alphabets/ Runes/Futhark, August 2022). https://omniglot.com/writing/runic.htm.

Curry, Andrew. *A War Diary Soars Over Rome.* (Trajan's Amazing Column. National Geographic). https://www.nationalgeographic.com/trajan-column/article.html.

Bülow-Jacobsen, Adam, *Archaeology and Philology on Mons Claudianus 1987-1993.* (Topoi. Orient-Occident. Persée - Portail des revues scientifiques en SHS, May 5, 2016). https://www.persee.fr/doc/topoi_1161-9473_1996_num_6_2_1691.

23
800 CE
MEDIEVAL LATIN
Nesbitt, Alexander, *The History and Technique of Lettering.* (New York, Dover Publications, 1957).

The 'Moutier-Grandval Bible'. (Digitized Manuscripts, Add MS 10546. British Library). https://www.bl.uk/manuscripts/FullDisplay.aspx?index=0&ref=Add_MS_10546.

Biggs, Sarah J. *A Carolingian Masterpiece: the Moutier-Grandval Bible.* (Medieval Manuscripts Blog. British Library, July 22, 2013). https://blogs.bl.uk/digitisedmanuscripts/2013/07/a-carolingian-masterpiece-the-moutier-grandval-bible.html.

The Harley Gospels: An Early Surviving Example of St Jerome's Vulgate. (Collection Items. British Library). https://www.bl.uk/collection-items/the-harley-gospels.

Lindisfarne Gospels. (Collection Items. British Library). https://www.bl.uk/collection-items/lindisfarne-gospels#.

Mark, Joshua J., *Charlemagne.* (World History Encyclopedia. https://www.worldhistory.org#organization, March 25, 2019). https://www.worldhistory.org/Charlemagne/.

Book of Kells. (Digital Collections. Trinity College Dublin). https://digitalcollections.tcd.ie/collections/ks65hc20t?locale=en.

Sacks, *Letter Perfect.*

Jeremy Johns, *Paper versus Parchment: Countess Adelaide's Bilingual Mandate of 1109.* (The Khalili Research Centre, Documenting Multiculturalism: Document of the Month, November 2018). http://krc.orient.ox.ac.uk/documult/index.php/outputs/38-paper-versus-parchment-countess-adelaide-s-bilingual-mandate-of-1109.

Ustick, W. Lee, *PARCHMENT' AND 'VELLUM,* (*The Library*, Volume s4-XVI, Issue 4, March 1936, Pages 439–443). https://doi.org/10.1093/library/s4-XVI.4.439

Thompson, Sir Edward Maunde, *An Introduction to Greek and Latin Palaeography.* (Internet Archive. Oxford : Clarendon Press, January 1, 1970). https://archive.org/details/greeklatin00thomuoft.

Loud, G.A., Metcalfe, A., eds., *The Society of Norman Italy.* (The Medieval Mediterranean: People, Economies and Cultures, 400–1500, Volume 38. Leiden, Boston, Köln: Brill, 2002).

Zenobia, *Saving Egyptian Heritage: The Old Italian Phosphate Company Colony in El-Quseir.* (Egyptian Chronicles, March 30, 2019). https://egyptianchronicles.blogspot.com/2019/03/saving-egyptian-heritage-old-italian.html.

24
1000–1500 CE
OLD ENGLISH
You've Got to Find What You Love,' Jobs Says. (Stanford News. Stanford University, 2005). https://news.stanford.edu/2005/06/14/jobs-061505/.

Sacks, *Letter Perfect*, 335-336.

Beowulf. (British Library). https://www.bl.uk/collection-items/beowulf.

The Bodleian First Folio. (Small Shakespeare Portrait. Bodleian Library). https://firstfolio.bodleian.ox.ac.uk/downloads.html#pdfs.

Tikkanen, Amy. *Runic Alphabet: Writing System.* (Encyclopædia Britannica, 2022). https://www.britannica.com/topic/runic-alphabet.

Steinberg, S.H., *Five Hundred Years of Printing*, 3rd ed. (Harmondsworth: Penguin Books, 1974).

Library of Congress Bibles Collection, Overview: Gutenberg Bible. (Library of Congress). https://www.loc.gov/exhibits/bibles/interactives/gutenberg/index.html.

Olocco, Riccardo, *The Venetian Origins of Roman Type.* (Medium. CAST, June 21, 2018). https://articles.c-a-s-t.com/the-venetian-origins-of-roman-type-a856eb3f0cb.

Electronic Beowulf. (Electronic Beowulf, fourth edition). https://ebeowulf.uky.edu/ebeo4.0/CD/main.html.

The Thirteen Books of Euclid's Elements. (Clay Mathematics Institute Historical Archive, May 8, 2008). http://www.claymath.org/library/historical/euclid/index.html.

The Editors of Encyclopaedia, Britannica. *Ninety-five Theses.* (Encyclopedia Britannica, 24 Oct. 2022). https://www.britannica.com/event/Ninety-five-Theses.

Jewish Marriage Contract, Ketubah. (The Library of Congress). https://www.wdl.org/en/item/4175/#q=marriage+contract&time_periods=500-1499&qla=en.

Simsir, Husamettin, *Varangian Guards and Their Traces in Istanbul: Runic Inscriptions in Hagia Sophia.* (University of Notre Dame's Medieval Institute, Medieval Studies Research Blog: Meet Us at the Crossroads of Everything, January 21, 2021). https://sites.nd.edu/manuscript-studies/2020/06/05/varangian-guards-and-their-traces-in-istanbul-runic-inscriptions-in-hagia-sophia/.

Larsson, M. G., 1989. *Nyfunna Runor i Hagia Sofia* (*Recently Discovered Runes in Hagia Sophia*). (Stockholm, Fornvännen 84, 1989).

25
1500 – 1650 CE
SPANISH
Carter, Harry, *A View of Early Typography Up to About 1600.* (Hyphen Press, by arrangement with Oxford University Press, 2002).

En Mexico : En casa de Antonio de Spinosa. (1571, January 1). *Vocabulario en Lengua Castellana y Mexicana*, Molina, Alonso de, d. 1585: Internet Archive. Retrieved November 15, 2022, from https://archive.org/details/vocabularioenlen00moli/mode/1up

Davies, *A is for Ox: A Short History of the Alphabet.*

College of University Libraries and Learning Sciences News. Research Guides. *The Beginnings of Printing in Mexico*, (n.d.). https://libguides.unm.edu/blog/the-beginnings-of-printing-in-mexico

Hessler, J. (2021, April 26). *Nahuatl as it was: An exploration of the Great Dictionary of Alonso de Molina. Nahuatl as it was: an exploration of the great dictionary of Alonso de Molina* | Worlds Revealed: Geography & Maps at The Library Of Congress. https://blogs.loc.gov/maps/2021/04/nahuatl-as-it-was-an-exploration-of-the-great-dictionary-of-alonso-de-molina/

Sacks, *Letter Perfect.*

Scribes and Manuscript Production After the Norman Conquest. (Medieval England and France, 700–1200. British Library). https://www.bl.uk/medieval-english-french-manuscripts/videos/1-scribes-and-manuscript-production-after-the-norman-conquest.

Steinberg, S.H., *Five Hundred Years of Printing*, 3rd ed. (Harmondsworth: Penguin Books, 1974).
Nadeau, Barbie Latza, *The Man Who Changed Reading Forever.* (Smithsonian Institution, November 6, 2015). https://www.smithsonianmag.com/travel/aldus-manutius-printing-typeface-typography-italics-venice-180956855/.

Saylor, Michael,*The Mobile Wave: How Mobile Intelligence Will Change Everything.*

(New York: Vanguard Press. Kindle Edition, 2013).

Linotype, *Stempel Garamond™ Font."* (Fonts.com). https://www.fonts.com/font/linotype/stempel-garamond/story.

Augustine, De Civitate Dei, 1467. (Southern Methodist University, Bridwell Library Special Collections). https://www.smu.edu/Bridwell/SpecialCollectionsandArchives/Exhibitions/InventionDiscovery/Italy/Augustine1467.

Johnson,Samuel. *A Dictionary of the English Language: A Digital Edition of the 1755 Classic.* (Edited by Brandi Besalke, December 6, 2012). https://johnsonsdictionaryonline.com/page-view/&i=2150.

Historiae De Gentibus Septentrionalibus: Olaus, Magnus, Archbishop of Uppsala, 1490-1557. (Internet Archive. Antverpiae : Apud Ioannem Bellerum, p10, January 1, 1970). https://archive.org/details/Historiaedegent00Olau/page/n5/mode/1up?view=theater.

Johann Gutenberg's Bible, 1454, (Harvard University, Harvard Library). https://iiif.lib.harvard.edu/manifests/view/drs:35522451$1i.

Erasmus, Desiderius, *Novum Testamentum Omne, Multo Quàm ANTEHAC Diligentius AB Erasmo Roterodamo Recognitu, Emedatum AC Translatum ... : Uná Cu Annotationibus Recognitis, AC Magna Accessione Locupletatis ... (1519)*: (Internet Archive. [Basileae : in Aedibvs Ioannis Frobenii], p125, January 1, 1970). https://archive.org/details/novumtestamentum00eras/page/n124/mode/1up?ref=ol.

Samuel Johnson's Dictionary, 1755. (University of Florida's George A. Smathers Libraries). https://johnsonsdictionaryonline.org/1755page/title-v1-1.

26
1650–1800 CE
AMERICAN ENGLISH
Spear, Michael, *The Linotype Machine: Thomas Edison Called It the 'Eighth Wonder of the World.'* (University of Richmond, August 15, 1996). https://facultystaff.richmond.edu/~mspear/lino.html.

Massin, *Letter and Image.* Translated by Caroline Hillier and Vivienne Menkes. (Studio Vista London. 1970, p18; quote originally appeared in *Le Potomak, 1913-1914: Précédé d'un Prospectus 1916).*

Richardson, Charles, *A New Dictionary of the English Language.* (Internet Archive. London, W. Pickering; New York, 1839). https://archive.org/details/anewdictionary-e00richgoog/page/n425.

The VVHOLE Booke of Psalmes. (NYPL Digital Collections. New York Public Library, 1640). https://digitalcollections.nypl.org/items/a5c31f84-060c-ffc6-e040-e00a18060180.

Davies, Lyn, *A is for Ox: A Short History of the Alphabet.*

Sacks, *Letter Perfect.*

Literacy Rates Continue to Rise from One Generation to the Next. (UNESCO Institute for Statistics, September 2017). http://uis.unesco.org/sites/default/files/documents/fs45-literacy-rates-continue-rise-generation-to-next-en-2017.pdf.

A Brief History of Hawai'ian Language Newspapers. (Building Upon Kahua A'o. College of Education, University of Hawai'i at Manoa, October 18, 2021). https://coe.hawaii.edu/kahuaao/hawaiian-language/.

Walch, David B. *The Historical Development of the Hawaiian Alphabet*, The Journal of Polynesian Study, No. 3, 1967), p 353 - 366. Church College of Hawaii. http://www.jps.auckland.ac.nz/document/?wid=3719.

Britannica, The Editors of Encyclopaedia. *Sanford Ballard Dole: President of the Republic of Hawaii.* (Encyclopedia Britannica, 5 Jun. 2022). https://www.britannica.com/biography/Sanford-Ballard-Dole

AFTERWORD
Zapf, Hermann, *Alphabet Stories: A Chronicle of Technical Developments.* (Rochester, NY: RIT Cary Graphic Arts Press, 2007).

Origin of the Bluetooth Name. (About Us. Bluetooth). https://www.bluetooth.com/about-us/bluetooth-origin/.

Lillehammer Winter Olympics, 1994. (Sarah Rosenbaum, Norway, 1993. Alliance Graphique Internationale). https://a-g-i.org/design/lillehammer-winter-olympics.

Chiuri, Maria Grazia, *Maria Grazia Chiuri's Letter From Rome: 'Fashion Has a Small Part, but Together We Can Make a Big Difference.'* (Vogue, April 15, 2020). https://www.vogue.com/article/maria-grazia-chiuri-dior-coronavirus.

Farra, Emily, *How Dior, Balenciaga, and More Are Finding Inspiration in the Past.* (Vogue, May 24, 2017). https://www.vogue.com/article/fashion-designers-looking-to-past-archives-inspiration-dior-balenciaga.

Discover Maria Grazia Chiuri First Cruise Collection for Dior. (DSCENE, June 7, 2017). https://www.designscene.net/2017/05/dior-cruise-2018.html.

Rice, Andrew, *Revealed: The Inside Story of the Last WTC Tower's Design.* (Wired. Conde Nast, June 9, 2015). https://www.wired.com/2015/06/bjarke-ingels-design-two-world-trade-center/.

The Battle Over Ground Zero. (BBC News. BBC, September 4, 2003). http://news.bbc.co.uk/2/hi/americas/3080778.stm.

Bringhurst, *The Elements of Typographic Style.*

GLOSSARY
https://www.merriam-webster.com/

Bringhurst, *The Elements of Typographic Style.*

Flask, Dominic, *Type Classification.* (Design is History). http://designishistory.com/1450/type-classification/.

Hern, Alex, *Don't Know the Difference Between Emoji and Emoticons? Let Me Explain.* (The Guardian, February 6, 2015). https://www.theguardian.com/technology/2015/feb/06/difference-between-emoji-and-emoticons-explained.

COLOPHON
Wadi Rum Protected Area. (UNESCO World Heritage Centre). http://whc.unesco.org/en/list/1377.

Boston Red Sox Cap Logo History. (American League, Chris Creamer's Sports Logos). https://www.sportslogos.net/logos/view/5360461946/Boston_Red_Sox/1946/Cap_Logo.

The Ancient Graffiti Project. (Ancient Graffiti Project :: Search Results). http://ancientgraffiti.org/Graffiti/results.

The Ancient North Arabian Scripts. (OCIANA: Online Corpus of the Inscriptions of Ancient North Arabia). http://krc.orient.ox.ac.uk/ociana/index.php/13-scripts/35-the-ancient-north-arabian-scripts

ADDITIONAL REFERENCE
Ambrose, G., Harris, P., *The Fundamentals of Typography.* Lausanne, Switzerland: AVA Publishing SA, 2006.

Bestley, R, & Noble, I., *Visual Research: An Introduction to Research Methodologies in Graphic Design, 2nd Edition.* Lausanne, Switzerland: AVA Publishing SA, 2011.

Bringhurst, Robert, *The Solid Form of Language: An Essay on Writing and Meaning.* Kentville, Nova Scotia, Gaspereau Press, Printers & Publishers, 2004.

Cahill, Thomas, *Sailing the Wine-Dark Sea: Why the Greeks Matter*, First Anchor Books Edition: Random House. New York, 2004.

Chappell, W. & Bringhurst, R., *A Short History of the Printed Word*, 2nd Edition. Vancouver: Hartley & Marks Publishers Inc., 1999.

Craig, James, and Scala, Irene Korol, *Designing with Type, 5th Edition: The*

Essential Guide to Typography. New York, NY, Watson-Guptill, 2006.

Davis, James C. *The Human Story: Our History, from the Stone Age to Today.* New York, NY, HarpersCollins Publishers. 2009.

Davies, W.V., *Egyptian Hieroglyphs.* London, The British Museum Press, 2002.

Dürer, A. *Of the Just Shape of Letters* (R. T. Nichol, Trans.,1535). http://www.gutenberg.org/ebooks/37103

Humez, A. & N. (1985). *ABC Et Certera: The Life & Times of the Roman Alphabet.* Boston, MA: David R. Godine.

Kemp, Barry J., *Ancient Egypt: Anatomy of a Civilization.* (New York, NY: Routledge, 1991).

Ostler, Nicholas. *Ad Infinitum: A Biography of Latin* Walker Books, 2008

Lawrence, D.H. (1997). *DH Lawrence and Italy*, Penguin Books, New York.

Meggs, P. B., Purvis, A.W. *History of Graphic Design*, 6th Edition. Wiley, New Jersey. 2016.

WEBSITES

http://www.codex99.com/typography/21.html
Art, design, and history

https://www.etymonline.com
Etymology

http://www.gutenberg.org/ebooks/37103
Dürer, A. *Of the Just Shape of Letters* (R. T. Nichol, Trans.,1535).
Project Gutenberg, over 60,000 free ebooks

http://artflsrv02.uchicago.edu/cgi-bin/efts/dicos/woodhouse_test.pl?keyword=^Rome
TEnglish-Greek Dictionary, Woodhouse Library, University of Chicago

https://www.perseus.tufts.edu/hopper/
Greek-English Dictionary, Perseus Digital Libary, Tufts University

MUSEUMS

Alexandria National Museum, Egypt

Archaeological Museum of the American University of Beirut, Beirut, Lebanon

British Museum, London, England

Coptic Museum, Cairo, Egypt

Egyptian Museum, Cairo, Egypt

Gutenberg-Museum, Mainz, Germany

Istanbul Archaeological Museum, Turkey

Jordan Museum, Amman, Jordan
Library of Alexandria Museum, Egypt

Metropolitan Museum of Art, New York City, USA

Museum of Fine Arts, Boston, USA

National Archaeological Museum of Athens, Greece

National Archaeological Museum of Naples, Italy

National Etruscan Museum, Villa Giulia, Rome, Italy

National Museum of Beirut, Beirut, Lebanon

National Museum of Prehistory and Ethnography, Rome, Italy

Nationalmuseet, National Museum of Denmark, Copenhagen, Denmark

Pigorini National Museum of Prehistory and Ethnography, Rome, Italy

Pompeii Antiquarium, Pompeii, Italy

Rashid Museum, Rashid, Egypt

Trinity College Library, Dublin, Ireland

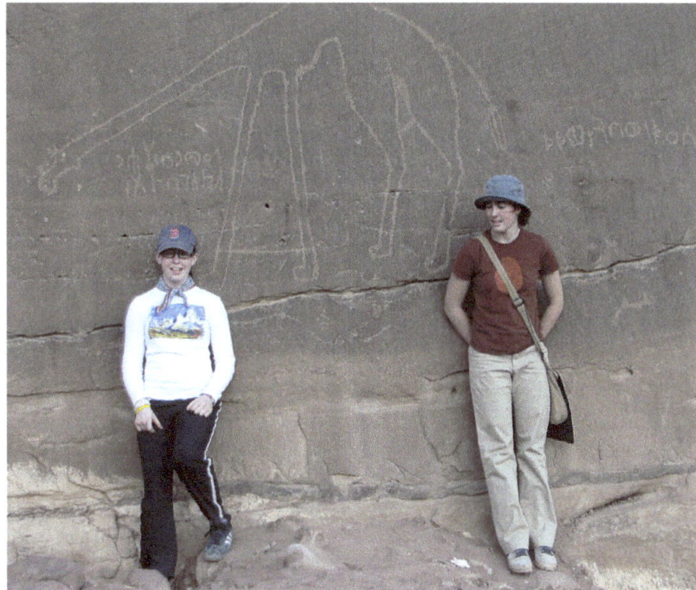

The author's daughters standing in front of a camel petroglyph (ca.10,000 BCE) and an example of Thamudic script (ca. 600–400 BCE CE) in Wadi Rum, Jordan, 2011. Carina, on the left, is wearing a Boston Red Sox cap. The stylized logo, a red "B" with white outline, has been used by the Boston Red Sox since 1947.

This book was designed by Colleen Comerford.

The text face is Avenir, French for "future," designed by Adrian Frutiger in 1987.
Greek text and Etruscan characters are set in Verdana,
designed by Matthew Carter and released in 1996.
Arabic text is set in Myriad Arabic, designed by Carol Twombly and Robert Slimbach
in consultation with Dr. Mamoun Sakkal.
When used for display, it is set in KufistandardGK (designer unknown).

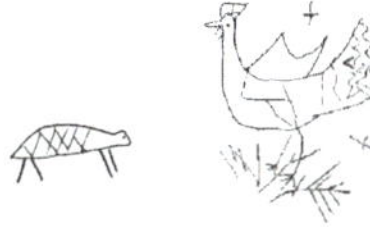

Drawing of an Animal (left); *Drawing of a Rooster* (right), Herculaneum, Italy, ca. 79 CE

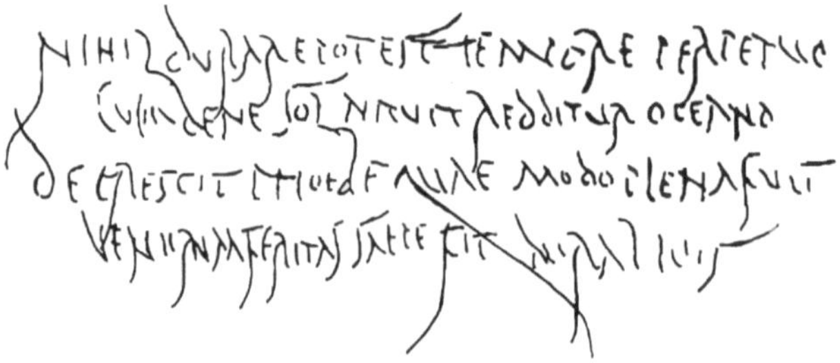

Latin, Graffiti/incised, ca 78 BCE, Pompeii, Italy.

NOTHING CAN LAST FOREVER: THE SUN,
WHEN ITS COURSE IS COMPLETE, HIDES ITSELF BEHIND THE SEA;
THE MOON, ONCE FULL, NOW WANES. THUS, LOVE'S WOUNDS SHALL HEAL,
AND FRESH BREEZES WILL BLOW ONCE MORE" GIULIO POLIBIO DOMUS

Translation Garcia y Garcia, 2005: Rome.